More Light
(Aa sar

Wilhelm Friedrich & Elisabeth Kärcher:
The Life and Work of a Missionary Couple
in Chuuk/Micronesia

Lothar Käser

VTR
Publications

© 2021

Bibliographic information published by the Deutsche Nationalbibliothek
The Deutsche Nationalbibliothek lists this publication in the Deutsche
Nationalbibliografie; detailed bibliographic data are available in the
Internet at http://dnb.dnb.de.

ISBN 978-3-95776-139-2

VTR Publications, Gogolstr. 33, 90475 Nuremberg, Germany
http://www.vtr-online.com

Translated from German by Geoffrey Sutton

Photo credits (cover): Archives of the Liebenzell Mission, Lothar Käser
Cover Design based on a design by
Design-Studio Henri Oetjen, Lemgo, Germany
Photos (interior): Families Kärcher and Wagner, Klaus W. und Ulrike Müller,
Lothar Käser, Alan and Louise Pipkin and archives of the Liebenzell Mission

Dedicated to the children of
Wilhelm Friedrich and Elisabeth Kärcher:
Hannelore, Waltraud, Anneliese, Ernst, and Helmut

Contents

Preface to the German Edition

It was Wilhelm Friedrich Kärcher's express wish that if any biography were written about him, it should only be published after his death.

Concerning his life and work there is a range of different sources. The most important ones are his letters from after World War II. There are personal letters, as well as newsletters to an extended circle of readers in which he reported on the progress of his work on Chuuk and on the surrounding islands. I will frequently quote from these, although occasionally I had to make some minor changes in the grammar, word order, and punctuation. Wilhelm F. Kärcher wrote many of his letters on the move, either by hand or on a small portable typewriter, sometimes even during a sea voyage, when often he did not have the time or leisure to formulate his texts beforehand or to correct them thoroughly.

Furthermore, there are a number of tape recordings recounting life experiences, in part intended for ERF Wetzlar, a German gospel broadcasting company, but also for relatives and acquaintances.

Some smaller publications from his pen bear autobiographical traits. The titles of these have been listed at the end of this volume in a separate bibliography.

Wilhelm F. Kärcher had communicated much concerning his work as a missionary by word of mouth or often spontaneously to his nephew Klaus W. Müller who made notes of the most important and impressive details. The material for chapter one about Wilhelm F. Kärcher's hometown Mühlhausen/Enz and the history of his family also comes from Müller.

Apart from a small number of letters, there also exists an extended diary written by Wilhelm F. Kärcher's wife Elisabeth. It comprises events from the 1930s to the 1950s, as well as being an important source for the duration of World War II, when the family survived the Japanese forced internment and the American bombing raids on Chuuk. Apart from a few pages at the end, it has been written in Gothic (Sütterlin) script. Besides this diary she also kept one for each of their three daughters, recording events from the early years of their childhood.

However, from the time of the internment and before, we only have very few personal testimonials about her husband. For safety reasons, he had burnt his diary records and letters which had kept on arriving for him from Germany; he feared they would fall into the hands of the Japanese military security services who could perhaps have used them against him as so-called evidence of spying activities.

It is not clear how Elisabeth Kärcher was able to keep her diary records and letters hidden during house searches by Japanese intelligence officers. There was one incident when she would have lost her cherished letters from her mother, if she had not fearlessly confronted the officers. This episode is recounted extensively in chapter 9.

Wilhelm F. Kärcher's reports in the bulletins of the Liebenzell Mission of Germany are a very rich source. Their distinguishing feature is that they help European and Western readers visualize the ways of thinking and the values of the island people in a vivid and uncomplicated manner.

The pictorial documentation poses a problem. Photographs from the first half of the preceding century have been produced with very simple techniques. Even with the help of computers they could hardly be improved.

For several years now there have been difficulties with the names of the islands on which Wilhelm F. Kärcher and his wife spent their working lives. Until around 1990 people used to talk (and write) about "Truk," the "Truk-Atoll," or the "islands around Truk." This terminology is also found in all ethnological, missiological, geographical, and historical publications printed up to that time. Along with the founding of the "Federated States of Micronesia" in 1979, the participating states replaced many appellations, place names, and spellings from colonial times with original and indigenous ones. This has to be kept in mind when doing research by computer and in related literature through libraries and the Internet. Thus, "Truk" was replaced by "Chuuk". German readers pronounce this new appellation "correctly" – i.e. like the islanders do – sounding the "uu" as a long "oo" (as in "cool").

Writing this biography would not have been possible without the dedicated participation of a number of people. Written testimonials and pictorial evidence were made available primarily by the daughters and sons of Wilhelm and Elisabeth Kärcher. I received important genealogical data and pictures of Elisabeth's family history from their nephews Werner Wagner in Puchheim and Karl-Heinz Wagner in Waltenhofen. Liebenzell Mission, too, has promptly and readily sent me pictures and allowed me to access records from their archives.

Going over the (German) manuscript demanded special attention. I am grateful to Waltraud Rist (née Kärcher) for her willing cooperation and efficient editing of the draft manuscript. I also want to express my appreciation to Esther Hahn and Elfriede Klenk, but first and foremost I thank my wife Gisela, who contributed to the success of this undertaking in various ways. She was the first to have to assess my original, and thus had to solve all those problems connected with a raw manuscript with its gaps, breaks, wrong choice of words, excessive formulations, and tangled sentence structures. Over and above that, she took care that I had the free space necessary for completing the manuscript speedily and without interruption. I was even released, generously and at her own suggestion, from washing and drying dishes during this time!

Not to be forgotten also are Waltraud Hoppenworth and Arthur Klenk from the publishing house Verlag der Liebenzeller Mission. They always advised me competently, and carefully prepared the (German) publication of this book.

Schallstadt,
in the fall of 2005
Lothar Käser

1

Home Background, Childhood, and Youth (1907–1930)

Wilhelm Friedrich Kärcher, who usually abbreviated his name to Wilhelm F. Kärcher, as is customary in the United States, and who will subsequently simply be called Wilhelm, was born on January 27, 1907, in Mühlhausen an der Enz (on the river Enz), in what is today Baden-Württemberg. Through its history and its people Mühlhausen a. E. is a village that had quite an impact on the later life of the missionary.

Mühlhausen an der Enz – Its History and Presence

The people of Mühlhausen call themselves "Mühlhäuser." In their mother tongue, the Swabian dialect of German, that is not only the correct but also the most appropriate form. So when I describe them as "Mühlhauseners" in what follows, I am just following a grammatical rule in written High German.

Mühlhausen is well known for being one of the most beautiful villages in Württemberg. The river Enz, a tributary of the Neckar river, leaves the northern Black Forest only a few miles upstream near Pforzheim, flows on from there through a valley with steep slopes of light-colored shell limestone, and forms a narrow loop of very picturesque landscape near Mühlhausen.

The rocky slopes downstream from the village, and the balanced climate that predominates, create favorable conditions for viticulture, which was presumably introduced to this area by monks a very long time ago. The products of the Mühlhausener winegrowers had made a name for themselves from early on.

Mühlhausen is a very ancient place, probably named after the numerous mills which were powered by the river for centuries. More than a thousand years ago, in AD 892, it is mentioned in a document as "Mulnhusa." It must have been around that time that monks brought Christianity to the pagan people then living in the Enz valley and built the first churches.

All through the Middle Ages, the population lived under changing feudal overlords, they suffered under unstable political conditions, and were sorely afflicted, especially during the Thirty Years' War (1618–1648). Until well into modern times the peasants of Mühlhausen were serfs.

Under Napoleon's reign, too, considerable sacrifices were demanded of the population. None of the young men from the village, who had been forced to participate in the campaign against Russia in 1812, returned to his hometown.

Communal life in those days was subject to strict regulations. Entertainment like dancing was forbidden, and dice and card games, and the practice of white and black magic were liable to punishment. Cursing ("taking the name of the Lord in vain") was looked upon as one of the main causes for divine affliction ("famine, dearth, pestilence, war, physical malformation, and other plagues"). Deliberate blasphemy was even punishable by death.

Political and economic conditions after World War I brought about big changes in Mühlhausen. As a result of general economic developments the mill lost its importance, especially after the loop of the river Enz (4.5 mile / 7 km long) had been utilized to serve an electrical power plant by the construction of an underground conduit for the water.

This water conduit also had another function; for the young men of the village it became the place for a trial of courage. Whoever could swim the 164 yards (150 meters) of the conduit all the way to the electrical plant was considered a "real man" from then on.

Until far into the twentieth century the village farmers carried on their agriculture in traditional ways, i.e. manually, with horses and oxen as draft animals. Neighborly help was taken for granted. The fact that agricultural land handed down to the next generation could not be divided *ad infinitum* had already become apparent earlier in village history. The farms were getting smaller and smaller, the farmers poorer and poorer. Having many children was the rule, but in the end only one of them could inherit the farm. The others had to earn their living elsewhere: the sons as craftsmen, merchants, or hired hands, the daughters as domestic helps in urban families, or as maidservants on other farms. Many emigrated to the States. With the onset of industrialization, the men were looking for work in the surrounding towns of Vaihingen, Dürrmenz, and Mühlacker.

In those days, important people in the village were the mayor, the State Church pastor, and the teacher. Whereas the village mayor (until later in the twentieth century) could be a local farmer, pastors and teachers brought with them an academic education and came from outside; they did not speak the Mühlhausener Swabian dialect and were, therefore, rather looked upon as strangers, even though they may have been highly regarded and respected.

Church and Spiritual Life in Mühlhausen

As briefly mentioned above, monks had started about 1,000 years ago to spread Christianity in southern Germany. In AD 794 a monk by the name of Alban appeared on the scene. He must perhaps be regarded as the patron of the first known church in Mühlhausen, because it was dedicated "to Albanus."

The Mühlhauseners had possibly started to build this church as early as before the turn of the first millennium. Originally, it had been a fortified church, surrounded by a strong wall, behind which the village people sought protection in times of turmoil.

Conrad Thumb von Neuburg, a nobleman from Württemberg, was a follower of the Reformation faith and introduced it to Mühlhausen.

In the course of time, morals became stricter, and religious education as well as attendance at Sunday services became obligatory. Whoever failed to comply with these duties was held accountable. Church pews were private property; they had to be purchased. This applied especially to the women, who thus secured for themselves a permanent seat in the church.

Approximately at the same time as the Reformation, general school education was introduced, of eight years' duration (*Volksschule*). As well as his class teaching, a teacher also had to work as the official church custodian – until 1899, when church administration was initially regarded as his main office. Likewise, it was part of his duties to keep the schoolboys "disciplined and in order" during church services. In the middle of the eighteenth century, during wintertime, up to one hundred and twenty children had to be taught for six hours, and in the summer for four hours, daily. Children who were mentally able learned "100 hymns and 30 to 40 Psalms" off by heart; all this over and above the mandatory school subjects.

Mühlhausen had several prominent State Church pastors over the course of time. The best known among them was hymn-writer Philipp Friedrich Hiller. He was born there on January 9, 1699, and was pastor in his place of birth from 1736 until 1748, just like his father who had held this office before him. Many of his songs found their way into generations of hymnbooks. His *Liederkästlein* (little box of songs) went through several editions up until the present time.

In the person of Philipp Friedrich Hiller, Mühlhausen was especially influenced by the Württemberg genre of Pietism[1]. Within this spiritual movement, one event was to gain special significance for the Kärcher family and for Wilhelm's life – an event that began shortly before the turn of the nineteenth to the twentieth century in northern Germany and found its continuation in southern Germany.

The Liebenzell Mission

In 1899, after some preliminaries in Kiel, the then so-called German branch of the China Inland Mission took up its work. This mission organization had been founded by the English missionary James Hudson Taylor (1832–1905). Its first German director was Heinrich Coerper (1863–1936), a theologian, who had previously served in various State Church parishes, among others in Heidelberg, Essen, and Strassburg. Soon after its beginnings in Hamburg, the work found a new home in Bad Lieben-zell, a town in the Black Forest, in 1903. It was called the Liebenzell Mission from 1906 onwards.

Rev. Heinrich Coerper placed the cross and resurrection of Jesus Christ firmly in the center of his theology. His preaching, influenced by Pietism, strongly emphasized personal conversion and sanctification. These gave direction to the intensive and extensive evangelistic and mis-sionary activities around Bad Liebenzell and further afield, emanating above all from the newly established seminary, its teachers and students. Meetings were held in the villages and towns of southern Germany wher-ever possible, also in private homes, often even in restaurants.

In many places this generated the momentum for people to assemble in so-called *Gemeinschaften*[2], since they wanted to be "serious (or decid-ed) Christians" as they considered themselves. These Fellowships met for an hour on Sunday afternoons or evenings; and soon this kind of meeting was commonly known as a *Stunde*[3], in the Swabian dialect, a *Schdond*, whereas the regular attendants of these meetings were called *Stundenleu-te*[4]. Fellowships like these developed over the decades in large areas of

---

[1] Pietism is a movement that originated in the Lutheran Church in Germany in the 17th century, stressing personal piety over religious formality and orthodoxy.

[2] A *Gemeinschaft* is, literally, a fellowship. In the context of German church life a *Gemeinschaft* is traditionally understood to mean a fellowship group that has its own meetings apart from normal State Church services.

[3] German for "hour".

[4] lit. hour-people.

southern Germany, organized by districts and supervised by preachers who had graduated from the Seminary of the Liebenzell Mission.

As early as before the end of World War I (in around 1917) the "Liebenzeller," as they were called, also came to Mühlhausen. They had been invited by a man named Gommel, a carpenter by trade. Like Wilhelm Kärcher, he too came from Mühlhausen. In the village of Möttlingen, close to Bad Liebenzell, he had "come to faith". In Pietistic parlance this meant that, at a particular time, he had made a conscious decision to live as a Christian.

Most notably, there was a certain seminary instructor who came to Mühlhausen frequently and had a lasting impact on the local Liebenzell Fellowship in its initial stages. This was Wilhelm Heinsen (1879–1959). As of 1912, he taught at the Seminary of the Liebenzell Mission and then became the first superintendent of the Association of Liebenzell Fellowships in 1933.

The Fellowship met in the living room of the Gommel family in a street called *Gässle*[5]. As more and more people attended these meetings, the room had to be enlarged several times by successively knocking down a wall and relocating it. In the end, a hall with steel girders (telescope jacks) had come into being, in which a coal-burning stove gave off a bit of warmth, causing occasional fits of coughing because of its long and loose-fitting pipes.

A person became a Christian by being converted. "To give your heart to the Savior," or "to get a pure heart," meant to become aware of one's guilt before God, to receive forgiveness, and to yield one's life to Jesus Christ and his guidance. Out of this, and with God's help, a change of heart and mind and moral conduct was the expected outcome; that is what people recognized as the most important event in their personal biography. As a consequence, the *Stundenleute* cleaned up their lives and their interpersonal relationships before God.

This social environment was to be of greatest significance for the childhood, youth, and the later life of the missionary Wilhelm Friedrich Kärcher.

The Kärcher Family

His mother, Karolina Kärcher, whom everybody just called Lina, was one of those who had put their lives in order before God and the congregation and who regularly attended the meetings in the *Gässle*. This was

---

[5] Swabian for "little alley".

not the only thing where she served as an example to her family. Her husband, Franz Kärcher, Wilhelm's father, attended the meetings but was somewhat reticent and diplomatic in the public expression of his Christianity: he felt obligated to the life and welfare of the whole village, he held various public offices, and he didn't want to make any enemies.

Wilhelm Heinsen, the aforementioned instructor at the Liebenzell Mission seminary, also used to visit the Kärcher family home. His personality, his upstanding character, his general knowledge, and his preaching must have made a considerable impact on the adolescent Wilhelm; but not only on him. In Mühlhausen, people were amazed that at every visit Wilhelm Heinsen evidently managed to greet almost all those of the Fellowship by name. To the question of how he could possibly keep remembering all the different names of those he had befriended, he had a surprisingly simple answer: One only needed to pray for people.

Wilhelm Heinsen's expositions of Old Testament texts had a special forcefulness to them. When he talked about the Tabernacle, people could listen for hours without losing interest.

August Reichardt (1853–1936) was the local State Church pastor at the time[6]. This *Pfarrer* also exerted a lasting influence on Wilhelm during his term in office. As an example of this influence, Wilhelm liked to quote later in his life a sentence that he had learned in confirmation class: "Faith is the trembling hand of the sinner put into the outstretched hand of the Savior." As a confirmand, Wilhelm had thought a long time about what this statement could mean, but couldn't understand it. Years later an event showed him its meaning. From the deck of ship in a storm, he saw a little boat being tossed up and down alongside. The people in the boat had trouble keeping their balance and were stretching their arms up in desperation, hoping to be grasped from above. At last, the ship's crew managed to haul them on board. The seamen leaned far out over the railing until the little boat rose up again, and then they gripped the people firmly by the arms. The little boat plummeted below them; but the people were now safe and secure. This made Wilhelm convinced that one had to

---

[6] The German constitution prescribes the separation of state and church; but the German State Churches form the historically established national church, comprised of the Protestant Lutheran or Reformed (or both of these united), or the Roman Catholic Churches; hence there is a distinction in the term "pastor," German: "Pfarrer" (lit. one who has, or is entitled to, a parish; title: Rev.) denoting pastors of state churches, and "Pastor" being used for leaders of non-state churches (although in northern Germany "Pastor" may be used for both).

stretch out one's arms and hands in faith, even in one's wavering faith, desiring nevertheless to be caught hold of; then the Redeemer and Savior would also powerfully and reliably take hold of one.

The Kärcher family was well-known and respected in the village. They were regarded as long established and thus a part of the traditional village fellowship over the centuries. Historically, their forefathers can first be found in Ludwigsburg. A certain Johann Andreas Karcher – not yet spelled Kärcher – lived there during the first half of the eighteenth century. However, his forefathers must have settled in Ludwigsburg long before that, since there are mentions of them, spanning several generations, in relevant local historical documents. This Johann Andreas Karcher is described as being an *Obermeister*[7], a term that no longer has an equivalent these days. He died in Markgröningen, a small town quite close to Ludwigsburg.

In 1769, his son Alexander Karcher, born in 1748, married Ursula Catharina Kientsch, whose father was a wine grower in Nussdorf. Alexander officiated as a legal clerk, which is possibly why he moved to Mühlhausen. This happened in the era when Mühlhausen came under the rule of the state of Württemberg. In his new hometown Alexander Karcher was also known as *Lammwirt*[8] and as *Beck*[9]. He died in 1816. The history of the Kärcher family in Mühlhausen begins with him.

Alexander and his wife Ursula had twelve children; the youngest, Johann Jacob, was born in 1794. Historical sources call him a "citizen" and a "baker." His son Christoph Friderich, born in 1819, did not call himself Karcher any longer but Kärcher; he was a *Gemeindepfleger*[10] and married to Friederike, née Bürle. Their second child, Jakob Friedrich, born in 1847, married Rosina Scheuhing, whose family had long been settled in Mühlhausen. On May 19, 1878, they had a son whom they called Franz Georg. The biography of Wilhelm and his family begins here, because this Franz Georg Kärcher was to be his father.

Franz Georg Kärcher (1878–1944) was a farmer and, as such, a reputable citizen of Mühlhausen. He was a member of the town council and on the board of local interest groups like "the Insurance Company" and "the Tobacco Company." He was known as a dutiful and straightforward man. In his younger years he used to work in the woods during the win-

---

[7] lit. an "overmaster" or someone "senior to a master".

[8] Owner of the "Lamb" inn.

[9] Swabian for "baker".

[10] Community administrator.

ter, together with other farmers, felling trees for the sawmill and for fire-wood.

Their route to and from work occasionally led them past the railroad gatekeeper's hut, which stood roughly two miles (c. 3 km) away from the village in the communal forest of Mühlhausen, right next to the "oak by the lake." One of the many village families called Müller lived there; they were called the "Railroad Müllers" for easier identification, a simple practice, widely used in many Swabian communities in the past, and occasionally even nowadays.

An intelligent young woman worked in this family as a domestic help. She was regarded as a beauty, and it was said of her that she talked "like a book." Her life story, even thus far, showed unusual features and, for Mühlhausen, perhaps even ones that took some getting used to.

Karolina Katherina Dieffenbach, as this young lady was called, did not come from Mühlhausen but from Nordenstadt near Mainz, where she was born on November 6, 1879, and where she spent her childhood and youth. For that reason she did not speak perfect Swabian, a flaw that those at home in the dialect only overlooked with reluctance, as they still do occasionally today.

When Lina (as her family and acquaintances called her) was six years old, her father died. This event not only decisively affected her childhood but also her future as a young woman. Families lacking a man as "head of the household" (as it was then called) to represent the family legally and in public, did not have an easy time. Women without a father or husband had a low status in society and were at the mercy of their superiors much more starkly than one could imagine nowadays.

After graduating from school, Lina started a job as a typist at the town hall in a village near Nordenstadt. One day it became obvious that, though she was not married, she was pregnant (aged just twenty). The father of her child was no less a person than the mayor in whose office she worked. For a woman in those days the shame attaching to an illegitimate pregnancy, and the consequences which in most cases a woman had to shoulder alone, had dramatic consequences. Lina saw the need to leave her hometown. Her little son, who was named Heinrich, remained behind in the care of her sister. Nothing was heard again of the father, nor was anything more said about him.

So Lina ended up in a railroad gatekeeper's house in Swabia, in an unfamiliar environment. This at first must have been very lonely for the young woman to whom fate had dealt such a bitter blow. Three more years were to pass before her life resumed a direction she actually desired.

The woodcutter Franz Georg Kärcher, who was somehow related to the "Railroad Müllers," was not unaware of Karolina Dieffenbach; their paths crossed from time to time on his way to work. Small wonder, then, that he started to get interested in her.

The next stage of this appealing love story reveals Franz Georg Kärcher considering the whole matter carefully. He wanted to be sure of what he was to do. First of all, he wanted to find out about this young woman's home background. Together with his friend he drove to Nordenstadt. What they were able to discover about the Dieffenbach family greatly impressed them both: a large farmstead, with two horses besides! The like was presumed only to be found at the country estate in Mühlhausen: ordinary farmers pulled their wagons with cows or oxen. Franz Georg was convinced that this family were "sound folk." He decided "to get serious" about Lina.

They were married in 1904 and then lived in a semi-detached house that Franz Georg Kärcher had already bought in the *Alten Steige*[11], one of several dwellings that had been built in the seventeenth century by the local lord of the manor.

Shortly after the wedding something happened that at the time was of great significance in Mühlhausen in raising the status of a fellow citizen, and thus also for the reputation of Karolina Kärcher: a railroad car arrived at the Illingen station, transporting the complete furnishings for a house, for a living room, bedroom, and kitchen. The Mühlhausener villagers were impressed – this Lina had brought "household effects" into the marriage! Now she was finally accepted; not only that – from now on people greeted her with respect.

Franz Georg Kärcher and his wife had five children together: four sons and one daughter. Including Heinrich, for whom Lina had had to leave her hometown, there were six children growing up in the family.

Heinrich, "born aside" (as "out of wedlock" was called) in 1899 in Mainz, was brought from Nordenstadt to Mühlhausen, was then adopted by Franz Georg Kärcher, and later earned his livelihood working primarily in brickyards.

Franz, born in 1904, was later to take over the farmstead from his parents. He had an appropriate education at the so-called "Winter School" in Vaihingen/Enz, and because of this worked from time to time on other farms. Physically he was quite different from his sturdily built half-brother Heinrich. One day, when both of them applied for a job, Franz

---

[11] lit. Old Uphill Road.

was rejected with the remark that he should go home and eat some more *Spaetzle*. These noodles made from flour are considered by Swabians a kind of national dish and, far more importantly, a source of energy when eaten in large amounts.

Wilhelm Friedrich Kärcher's birthplace in Mühlhausen/Enz

Wilhelm Friedrich Kärcher, or simply Wilhelm, was born on January 27, 1907, in Mühlhausen. He got his name from the fact that he was born on the same day as Wilhelm II, the German Emperor at the time.

In 1909, the fourth son Karl was born. He later became a shoemaker.

Two years later, in 1911, a sister by the name of Frieda joined the four brothers. With so many older brothers she as a girl could have reckoned on having an impressive squad of protectors. But to her that was indeed only partly true: she sometimes regarded the preponderance of boys in the family as an imposition. Later, she complained about always having "to clean up after her brothers," as she called it. Franz is said to have retorted with the comment that this was, after all, the reason they had "taken her in" as their sister.

The brothers had to take turns as children to watch over their little sister. They did not really like doing this. Occasionally, they thought up the most outrageous ideas. One day they put little Frieda in a cart and hitched a goat to it. The frightened animal, not used to pulling a cart, got panicky, darted off with the unfamiliar vehicle and landed, together with the little girl, in a manure pile.

Such scenarios sometimes caused their mother to wish her sons would "go to where the pepper grows"[12].

Later on, Frieda went "into service," as was the rule with young women at the time. Initially, she worked for the owners of the house and estate and after that for a family in Stuttgart, where she learned home economics. One of her greatest desires, to learn to play the piano, was never fulfilled. It would have been beyond the family's financial means.

In 1920, i.e. all of nine years after Frieda, Ernst came along as a sort of afterthought. He stayed at the parental home until he was conscripted as a soldier in World War II.

In the Kärcher family things were always lively. Their daily work was rarely better than hard; but despite that, they often played musical instruments and, even more frequently, sang together, mostly accompanied by mouth organ and guitar. The children were regarded by the neighbors as open-minded, happy, and humorous; in short, as pleasant young people who got along fine with everybody and who could be depended upon. Their mother's difficult past was no longer significant.

The Kärcher Family (left to right): Karl, Wilhelm, Lina, Heinrich (added later), Frieda, Franz Georg, Franz; Ernst is missing from the picture

---

[12] meaning something like "would keep out of sight!"

Lina Kärcher always kept in touch with her family in Nordenstadt. During her visits she was usually accompanied by one of her children. Her nieces and nephews likewise loved visiting Mühlhausen in the difficult years after World War I even for an extended period, since the Nordenstadt folk were not as well off as those in Mühlhausen. The nieces and nephews had a good relationship with each other.

Franz Georg Kärcher, the father, and Heinrich (who was approaching twenty towards the end of the War), had both experienced World War I as soldiers. They returned to Mühlhausen safe and sound.

Wilhelm Friedrich Kärcher's Early Years Around His Hometown

Wilhelm attended community school in Mühlhausen and, towards the end of his school time, confirmation classes. He was given Psalm 34:8 as his confirmation verse: "Taste and see that the Lord is good; blessed is the man who takes refuge in him;" in addition, two lines from a hymn by Georg Neumark (1621–1681): "He who trusts in God's strong hand, will not have built his life on sand."

The day of his confirmation – he confided years later at his commissioning service in Bad Liebenzell – did not leave any big impression on him. Only later did he become aware that the call to follow Jesus had been meant for him personally, Wilhelm Friedrich Kärcher.

On the other hand Wilhelm himself recounted in later years that the issue of his life's direction and goal had been on his mind from an early age. It was the first question in the catechism he had to learn as part of his confirmation knowledge: "What is to be man's chief care in life? Answer: That he may have certain hope of eternal life. As Christ (Matthew 6:33) says: 'But seek first [God's] kingdom and his righteousness, and all these things will be given to you as well.'"

This question worried him at times rather deeply; thus, for example, when one of his fellow students in the confirmation classes succumbed to pneumonia and died. For the rest of his life he remembered seeing Oskar lying dead in his coffin, and the question would come to mind forcefully: "What is to be man's chief care in life?"

Quite how much he struggled to find an answer to this question, not only for his own life, but also for the appropriate wider consequences, is shown by his emotions during a folk festival in the neighboring village of Rosswag. After the catechism classes, which the newly confirmed young people still had to attend a while longer on Sunday afternoons, the adventurous among them longed for some "action."

One day the opportunity for such action arose in Rosswag; Wilhelm remembers the swing boat, music, people, and hullabaloo. He told his mother that he wanted to go. She was just getting ready to go to the *Stunde* at the Liebenzell Fellowship. She didn't say anything. But her son had the definite feeling that she prayed for him at that moment.

He was aware of the fact that the people meeting at the Fellowship cherished that "certain hope of eternal life" that was so often talked about during confirmation classes. And when he found himself at the folk festival, he couldn't rid himself of the question: What would happen if Jesus returned that very moment, as taught by the confession of faith? The thought that neither his friends nor he himself might not be allowed to go with Him, really depressed Wilhelm.

Certainly, in later years, Wilhelm was not of the view that Christians had no right to seek pleasure nor to enjoy life, nor that they were out of place at such festivals. He never felt even remotely beholden during his lifetime to the warped ideal of the grief-stricken seeker after God. Just then, however, it was clear to him in Rosswag that he should actually be at the Fellowship in Mühlhausen, alongside his mother. He knew that this was what she really wanted. An hour later, to his mother's surprise, he was back home again.

He remembered from the days of his catechism classes his pastor telling a story about a baker. The baker had become very ill and lay dying. On and off, as he sank into delirium, he talked about some "brick flour," which his wife just couldn't understand. One day, when her husband had regained consciousness, she mentioned it to him. He told her that at one period in his life he had also sold saffron. In order to bulk up the spice he used to grind old bricks to a fine dust and mix it with the saffron he was selling. Now faced with death, he felt enormous guilt at having deceived his customers.

One day – it was about one year after Wilhelm's confirmation – an evangelistic campaign was being held at the schoolhouse. The speaker was the aforementioned Liebenzell Seminary instructor Wilhelm Heinsen. When he challenged his listeners to clean up their lives with God, fourteen-year old Wilhelm went to him to talk about his life's problem. He recounted this himself as follows:

"After the First World War, Herr Heinsen used to hold many blessed evangelistic campaigns here and there. He attached great importance in counseling to talking things through. As a boy I also was spoken to directly by his preaching and went to see him in his room. After confessing my sins, he took his well-worn Bible and opened it at several places in

the Old and New Testaments; for example at 1 John 1:9, 'If we confess
our sins, he is faithful and just and will forgive us our sins and purify us
from all unrighteousness.' Or Micah 7:19, 'You will ... hurl all our iniq-
uities into the depths of the sea.'

"Herr Heinsen then asked me, whether I still knew from school how
deep the ocean was at its deepest place. 'Nine thousand meters or more,' I
replied. Heinsen answered, 'Okay, and now I ask you: Who would go
down there to bring up your sins again, if God has hurled them into such
a depth?' I considered it a bit and said, 'I don't think anybody would.' –
'Can you believe that now?' I didn't have the courage to say yes. He repeated the question. Finally, as I saw the open Bible in his hand, I answered, 'I believe, because the Bible says so.' Pointing to the Bible, like
a schoolmaster wanting to instill something in his student, he said very
urgently, 'Always believe what is written in the Bible, the Word of God!'
Then we knelt down and prayed. When we got up, I was assured of my
salvation" (Pagel, 1989:127).

The fact that the Fellowship met at times other than for the Sunday
church services, did not particularly make others sympathetic to their
cause, but made them somehow suspicious: "They are just pretending to
be something better," they said.

There were various ways of getting to the meeting place in the *Gässle*,
but there were also places where everybody had to pass by. At these, on
the way to the *Stunde*, one would be open to special scrutiny. Curiosity
hid behind window curtains, and everybody in the village knew who was
going to the *Stunde* and how regularly they did. Sometimes open hostility
was expressed by those who were not well disposed to the *Stundenleute*
for other reasons. They were ostracized, and the younger villagers especially would often excel in disgraceful behavior: they would lie in wait
for some of their peers and rough them up. Nowadays, this would be
called mobbing or bullying. Secretly, however, many villagers respected
the "pious ones," as they were called. Their integrity was well known and
appreciated, even if people constantly put them to the test.

Wilhelm's joy about "the new life" that he had just embarked upon
did not remain unclouded. There were his friends Karl, Paul, Gustav and
Gottlob. He always met them on Sundays and they were usually "up to
something," as people would say a bit euphemistically.

At first, they were simply indulging in boyish pranks that sprang from
their longing for new experiences. In the Mühlhausen of that time there
wasn't much going on to amuse children. After confirmation, things were
a bit different. The young fellows felt more grown up. The outward sign

of this were the long pants they were allowed to wear for the first time at confirmation.

Once in a while it so happened that the five friends were quite illegally picking strawberries in someone else's garden. They started smoking. One of them even stole his father's cigars for this purpose. It was very clear to Wilhelm that he just could not participate in such activities any longer, not merely because he and his friends felt so nauseated after smoking the cigars that they couldn't help vomiting, but because in no way did he want to jeopardize or lose the assurance of salvation he had gained. His decision to stand up to his friends was a hard one, and they promptly attacked him. The Sunday whistle-blast, which used to signal their readiness for joint adventures, ceased abruptly from then on. He had lost them as friends.

But he won others, including his mother and his older brother. The fact that in those days there was no distinctive Christian youth work, where one could take part in age-appropriate activities, did not make it easy for him. The Fellowship services mostly involved much older people, and the Bible messages were about topics that were not relevant, or not yet relevant, for the life issues that children and young people were encountering as they grew up. Yet, here too, there were a few young people who had the same interests as Wilhelm. They managed to meet five times a week for various occasions, including two choir rehearsals, one a mixed and one a male choir.

After graduating from his seven-year general school education, Wilhelm went for a year to a "college of further education," as it was called, and started his apprenticeship as a carpenter with the Dietrich Company in Mühlacker in 1921. At the same time he attended a vocational school.

He thought of his professional training as something special. After school, others had to start earning money right away, simply as unskilled laborers at the brickyard in Mühlacker. But along with this apprenticeship, a personally difficult period in his life started.

His master carpenter was an "unbeliever," as he called it, i.e. he was not at all a Christian, as Wilhelm understood it. It was similar with his work colleagues and their way of talking about matters of faith and being a Christian.

External circumstances in his new working life posed another difficulty. In the morning he had to walk for an hour to get to his job. Then came eight and sometimes ten hours of work. Construction cranes were still unknown. The carpenters had to heave the beams up the building on their shoulders. And when the work stopped, the dead-tired apprentice still had a one-hour walk home. In spite of this, he seldom missed a meeting of the Fellowship.

That the apprentice wanted to be different in his person and life from his colleagues, was not only quickly noticed by them, but it blatantly incited them to "pay him back." And the mobbing came rather swiftly.

In later years, Wilhelm used to comment that such things are part of Christian discipleship; scorn and derision of this kind must be endured. Such behavior, however, must have been specific to Germany, because it was not usually the case on the South Sea Islands or in America that Christians who took their faith seriously would be vilified by those who also called themselves Christian, but who limited their Christianity to paying church taxes[13].

For himself, he saw that the solution to the problem lay in proving that he was not a slacker, neither when it came to enduring insults nor in his willingness to work hard. And work hard he did. After the lunch break he was, of course, the first to get back to his job, and usually the last to leave. His first report card from the vocational school contained testimony of approval, the second conveyed praise, and the third year brought him a prize of a book worth twenty Reich marks[14], an incredible award for an apprentice in those years. His master couldn't help but acknowledge this achievement. As each year of his apprenticeship passed by, Wilhelm was taken more seriously, and in time the insults, discrimination, and teasing grew less and less.

This willingness to achieve, so evident in Wilhelm's first years of his working life, was sustained throughout his whole later life, and it determined his ministry as a missionary.

After his apprenticeship as a carpenter, Wilhelm took up a new job in Bietigheim. He commuted there daily by train from Illingen. This meant a walk to the station of two and a half miles (4 km) every morning, and back again in the evening. As unusual as it may sound, compared with others, he was much better off. Many from Mühlhausen, who worked in Pforzheim, regularly covered a total distance to work of almost 10 miles (15 km) on foot every morning, and in the evening they had to walk the whole way back again. On top of this, they often had to help with farm chores in the evening. So did Wilhelm: He fed the cattle and cleaned out the stable, and all of this was taken for granted.

---

[13] as is done in Germany.

[14] German currency between 1924 and 1948; 20 RM at that time were roughly $80 at today's value.

Wilhelm Friedrich Kärcher as journeyman carpenter

One day in Bietigheim he was busy constructing a roof truss, when he noticed a man in dark clothing, with a briefcase under his arm, who passed by the construction site every day. Wilhelm inquired about him and learned that this was the preacher at the local Fellowship. The young carpenter was not very impressed with him, least of all with his activity as a preacher. Wilhelm just couldn't see any "useful" work in that.

His life as a young adult was determined and overshadowed by the economic and political confusion during the recession of the Weimar Republic[15]. Nevertheless, he considered himself a fully-fledged Mühlhausener, meaning he felt himself tied into the social structures of the village, from which one could only escape by leaving forever. Young people who dared to break out without leaving were inevitably suspected of wanting to be something better than others.

The village community was firmly integrated into the communal life and suffering. That had its advantages. No one who had fallen on hard times through no fault of his own had to deal with it alone. On the other

---

[15] Name of the German republic from 1919–1933, proclaimed in the city of Weimar.

hand, such individuals might see their freedom considerably curtailed. Being, or wanting to be, different had repercussions. Whatever was not in harmony with the thinking pattern of the village community was simply not tolerated. Everyone knew each other; anything exceptional was aired publicly, to say the least. People were afraid of this. To become the talk of the village was an unbearable thought. The most important consideration regarding one's own behavior in public concerned the question of what "people" would say. This kind of social control determined an individual's life to quite an extent.

In retrospect, though, one also gets the impression that life in Mühl-hausen during the first half of the twentieth century was characterized by quiet contemplation. Modern means of communication were still non-existent. Whatever happened or was arranged officially was not shared with the villagers in written form by a community bulletin, but by word of mouth. It used to be "rung out." This was done by the town crier, a man who would walk through the streets once a week, wearing a uniform cap and ringing a bell. He would stop at the crossroads and shout out the news to the people. Whenever he rang his bell all the windows in hearing range would open. Those who were not able to hear the information clearly, would ask their neighbors.

If someone fell ill, the whole village knew about it, asking concerned questions about the patient's well-being. Deaths were mourned by the whole village community, and funerals were attended by whoever could come, and there were always many.

The same was true, of course, of weddings. If an engagement was in the offing, all family relationships were traced back as far as possible in order to ascertain whether the two were really suited for each other. On the wedding day, the bridal couple, relatives, and all the wedding guests formed a sort of procession, going from the bride's house to the church. The Mühlhauseners stood on the side of the road like an honor guard. Schoolmates and friends of the wedding pair called out happy sayings to them. The white wedding dress and veil stood for the "purity" of the young woman. This was strictly observed. It sometimes happened, in the case of a bride whose lifestyle did not correspond to this ideal, that enraged Mühlhausener women would rip the veil off her head right in front of the church.

Whatever else, ethics and moral convictions were strongly influenced by the church. That is also why the custom of attending the Sunday service was taken for granted.

Just like in all rural communities in those days, the mentality of the Mühlhausen folk was determined by a corporate identity. It was "us against them" – "them" being the people from neighboring villages like Rosswag or Lomersheim. They were considered to be different, think differently, and talk differently. They were strangers or at least "non-Mühlhäusers," from whom one could not easily expect anything as good as that from one's own people.

It was this exact same mentality that characterized the societies in the South Sea islands. What could have better prepared the later missionary Wilhelm Friedrich Kärcher for his eminently successful ministry among the islanders of Chuuk than to grow up in a village like Mühlhausen? After all, his character and personality had been formed in the mindset of this social environment. All his life he freely and in all modesty acknowledged that he hailed from the simple background of a farming village. He regarded his childhood and youth in Mühlhausen of great importance for his later work; it was a good preparatory schooling for the South Seas.

2

From Craftsman to Missionary
(1930–1936)

A Difficult Decision

Let us remind ourselves: Wilhelm Kärcher, when he was a carpenter on a construction site in Bietigheim, had not really liked that preacher dressed in black whom he had observed occasionally from the roof truss. So he didn't see in him anything special to emulate for his own future. At some time his attitude must have changed.

As a carpenter he did not only work to earn money. "I liked my trade so much, so much!" he used to say. For six years he remained as journeyman with his firm. During the first four years he must have been sure that the carpentry was his calling in life. But after that, a change took place in his thinking.

This development began at a meeting on the "Mission Hill" in Bad Liebenzell in which he took part. One of the speakers had been speaking about the Great Commission of Jesus Christ in Matthew 28:18–20 and had challenged those in the audience who felt that this applied to them to raise their hand. Our young carpenter was not ready to do this. But apparently he started at that moment to consider whether God had perhaps different plans for him than a life as a carpenter. From then on, the question whether he should become a missionary seems to have been constantly on his mind, and he found it hard to come to a decision.

He struggled in his heart and tried to solve the problem by talking himself into believing that it would be enough for him to give his tithe regularly for the work of the Liebenzell Mission. But he couldn't come to terms with himself about it.

The struggle lasted for two years. In order to finally find peace he decided to take one first step. He contacted the Liebenzell Mission in writing.

The letter he received from the leadership of the Mission in reply confirmed his opinion that he had now done what he could and would surely be able to let the matter rest. In fact, the leaders had informed him that he could not be accepted at the present time. Nevertheless, they wrote, he should apply again the next year.

The way things had gone led him to the conclusion that he didn't have to be concerned anymore about solving the question of his future calling as a missionary. He wanted to see God's will behind the fact that he did not have to take the initiative in this situation again, but that others might feel bound to. In his case this proved to be correct. In later years, therefore, he strongly argued the point of view that in such a decision no one could simply tell a person what to do; God would have to work this out in people's lives and arrange their personal circumstances accordingly.

Indeed, without any effort on his part, a letter soon reached him, summoning him to present himself to the German Tent Mission on May 1, 1930. They were due to hold an evangelistic campaign in Bietigheim. In the fall he would then be able to enter the Seminary of the Liebenzell Mission.

At last, he was absolutely sure of things.

A Conversation with the Boss

With it, however, Wilhelm faced the situation of seeing through what had been started. He did this by giving his notice. When he disclosed to his master carpenter that he would be "going into mission work," the latter just guffawed: "Go on, you can't be serious!"

But after Wilhelm had made his boss understand that the decision to resign from his job was final, the master began to press him: "Kärcher, I have more experience than you do. I know that you will soon be fed up with that pious bunch!"

He even offered him the opportunity of returning in that case to his job: "If you find you've had enough, just come back to me!"

But Wilhelm stuck to his decision, collected his pay, and went. On October 21, 1930, he entered the Seminary of the Liebenzell Mission to begin his four-year training as a preacher and missionary. At the time he was twenty-three years old.

"The King Has Called Us!"

Later in his life he remembered an event in connection with his decision, one he had witnessed as a child at the beginning of World War I.

It was around midnight one day when he was standing at the station in Mühlacker watching the recruits getting on the train to go off to war. Little Wilhelm must have caught someone's attention because he was suddenly lifted up and handed through a window into a railcar. The young soldiers showed him their brand-new outfits. Outside, in the station, children and mothers stood in great apprehension, saying their tear-ful farewells to the soldiers leaving for the frontlines, giving them last words of advice and caution to help them on their way.

"Then there were shouts, and whistles blew. I was quickly shoved out of the window, and the train started to move out into the cold, dark night, accompanied by loud and joyful patriotic singing. So they went off in the certain knowledge: 'The king has called us.'"

These were the words Wilhelm used many years later from memory during an interview at the German Gospel Broadcasting Company (ERF) in Wetzlar, and he continued:

"After fighting hard battles for long months, a few of these soldiers came back on furlough, and many of them never returned. In the village there was always great joy on welcoming a soldier home; and how we young guys looked up to these soldiers! The days of furlough went by far too quickly. And then something happened that I thought was strange. When the soldiers went off to the front for the second time, they didn't sing with such enthusiasm as at first. I even got the impression that they found it really hard to go back to war. And yet, they went back again, well knowing what awaited them. Why did they not simply stay home? Why did they climb up the *Steige* again in Mühlhausen and look wistfully back at the village? — Because the king had called them!"

Wilhelm Kärcher felt exactly the same as the soldiers, after he had made up his mind to go to the Liebenzell Mission Center. But there was also a difference. The King, whose call to service he wanted to follow from now on, had not just said, "All authority in heaven and on earth has been given to me" (Matthew 28:18), but – as the prospective missionary stated – the King Himself would go with him.

And this is what Wilhelm Kärcher was to experience in his life time and again.

The Missionary as Carpenter and Handyman

There had been no difficulties with his application to the Mission. One important reason why he was accepted had to do with his profession. The Liebenzell Mission had just started to build a guesthouse, the so-called "Pilgrim's Rest." Construction workers were needed for that. In order to complete the building speedily it was necessary to curtail classes during the building period. Seminarians with special professional qualifications were sometimes even forced to miss classes on certain days because the Mission could not do without their expertise and their help.

In those days, it was almost taken for granted as part of the missionary image that a missionary would be skilled in a trade. For his later ministry it was, in most cases, absolutely vital that he could first build a house at his future place of work. Power tools, as we know them today, were non-existent. Given the conditions on the mission field, generators for electrical power were out of the question. Most of the work had to be done by hand.

Incidentally, the fact that missionaries were craftsmen gave rise to an interesting selection procedure. They came from a certain stratum of society. In the middle-class parental homes where they had grown up they had encountered specific moral values regarded as important, even today: a simple lifestyle, thriftiness, diligence, punctuality, self-discipline, goal setting, time scheduling, and several others. Since missionaries often came from Christian homes, matters like humility, self-denial, and modesty in sexual matters were altogether taken for granted by those wanting to be serious Christians. Moreover, as craftsmen they did not question the hierarchical structures commonly practiced in the workshops. They knew that the work would be accomplished effectively, just as they had experienced it during their apprenticeship and the first years of their career. The master craftsman was the boss, after him came the journeymen, and finally the "apprentice lads," as the trainees were called in those days.

Values and moral concepts are, by nature, deeply anchored in people's subconscious, and they significantly determine their behavior towards their fellowmen. So they also determine the missionaries' behavior towards people in foreign societies whose moral concepts often have a different situational focus and present in a totally different form.

With his background as a craftsman the missionary in the first half of the twentieth century was a representative of his own social stratum in Germany. This mindset had its justification, but it could also lead to tensions on the mission field because the person concerned was not conscious of it: he took it for granted that his own world of values was better and desirable for everybody to have. When these new and different values which he wanted to introduce into a strange society were at times accepted only hesitantly, he tended to perceive it as unusual. Or else he quite often scorned this rejection, interpreting it as a hardening of the heart on the part of the "natives" who, against better judgment, were just not willing to accept the missionary's values and orientate their lives accordingly. Much of what Wilhelm Kärcher thought, did, and wrote at the beginning of his activities in the South Seas was conditioned by just such an attitude, as we shall see.

On the other hand, on the mission field the missionary as craftsman was basically the one with the best education. No wonder, then, that he found himself in the role of the "boss" who would tell the "natives" what to do. In those days, that may certainly have been sensible behavior, for without this there would not have been any development in many cases, neither in the area of economics nor in that of religion; and the same was true of the South Seas.

Training at the Seminary of the Liebenzell Mission

After he had stowed away his few belongings in Bad Liebenzell and settled himself down, he felt deeply satisfied. He was very sure of having done the right thing. Two years of indecision and inner struggle over the question of his purpose in life had come to an end. He now found it easy to recognize the will of God in the new plan for his life.

At the same time he found his new circumstances to be very regimented. Life in the institute was so totally different from the freedom and independence he had previously enjoyed. In retrospect, he therefore called the years until 1934 "a kind of storm-and-stress period."

Deficits

The training program for future missionaries at that time was essentially limited to acquiring a thorough knowledge of the Bible and an aptitude for preparing and preaching sermons. A knowledge of ethnology, cultural anthropology, and general linguistics was not considered necessary for working on the mission field.

"Total commitment to the Lord, humility, and obedience" were considered to be paramount. The Liebenzell Mission leaders – as was the case with other missionary organizations – were convinced that South Sea missionaries primarily needed to possess practical skills in building houses, churches, and in handling boats.

For this reason, important basic information, which would have enhanced their work significantly – and which was even available in scientific publications at that time – were unknown to future South Sea missionaries. Thus, for example, nobody was acquainted with the standard works on "Mana" and "Tabu" (taboo) that Friedrich Rudolf Lehmann had published (1922, 1930). These two concepts determined religions in Oceania – and they still do today. To the extent that a missionary who thinks within his or her European-Western mindset and lacks familiarity with them is neither able to understand South Sea islanders and their animistically oriented frame of mind nor able to proclaim the message of Christ in an understandable way.

Wilhelm Kärcher, too, was to get acquainted with this issue and many other altogether differently focused mental pictures of the people on his future mission field; yet that not until he finally arrived there, and then rather by chance than systematically. Other deficiencies he had to grapple with will be mentioned later in this book.

Internship in Southern Baden

After finishing his training at the seminary, he came to Emmendingen, a small town close to Freiburg im Breisgau, for a practical trial period of two years. This practical training of graduates in a Fellowship circuit was in those days called "probationary service"[16].

Reflecting later in his life on his economic situation at that time, and making comparisons, he spoke about people's poverty, and the poverty of mission organizations. Nobody owned a car. After four years of training, his income was barely 25 Reich marks a month, that is 85 pfennigs per day[17].

At that time, his poverty represented a certain challenge to him, as he freely admitted. Had he worked in his trade as a carpenter, he would have received a downright princely salary by comparison. Yet he did not regret it. He sensed that God had enriched his life and for that he was glad. Much later, he gave material proof of this to someone who interviewed him; he told that person, "There is an Audi outside, and it belongs to me!"

The South Seas as His Future Field of Service

On September 6, 1936, Wilhelm Kärcher was ordained at the Fall MissionFest in Bad Liebenzell and commissioned as missionary to Chuuk, a group of islands in the Micronesian Carolines.

As the text for his address he had chosen Psalm 34:8: "Taste and see that the Lord is good; blessed is the man who takes refuge in him." That had been his confirmation verse. To this he added the significant lines from poet Georg Neumark's (1621–1681) hymn *Wer nur den lieben Gott lässt walten*: "Who trusts in God's almighty hand, will not have built his life on sand."

The day of his confirmation, as he said in his message, had not left any special impression on him. Only later had he become aware that Je-

---

[16] German: *Probedienst.*
[17] Roughly $3.40 a day at today's value.

sus' command to "come and follow me" really had been meant for him personally, even then. He expressed it as follows: "On the basis of God's Word I have gained assurance of salvation to this day, and in the rock of Jesus Christ I was able to anchor my life as a young person." He had made this statement apparently with great emphasis. In the summary of his message, which can be found in "China's Millions" – the news bulletin of the Liebenzell Mission in those days – it is printed in bold.

For him as a carpenter it was certainly clear what was meant by sand and building on it. A little later, on the sandy islands of Micronesia, his future place of work, he was able to actually see it with his own eyes.

But what it means to taste and see how good the Lord is, and to also understand it as a blessing to take refuge in Him – or, as it says in German, to trust in Him – that was to become a severe test, a nightmare, which would be difficult to endure for Wilhelm Kärcher and his family a few years later, requiring unimaginable stamina on their part.

A Strange Encounter

In the course of the convention when the young missionary was being consecrated to the ministry, something strange happened; and after his arrival on Chuuk a few months later it was even to have some kind of sequel.

Together with him on the podium was Sr. Elise Zuber (1876–1945). She had already worked on Chuuk for a number of years and was being sent out again for another term of service.

Apparently, Elise Zuber was firmly convinced that another missionary on Chuuk would be totally superfluous; and she shared this opinion expressly with Rev. Ernst Buddeberg, the mission director at that time. She definitely wanted nothing to do with Wilhelm Kärcher. In any case, she did not say a single word to him. Was she so sure that he would not come to Chuuk, after all? But, as so often, things would work out very differently. It was only a short time later that the two would meet again – under totally changed circumstances!

An Existential Question

One of the big problems for the future missionary was the question of finding the right spouse. Wilhelm Kärcher, the seminarian, abided by the strict rule that he would not have any relationship with a woman before graduation. But now this had to happen rather quickly because the time was short. He was to be sent out in the coming year. He had barely four months left for his search.

In those days, people were still of the opinion that such an issue could hardly be left to the decision of a young man on his own. To find "the right one" required the counsel of men with relevant experience and insight. They were not just given the right to have a voice in such an important matter but also an obligation. Such men were indeed to be found in the leadership of the Mission. They had, in fact, already looked around and had laid their eyes on a young lady whom they deemed to be a suitable future Mrs. Kärcher.

It is hardly surprising to learn that, at this point in time, Wilhelm too had not been idle and had met a young woman whom he could envisage becoming his wife. What he didn't know as yet was the fact that it was exactly the same young woman that the mission leaders had favored for him.

3

Elisabeth Wagner

Home Background, Childhood, and Youth

Elisabeth Wagner was born on November 22, 1912, in Immenstadt/Allgäu, as the first child of the master baker Michael Wagner (1879–1960) and his wife Marie (1883–1969). Her parents' home was in Waltenhofen, a village southwest of Kempten on the western slopes of the Iller valley. Her parents owned an inn with a bakery. Elisabeth, who was musical and interested in music, occasionally entertained the guests in her free time by playing the piano.

Concerning her childhood and youth in her beloved Allgäu mountains she sometimes wrote that they had been happy times, under the care of loving parents who wanted her best, in the company of her three brothers: Fritz, born on November 23, 1910; Ernst, born on May 2, 1914; and Karl, born on December 28, 1916.

Karl, Ernst, Elisabeth and Fritz Wagner

She finished her schooling on March 29, 1928, having attended secondary school at St. Maria Stern Junior High Girls' School in Immen-
stadt. Her graduation diploma – which names her Elise Wagner – depicts
her as a good student (showing grades such as "excellent diligence and
excellent behavior; religious instruction and physical education excellent;
singing commendable, etc.").

Away from Home

Immediately afterwards, the sixteen-year old went to Berlin. Here she
lived at first with her aunt Elise Grentz ("aunt Lies"), whose husband
Ernst ran a trucking company in Wrangelstrasse, no. 84. Elisabeth
worked in the office.

In April 1931 we find that she had "taken a position," as it was called
in those days. This was in a well-to-do upper-class family of the time
("Reichsbankdirektor[18] E. Bulling, Am Hirschsprung no. 12") in Berlin-
Dahlem, where she worked as housekeeper until 1936.

Soon after her arrival in Berlin Elisabeth had joined a Christian girls'
group. To be sure, her aunt was a bit astonished that her niece had given
up her previous interests within such a short time and was now focused
on her newfound friends. But she did not object.

In the diary that she began on August 30, 1936, in Waltenhofen, Elisabeth called the group her "Klub"[19], meant as an acronym. The word is
made up of the initial letters of the invitation "Komm, lass uns beten"
(come, let us pray). During the first half of the thirties, she apparently
came to a deliberate decision in this "Klub" to live for Christ, and its
members were to accompany her even further in life, even though in a
more distant way.

As can be seen from this diary, by 1929 she had already thought about
entering Christian ministry, given that she had developed an interest in
foreign missions. But for several years she could not bring herself to take
any decisive step in this direction with full conviction.

An Important Decision

At the beginning of the thirties, Elisabeth Wagner had attended a
meeting addressed by Hedwig von Redern (1866–1935), the co-founder
of the German Women's Missionary Prayer League (*Deutscher Frau-*

---

[18] Director of the National Bank of the Reich.
[19] German for "club".

enmissionsgebetsbund – DFMGB). During this "Missionary Sunday," as she called it in her diary, she knew for certain that she should be a missionary.

Initially, her parents did not grant their consent. She understood their negative attitude; after all, she was their only daughter. So she would be patient. That meant five years of waiting. But during this time, her inner ear again and again heard the words from Isaiah 66:19 permeating her thoughts, "I will … send some of those who are saved to the nations … and to the distant islands that have not heard of my fame or seen my glory. They will proclaim my glory among the nations."

What is impressive and, at the same time, remarkable is this: she was sure that her journey would lead her to the South Seas. It may be that in Berlin she was more consciously and more frequently confronted with the fact that Germany had previously possessed colonies in Oceania (up to and including World War I); or that she as a southern German knew the Liebenzell Mission as a South Seas mission. In any case, it was indeed to be the South Seas where she later found her calling, but in an altogether different manner than she had previously thought – not as an unmarried missionary but as the wife of a missionary.

Her intention of preparing herself for missionary service apparently took shape towards the end of 1933. It was then that she was seriously planning to study nursing. At that time this meant, in fact, that she would become a deaconess. This resolution seems to have come about in her "Klub." It filled her mother with apprehension. She was afraid that her daughter had simply made a rash decision, that it was some kind of flash in the pan. In a letter from Berlin-Dahlem, dated January 10, 1934, Mrs. Bulling tried to allay Marie Wagner's misgivings: The "Klub" could well be the source of influence, but its director ("Fräulein Meister") was a respectable woman, "deeply affected by religion," who would never pressure anyone:

"if she were not honestly convinced that a real calling was present. And if it should indeed come to that, then, dear Mrs. Wagner, you will just have to submit to the Lord. Is it not much better to see your child in such a profession than for her to be frivolous and bring shame and dishonor to you?"

Those were clear and forceful words.

The letter ended with a reference to the impression Elisabeth Wagner had, so far, made on her employers: "If Lisel should ever leave us, we would not only be losing a domestic help but a beloved member of the family."

In mid-1936, Elisabeth's plans had matured. A further letter by Frau Bulling, this time to the leadership of the Liebenzell Mission, indicates this. And since the letter shows how much Elisabeth was appreciated in the Bulling household, we will reproduce the wording here:

Dahlem, 13 May, 1936

Dear Reverend,

Your esteemed letter caused great joy among us because Lisel has now arrived at her desired objective, and we are wholeheartedly glad for her. On the other hand, this speedy calling has also caused us some dismay, since it would upset all our summer plans. We are leaving by mid-June; our accommodation has already been booked. Even if I could find another domestic help by then, which is very difficult nowadays, I would not know her sufficiently well that I could entrust her with the care of the whole house for weeks on her own. Moreover, I have invited a houseful of guests for the Olympics on the assumption that Lisel would assist me in her calm and purposeful manner of working. It is impossible for me to cancel these invitations. If Liesel [!] were to leave me in this vulnerable position, I would be greatly inconvenienced. We have now worked together in a trouble-free relationship for five years. Lisel is indeed a human being to be treasured, especially today in this corrupt world. I would find it very difficult to lose her, for she is absolutely dependable, industrious, and faithful down to the smallest detail, and all of this in a refreshing, pleasantly cheerful disposition. I am sure that in due course you will have in her an esteemed co-worker.

I hope, dear Reverend, that my appeal to you is not in vain; I beg to request that you leave Lisel with me a while longer, for those few more weeks.

With my heartfelt gratitude and best wishes for your missionary endeavors, I am,

Yours truly,

Frau R. Bulling

Elisabeth's employer even suggested to the *Zentrale der Hausfrauenvereine Gross-Berlin* (Center of the Association of Housewives in Metropolitan Berlin) that they award her with a prize for her achievements. She also wrote a letter of appreciation that Elizabeth could be proud of. In it Frau Bulling emphasized especially the blessing of Elisabeth's influence on the daughter of the house:

Berlin, 27 March 1936

To the Center of the Association of Housewives in Metropolitan Berlin
Berlin W 35
Am Karlsbad no. 12–13

Letter of Appreciation

In the past 5 years of service, Fräulein Lisel Wagner, b. 22 Nov., 1912, in Immenstadt/Allgäu, has gained our undivided appreciation through her absolute honesty, conscientiousness and loyalty; through her untiring and undaunted labor; through her great competence in all domestic matters; and – last but not least – through her constantly friendly and cheerful disposition.

I would, moreover, like to emphasize especially the blessing of her influence on our daughter (now aged 10) and also point to Fräulein Lisel Wagner's exemplary moral and religious pattern of life.

Frau R. Bulling

On September 3, 1936, Elisabeth Wagner joined the Liebenzell Mission.

On the "Mission Hill" in Bad Liebenzell

The first days as "Sister" Elisabeth in Bad Liebenzell must have been hard for her. She felt unhappy and did not find it easy to adapt to her new situation. Nevertheless, she did not lose her sense of humor. With a certain self-mockery she wrote in her diary that her tears had been flowing down the "Mission Hill" for days and nights, and that she longed for the "fleshpots of Egypt." By this she presumably meant her varied life in Berlin, which in retrospect seemed so glorious, especially since, to start with, she had to work in the mission center's kitchen.

But only a short time later she had a totally changed attitude towards her new situation. She especially liked the classes with Rev. Heinrich Hertel (1892–1966); and her mood was lifted when she saw how people were concerned for her well-being. For example, one day she was called into the mission administration office to receive 10 Reich marks, which had been collected for her by her "Klub" in Berlin.

An Interview with Dramatic Consequences

From mid-December 1936 to the beginning of January 1937 we note in Elisabeth Wagner's diary that an event had occurred to really trouble

her. For three weeks afterwards she was unable to make any further entries. What had happened?

Under the entry for January 6, 1937, we find the following description
of events:

"I am sorry to say that only now can I begin writing again. In the
meantime I have become ... engaged to be married! Sometimes it seems
to me like a dream, but the ring on my finger confirms the reality of it.
How could it all have happened so fast?

"On Wednesday, December 16, I was called in to see the pastor [Rev.
Buddeberg]. He was very friendly and asked about my family situation.
All of a sudden he became very serious and said, 'Dear Sister, I have
taken on a special assignment. A young brother, who is to be sent out
shortly, is looking for a life partner, and he asked me to inquire of you,
whether you would be willing to go with him.' So I sat there and really
had to struggle with my tears."

What she did not yet know was the following: Wilhelm Kärcher had
tried to resolve the problem of preparing to leave for the mission field
still without a life partner, by asking the mission director to mediate. It is
not quite clear whether he had mentioned the name Elisabeth Wagner. In
any case, the mission director had declared his willingness to function as
mediator because he knew that Elisabeth had joined the work with a view
to going to the South Seas as a missionary.

The classic fate of a future missionary wife, one which was not even
rare until the first half of the twentieth century, had caught up with her.

How Does One Become the Wife of a Missionary?

The young women who married missionaries in those days embarked
on marriage under very special conditions. The usual procedure was for
the mission leadership to start their search by sending a letter to the leaders of churches and fellowships in the hinterland linked to the mission
organization concerned. The letter requested them to name suitable young
women who by their upbringing, personality and education would make
good missionary wives. After extensive information had been completed
and compiled in a file of written reports, the named young women were
asked to appear before a mission committee. The committee would inform them, or rather confront them, with the fact that they had been se-
lected to marry a certain missionary. The women were almost always
totally unsuspecting. Only at that moment did they realize that for months
people had been writing about them and that detailed personal files had

been kept on them. Only rarely had they ever set eyes beforehand on the man picked out for them.

One can well imagine the conflict of conscience and dilemma of deci-sion-making burdening these young women. On the one hand they found it depressing to have to promise marriage to a man whom they didn't know; and on the other hand, if they said no, they would probably be blamed for not wanting to follow the will of God who so obviously had called them into his service on the recommendation of the mission leadership[20].

Elisabeth Wagner, too, was completely unsuspecting, but then again not totally unprepared. Her diary suggests that her intended husband had not only made a good impression on her during their occasional encoun-ters, but that she even felt a certain affection for him …

Elisabeth Wagner (middle, front row) as junior deaconess

For his part, Wilhelm Kärcher describes these occasional encounters more explicitly: he had noticed this young woman and found her likeable. Once he had had to do some work in her immediate proximity. She had been working with a hoist and could not figure out the ropes. Luise Bud-deberg, the mission director's wife, had come by and requested that he help Elisabeth. That was the first time the two of them had personally spoken with each other.

Despite her sympathies for Wilhelm Kärcher, her interview with Ernst Buddeberg (heading the work of the Liebenzell Mission during that time) must have put her on an emotional roller-coaster. His words to her had taken her completely by surprise. She was in total disarray. Her new situation in life almost crushed her. Her diary for that night records that she felt "more like dying than like living", that "everything had been taken away" from her. All night long she felt torn this way and that way. Now she simply had to come to terms with it and find some peace. That would take time.

Nonetheless, she immediately pulled herself together and wrote an express letter to her parents whom she had to ask for permission, as she mentioned in her diary. This letter was worded as follows:

Liebenzell, December 16, 1936

My dear parents,

This time I have to approach you with a request that will, perhaps, dismay you somewhat at this moment. Today, I was called in to see the pastor, and he told me that a brother had asked him to find out whether I would be willing to go to the mission field with him. He is leaving for the South Seas this very spring. I would then follow him in about 2 years' time. I already know this brother a little bit, since I meet him on a daily basis. I have a very good impression of him; the pastor also commends him highly. Tomorrow I am supposed to go to Tübingen for an examination to see whether I am suitable for the tropics. Now I would like to ask you whether you will give your consent to this. After all, I have sensed this coming for a long time and anticipated something like this happening. Please let me know by return mail since the matter is now somewhat urgent. But, please, do not say anything to anybody as yet. Greetings with much love,

Yours ever,

Lisl

On the very next day, i.e. on December 17, she left for Tübingen in the early morning to be examined at the Paul Lechler Hospital as to her fitness for the tropics. The results turned out positive.

It was very unusual that Elisabeth did not have the crucial meeting with Wilhelm Kärcher to discuss their situation until the following Tuesday, that is almost a week after her interview with the mission leaders. The occasion for their conversation had been prearranged and was, therefore, initially a little embarrassing. From today's perspective there were some grotesque features about the scenario; Wilhelm himself described the situation as extremely awkward – for both partners – when he talked about it later.

The room – once again the director's office – was accessible via two doors. Wilhelm came in through one, and Elisabeth through the other, accompanied by Frau Buddeberg who then left the scene discreetly. "Fräulein Wagner," as Wilhelm still had to call her at that stage, sat down on the sofa.

He sat down on a chair opposite Elisabeth. Between them stood a table. After a short, uneasy silence, Wilhelm spoke first and asked, "Would you be willing to go with me to the South Seas as my wife?" Her answer was very direct, "Yes, but God must take priority in it all." By this she meant that Wilhelm, as her future husband, would take second place behind their planned mutual endeavor as missionaries.

That statement later proved remarkable in several respects. It not only described her own attitude clearly and precisely, but also corresponded with Wilhelm's own ideas, as became obvious later on.

By the same token, she also sensed "total harmony, and that gave me confidence." The inner unrest which had plagued her now for almost a week disappeared noticeably. From now on she was able to accept the life plan as it was unfolding. Nevertheless, the following weeks proved extremely turbulent for her.

Elisabeth and Wilhelm Get to Know Their Future In-Laws and Their Families

Elisabeth's parents' written consent to the marriage seems to have come quickly; hardly a week had gone by after that first extensive conversation when on December 22, 1936 Wilhelm wrote a letter – recognizably by his most beautiful "Sunday handwriting" – to his future in-laws, in which he thanked them for their trust so obviously shown him and invited them to come to Mühlhausen for the engagement to be celebrated on Christmas Eve. Their attendance was all the more important and desirable since they would not be able to be present at the wedding, which would "then presumably not take place until far into the future."

On the following morning, Wilhelm and Elisabeth traveled together from Bad Liebenzell to Mühlhausen. On the way they bought their rings in Pforzheim and organized their engagement announcements.

Elisabeth was cordially welcomed by Wilhelm's parents in Mühlhausen. With her own parents later in Waltenhofen the response was to be totally different.

Elisabeth Wagner and Wilhelm F. Kärcher as engaged couple

In journals and letters it is not clearly discernible, but still quite evident, that Michael and Marie Wagner were not present at the engagement celebration in Mühlhausen, for the day after Christmas Elisabeth and Wilhelm set out to travel from Mühlhausen to Waltenhofen.

Her first visit with Wilhelm to her parents together started in a tense atmosphere. Of Elisabeth's three brothers Ernst had a special relationship with her. He was the one who picked them up at the station.

It seems he was wearing uniform, because in a letter that Wilhelm wrote two years later, on December 26, 1938, from Lúkúnooch in Micronesia, he remembered the scene with the following words: "That time, Ernst picked us up wearing a saber, out of respect for the bridegroom." This sounds humorous, but on the day itself Wilhelm had found the situation depressing. He had the feeling his future brother-in-law wanted to signal that he regarded him as any Tom, Dick or Harry coming to steal his sister. In any case, at the station Ernst was attentive only to Elisabeth and hardly noticed Wilhelm; brother and sister walked on ahead, and Wilhelm carried the suitcase about thirty meters behind them. Not once did Ernst look back at him. On the way Elisabeth begged her brother to put in a good word for Wilhelm with their parents. He did not do so. It was too difficult for him.

An atmosphere charged with animosity – one that neither Wilhelm nor Elisabeth had anticipated – awaited them in the Wagner home. Elisabeth's mother was known to be a resolute woman. She had been employed in Paris – an extraordinary circumstance in those days – and could speak perfect French. To start with, Marie Wagner eyed her daughter's fiancé from top to bottom. Though Wilhelm had the impression that his future mother-in-law would accept him soon enough, he was to be disappointed – at least for a number of days.

The Wagner family (from the left):
Marie, Karl, Fritz, Elisabeth, Ernst, Michael

Things hit Elisabeth even harder. She was confronted by the accusation that she must have known "about it all" for a long time already: their marriage plans were nothing but a ploy to keep parents excluded etc. Elisabeth recorded in her diary that her parents were absolutely furious.

In Mühlhausen, too, the unexpectedly difficult situation seems to have had its repercussions because, on January 6, 1937, Wilhelm's mother Lina sent a letter to Waltenhofen, in which she tried to calm things down. She pointed out that she and her husband had experienced matters in a similar way, although not quite as dramatically, because she had known about Wilhelm for some time already, and about the fact that he was supposed to get engaged before his departure. She also reminded them that Elisabeth had obviously been able to decide to take this step very quickly and joyously, and that it was "a glorious thing" – was it not? – "to be allowed to serve the Lord." Would it not be best, therefore, for both families to "support them in this matter?"

And indeed, after a short while, the Wagner family's fury did abate. Elisabeth's parents were in the end even relieved to think that their daughter did not have to leave for the South Seas alone.

However, by the time Lina Kärcher wrote her letter, in which she called for reconciliation, the engaged couple had already said their fond farewells to each other prior to a long separation.

Waltenhofen/Allgäu, hometown of Elisabeth Kärcher

4

Wilhelm Kärcher's Journey to the South Seas

Farewell from Europe

The engaged couple's visit to Waltenhofen lasted only a few days. Wilhelm and Elisabeth spent the turn of the year in Mühlhausen. Their time was filled with packing suitcases and saying farewells to relatives.

On the morning of January 2, 1937, his mother chose for him Psalm 121, a Song of Ascents (i.e. a blessing given to a pilgrim embarking on a dangerous journey) to accompany him on his travels: "I lift up my eyes to the hills – where does my help come from? My help comes from the LORD, the Maker of heaven and earth. He will not let your foot slip – he who watches over you will not slumber; indeed, he who watches over Israel will neither slumber nor sleep. The LORD watches over you – the LORD is your shade at your right hand; the sun will not harm you by day, nor the moon by night. The LORD will keep you from harm – he will watch over your life; the LORD will watch over your coming and going both now and forevermore."

A car took him to the station in Mühlacker. Elisabeth and some of his relatives accompanied him.

Besides many other formalities he had to see to before his departure, he also needed to apply to the *Wehrmacht* authorities (the armed forces of the Third Reich) for permission to leave the country.

While they were slowly driving up the *Steige* to get to the Mühlacker road from the Enz valley, Matthew 10:37 came to his mind. There Jesus says, "Anyone who loves his father or mother more than me is not worthy of me." This was exactly what he was obeying now. It really hit him hard. He could not foresee that it was to be a farewell forever: he would not meet either of his parents again in this earthly life.

His route took him first to Bad Liebenzell. The next day the young missionary had his farewell service. Wilhelm Heinsen, one of his teachers at the seminary, gave a message on Romans 8:31, "If God is for us, who can be against us?"

In the morning, the brass band had struck up the missionary hymn *"Zieht fröhlich hinaus zum heiligen Krieg"* (similar to "Onward, Christian Soldiers, marching as to War"). To us these days this sounds rather warlike. But in those days a statement like that had nothing martially aggressive about it, and certainly did not mean that a missionary was entering upon some kind of Christian *jihad*, fighting presumed enemies of the faith in faraway places. Nevertheless, though life as a missionary was certainly not like a warrior's, it was always a kind of a battle. Wilhelm Kärcher, too, was to struggle through many such battles.

The brass band accompanied him down the "Mission Hill" to Bad Liebenzell railway station. From there he planned to travel to Berne in Switzerland via Pforzheim, Karlsruhe, and Basel on that same day. Acquaintances from the Fellowship regions of Emmendingen and Freiburg in Upper Baden, where he had worked during his practical internship, had come to Freiburg main station to say good-bye to him during the few minutes of the train's stop-over.

In Berne he stayed overnight with Rudolph Mäder and his wife. Both of them had worked on Chuuk as missionaries from 1907 on until 1934, with a longish break in the middle.

From Berne the train went on through the Simplon Tunnel to Milan and finally Genoa. Until his ship sailed he stayed in a sailor's mission hostel. There, he made the acquaintance of four Sisters of the Rhenish Mission (the *Rheinische Mission* of Germany) who were on their way to Indonesia. Probably on January 5, he took a berth in a cabin on the steamship "Stuttgart" that was to take him to Shanghai via Singapore and Manila.

From Genoa to Shanghai

Originally he had booked a cabin amidships. It turned out to be very narrow, especially as he found it occupied already by two gentlemen – two "chubbies," as he remarked sarcastically. Wilhelm could see that his presence would only make the living space even more crowded. So he moved into a cabin offered to him in the stern of the ship. This also had the advantage that people left him in peace throughout the whole voyage.

For the two-month trip ahead of him he only had 70 Reich marks in his pocket. Half of it he later gave away to missionaries on their way home from China who were in financial straits.

The great ocean voyage began at six o'clock in the evening, on a dark, cold winter's night. The wind was howling around the ship.

"I was now at sea for the first time, but not much of it was visible. Only when I retired to my cabin did it hit me that a totally new episode of my life had started at this point, similar to when Abraham obeyed God's command and left his home country to go to an unknown, faraway country of strange and different people. That it was God who had led Abraham on this journey was probably always a great consolation to hold on to. This certainty informs every missionary's heart if he embraces the adventure of serving his Lord and Master far away on the sea of nations, often in a remote and lonely outpost. If he is not assured of this, he will probably be buffeted by life's billows and some day, somewhere, stranded like a shipwreck, as happened to Lot and his family" (1950:6).

The voyage that was to last four weeks was for Wilhelm an unforgettably beautiful time. The day after the ship sailed from Genoa they could see Mt. Etna, the volcano on Sicily, as the "Stuttgart" sailed past the volcanic island of Stromboli and out into the Mediterranean Sea.

By January 8, the ship was passing along the northern coast of the island of Crete, where the Apostle Paul had miraculously survived a shipwreck on his voyage to Rome (see Acts 27).

In Port Said, at the delta of the Suez Canal, he was greeted cheerfully with *"Heil Hitler!"* by the Arab merchants. During the passage through the Red Sea and along the Sinai, he reread with great interest the story of the wilderness wanderings of the people of Israel, understanding it in a completely new way.

During this time he experienced a very gratifying encounter: "On January 12, shortly before 10 o'clock, just as I was bidding good night to a Norwegian missionary and a Scotsman who had been my table companions, the latter struck up a conversation. He knew I was on my way to the South Seas and what my assignment was to be, so he asked me for my address there; he would write to me from time to time from Singapore, and would I inform him likewise about our work on the islands? He went on to tell me that, on the surface, he had everything: a nice family and a flourishing business; but he was an unhappy person inside because, as he said, 'I have no peace with God.' We talked for a long time, as well as I was able to do in my English, about the one thing that was necessary; and he was very honest."

This episode highlights something remarkable in Wilhelm Friedrich Kärcher's biography, for which we cannot find an explanation anywhere: He had obviously never attended language studies in England.

For us today it would be completely unthinkable to let a missionary to the South Seas leave without having provided the opportunity for him or her to gain adequate competence in spoken English. Even in those days, the lack of language skills meant a considerable impairment of one's ability to communicate. People who knew next to no English were simply not effective and had to somehow muddle through as best they could. Wilhelm Kärcher sensed this, too, and not just in connection with English, as we will see shortly. Even in his later years he still felt that his preaching was clumsy whenever he had to do so in English. All the more impressive are his efforts to lead a counseling session with the few language skills he had gained from his seminary teacher Susie F. Thompson (1874–1958), a feat he managed during his voyage to East Asia. ("Miss Thompson," as everyone called her, taught English classes at the Liebenzell Mission Seminary from 1926 until 1939.)

January 14 was the first dramatic incident in Wilhelm's journey. The "Stuttgart" met a Dutch freighter that had signaled by radio that a doctor was needed. A passenger with appendicitis had to be operated on immediately. The "Stuttgart" was indeed able to help. The physician was ferried across in a lifeboat, and after a four-hour stopover the appendectomy was successfully carried out. The voyage could now continue.

On January 20, he wrote a postcard to his future in-laws in Waltenhofen. It reveals how peculiar and even distant the relationship still was between them. He addressed them in the polite form (comparable to "Sir" and "Madam") but ended with the familiar "Yours, Wilhelm."

In Singapore, where he must have mailed his postcard, he saw for the first time how people behaved when they worshiped in a strange religion. He spoke of the many grotesque idols of the Buddha, to whom people (mostly women) were kneeling.

During a sightseeing walk in the city he apparently mistimed his way back. He had gone much farther from the harbor than he thought. To reach the ship in time, he ran like mad and in so doing aroused the attention of a whole row of rickshaw drivers; they immediately pursued him, sensing a big fare to be gained from a rich passenger. But he wanted to save money – since by now he had only very little left. Shortly before the ship's siren began to wail, he managed to get back on board.

On January 30, the "Stuttgart" performed an on-board flag ceremony. The reason: Adolf Hitler was giving his so-called *"Führer's* speech." But it did not get through to Southeast Asia. Atmospheric interference was so strong that all that could be heard through the loudspeakers were hoarse distorted voices. Not one word could be understood.

He seems to have especially appreciated his future brother-in-law Karl. A postcard from February 3, written on the East China Sea and mailed from Shanghai, was expressly addressed to him and full of all kinds of wisecracks: It was very hot, he wrote, and the climate was not at all favorable for skiing.

In the Far East

In the meantime February had come. The "Stuttgart" had reached the delta of the Yangtze Kiang and the port of Shanghai. That was the end of one voyage. The young missionary now had to change to the Japanese steamer "Chichibu Maru." Because of the dense fog it was several hours before the ship could cast off; and shortly after that, the ship ran aground a sandbank, where it remained stuck for three hours, until the rising tide set it free again and it could reach the open seas.

The "Chichibu Maru" was scheduled to sail via Kobe to Yokohama. Many passengers wanted to continue their voyage from there via Honolulu to San Francisco. Wilhelm's cabin mate was a Russian; not the only thing which reminded him that he was now in "foreign" territory. The ship was part of Japan; on the "Stuttgart" he had still been on German territory.

Moreover, on the "Chichibu Maru" he got acquainted with another Swabian who had been living in Kobe for twelve years and who was overjoyed to be able once again to converse with someone in his own mother tongue.

On February 10, as they entered the port of Yokohama, he was met by the Liebenzell missionaries Ernst Lang (1897–1989), Bernhard Buss (1902–1992), and Otto Mosimann (1903–1997).

In Japan, he was already very close to his future field of service – not just geographically. Since the end of World War I, the Japanese had administered the Micronesian Marianas, Carolines, and Marshall Islands as League of Nations Mandates. Consequently, for him as a non-Japanese wanting to travel there to work, there was a lot of red tape to go through.

First of all, he had to wait for his possessions to come. These were stowed in several wooden crates on another ship, the "Gneisenau," and soon arrived.

Then he went about getting a berth for himself on the ship that was to transport him to Chuuk.

Bureaucratic Red Tape and Its Simple Solution

The Japanese official he had to deal with over his passage from Yokohama to Chuuk claimed that there was no more room for him on the "Yamashiro Maru." For all of nine days Wilhelm tried doggedly to wrestle a cabin from the obstinate fellow. In vain! Then Ernst Lang who was assisting him and who had frequently encountered such problems with Japanese officials, advised him to try out a "present" on the unwilling official. If you wanted to achieve something in Japan, this was the most elegant way of oiling the wheels, by first "greasing the palm."

Now it was hard to know what to do. Where on earth could he find a suitable present?

Facing this situation Wilhelm remembered that in Germany someone had said good-bye to him and slipped him a small container the size of a matchbox. He had almost forgotten about this parting gift. He had not even unpacked it but simply put it among his belongings. What did he discover when he opened the packet and took off the lid? To his great surprise, two elegant golden cuff links, embedded in velvet lay before him.

Then and there, a canny idea occurred to him. What on earth could he do with golden cuff links on Chuuk? He would mostly be wearing short-sleeved shirts, anyway, for which no cuff links were needed. It was actually quite senseless to give a present like that to a future missionary! Was it really? Not at all! Wilhelm realized in a flash what a blessed effect these cuff links could achieve as a "present" to an unwilling official. So he asked Mrs. Lang to wrap the valuables attractively, attach a nice ribbon to the box, and have Mr. Lang present it to the official with perfect courtesy, bowing several times, and handing it over to him with both hands in further gestures of humility: This was a gift that his passenger Kärcher had brought for him from Germany.

When the official unwrapped the present, his eyes opened wide – he would see what he could do. When passenger Kärcher called on him again several hours later, he was greeted with these words: "We do have a free cabin. You can come on board."

Now, one might think that an act like that constituted a minor case of bribery of an official; the facts were undeniably similar. However, Wilhelm himself had a completely different understanding of the whole process: he remembered that there was an Old Testament precedent. Genesis 32 reports what Jacob did when he had to meet up with his brother Esau again following a lengthy time of separation, after he had tricked him out of the blessing of the firstborn: Jacob sent someone ahead with a present calculated to reconcile his brother. Esau responded positively to this gesture and everybody was happy.

The Voyage to the Carolines

Ten days after his arrival, the steamship "Yamashiro Maru" sailed from Yokohama, bound for Palau. There were storms at sea, and the voyage lasted from February 20 to 26. With him on board were quite a number of rather exotic figures: pearl divers seeking their fortune in the South Seas.

The Palau islands with their tropical vegetation reminded Wilhelm of beautiful bouquets. In Koror he was greeted by co-workers from the

Liebenzell Mission. He lived with Wilhelm Siemer (1904–1991) and his wife Martha (1909–1961), and this was his first experience of the simple life missionaries had to lead in those days. He never seems to have entertained any illusions as to what awaited him. In any case, writing about his impressions of Palau he said:

"Someone in Germany once asserted that missionaries live in beautiful big log houses. But I have found things to be somewhat different. Sure, they have nice wooden houses, and from the outside they are quite photogenic, but inside you have to tread carefully for fear of the pictures falling off the walls."

This slightly sarcastic comment is found in a longer report, dated April 3, 1937, which he must have written during the last 1,100 miles or so (1,800 km) between Palau and Chuuk. He begins with Matthew 28:18, "All authority in heaven and on earth has been given to me." These words of Jesus formed the lectionary in the Moravian Brethren's *Daily Watchwords* for January 1ˢᵗ, the date he had said farewell to his fiancée and his relatives and friends in Mühlhausen three months before.

The night before his arrival on Chuuk, a Japanese banquet, a "Sukiyaki Dinner," was served on the "Yamashiro Maru;" and on the morning of March 4, Wilhelm Kärcher could hear the anchor chains rattling through his drowsiness. After a voyage of a little more than two months he had landed safe and sound in the harbor of Tonowas Island.

What awaited him, he didn't know. But he was sure that it was God who had led him to this place, into a world and among people whose thinking, emotions and will were totally different from the pattern of European and Western society with which he was familiar; which he had indeed consigned to the past for a long period to come.

He could hardly wait to get to know the life of the people on the islands of Oceania, to bring them the gift which filled his whole being – the gospel of Jesus Christ as handed down in the Old and New Testaments.

5

The South Sea Islands as Living Sphere

The Pacific Ocean

If from the depths of the universe a spaceship approached our planet, the first thing on its surface that the crew would notice would be the Pacific Ocean. The extent of the earth's largest ocean from west to east spans more than one third of the world's circumference. Its dimension, fifteen times bigger than Europe, covers more than a third of the earth's surface. The Pacific Ocean is the deepest of all the oceans; its greatest depth exceeds the height of the Himalayas by far. If all the earth's land area above sea level were superimposed on the Pacific Ocean there would still be room for more. Land is almost absent here. Apart from New Guinea, the percentage taken up by the islands of Oceania in this unimaginably large expanse of water is less than 0.001%. The Pacific Ocean is a world of islands.

Micronesia

Oceanian studies, the science relating to the cultures and languages of the people living in the South Sea Islands, divide Oceania into three sizeable areas: Polynesia, Melanesia, and Micronesia. Polynesia covers the eastern part of the Pacific, constituting with Hawaii, New Zealand and Easter Island the vertices of the so-called Polynesian Triangle; Melanesia is grouped around the island of New Guinea in the southwest of Oceania; and Micronesia is situated in the northwest of the Pacific Ocean.

Micronesia is over 3 million square miles (almost eight million sq. km). Here, too, most of the area is covered by ocean. The "small islands," as the name Micronesia signifies, together scarcely total more than 770 square miles (or 2,000 sq. km), less than the area of the *Saarland* in Germany, or less than half of the State of Rhode Island. In reality, they are scattered across an area of water larger than the United States and are only a little less extensive than the European mainland. Hardly more than a hundred of the islands are inhabited.

Even the location of Micronesia within the Pacific Ocean is known only to remarkably few Europeans today. And yet this area has some significant geographical and geophysical distinctives. Southwest of the Marianas, about halfway between Guam and Yap, is found the greatest ocean depth known: the Challenger Deep. Not discovered until 1960, it is almost 36,000 feet deep (about 11,000 m). Besides Chuuk, several other Micronesian atolls also belong to the largest on earth. Kwajalein in the Marshall Islands, for example, is the longest ring reef or coral atoll, and Nómwun Wiité has one of the largest lagoon areas.

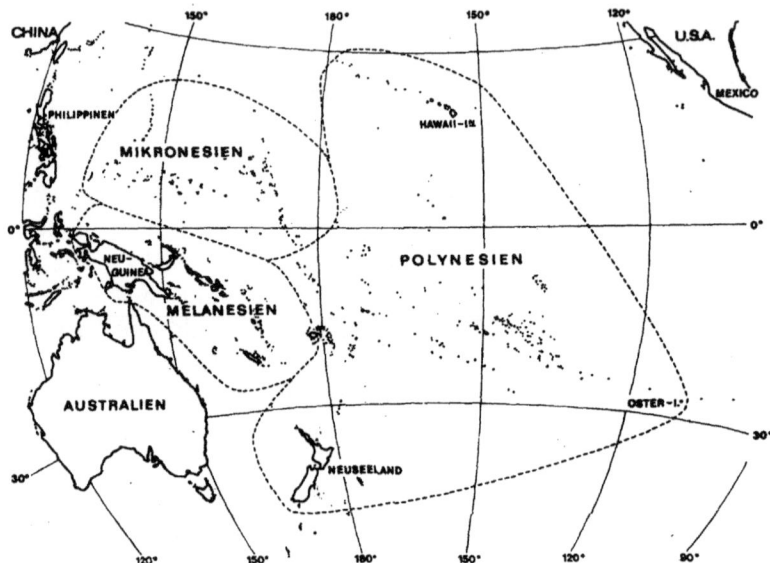

Oceania and its three culture areas

But that is not all. World history has been written in Micronesia. In the early morning hours of August 6, 1945, a high-flying single airplane appeared over the southern Japanese city of Hiroshima. Minutes later, a glaring flash of lightning lit up the sky; but nobody at that moment could tell what caused it. Within seconds, the lightning developed into a glowing fireball, from which a mushroom cloud rose into the sky. In a few minutes, the force of the atomic explosion had killed 70,000 people and severely injured almost as many. The aircraft, an American bomber of the type B-29, had started from the small Micronesian island of Tinian in the Marianas.

Northwest of the Marshall Islands, not far from Chuuk and Pohnpei, are two lonely atolls whose names went around the world in the early fifties of the past century: Bikini and Eniwetok.

On November 1, 1952, the little island of Elangelap north of the Eniwetok Atoll was bathed in radiant sunshine. The air was stifling and white banks of cumulus drifted slowly westward. The atoll was devoid of people. Out on the ocean several American ships lay anchored, miles away from the land. Suddenly a gigantic white fireball emerged out of the almost circular lagoon, reaching a diameter of more than three miles (about five km) within seconds. For hundreds of miles the sky above the ocean was dazzlingly bright. American scientists had just detonated the first hydrogen bomb in history.

The Carolines

This is the name for approximately 500 islands on the southern perimeter of Micronesia, forming a flat curve bent slightly to the north. They are distributed across a swath from west to east about 1,900 miles (over 3,000 km) wide. Almost exactly in the middle, which is also the middle of the western half of the Pacific, is Chuuk; and this was where Wilhelm Kärcher was to spend the most eventful and dramatic part of his life as a missionary among the South Sea islanders.

The Caroline Islands (acc. to Petersen 2009:8)

The South Sea and Its History

The distance between Mühlhausen and Chuuk, taking the western route, is 12,500 miles (20,000 km). It is staggering to think of the risks and hardships a discoverer like Columbus had to endure when he was looking for the westward route to India from Europe, whereas we today would need but a few days at the most! At that time he had no idea about the South Seas islands. He had assumed that there was only one ocean, i.e. the Atlantic, westwards between Europe and the Far East. When it became known that Columbus had, in reality, not reached India but an altogether new continent, the search for the coveted riches of the Far East in the westerly direction had to start all over again.

About twenty years after the discovery of America, the Spaniard Vasco Núñez de Balboa, a conquistador and gold seeker in the service of the Spanish crown, stood with his soldiers on a little elevation on the Isthmus of Panama and looked towards the south. The ocean lying there before him made a great impression on him. Never before had a European set eyes on it from the New World. From that day on, Balboa was known as the discoverer of the Pacific Ocean. And since he had directed his gaze southwards on seeing this ocean for the first time, he named it *"Mar del Sur,"* the "South Sea."

Seven years later, Ferdinand Magellan (Fernão de Magalhães), a Portuguese who was likewise in the service of the king of Spain, stood at the prow of his sailing ship "Trinidad" and, filled with eager anticipation, looked to the northwest. More than a year before he had started out from Spain with a convoy of five ships, sailing westwards to reach the Molucca Islands, which he assumed to be not far beyond the New World. Magellan had already had to overcome difficulties during the voyage along the east coast of South America. According to his thinking, he and his crew should actually have long since found the way to the South Sea which Balboa had seen from Panama. For over a month they had struggled day and night in wind and weather between the southern tip of South America and Tierra del Fuego. At times the difference between high and low tides had been 33 feet (10 meters), and more than once treacherous tidal currents threatened to devour them or ran them aground in narrow straits. Unimaginable gales had been raging. But on November 13, 1520, the sea became calm. Magellan was sure he had found the passage to the unknown ocean. The horrors of the strait that today bears his name lay behind him. For that reason he named the peaceful, sunny, and seemingly stormless sea lying in front of him *"El Mar Pacifico,"* the "peaceful" or Pacific Ocean.

Magellan had no idea how gigantic the emptiness was which he had ventured upon. For ninety-eight days he and his crew sailed northwest. Scurvy was taking its terrible toll and food became scarce. They were able to survive by eating the rats on board and soft-boiled leather and sawdust. At last, they again came across inhabited land. After a voyage of almost four months, Magellan dropped anchor in a bay off the island of Guam. He had found the Marianas, a group of islands in Micronesia.

On January 17, 1565, the Spanish galleon "San Lucas" was about 7° north and 152° east in the Pacific on a westerly course. The sea was turbulent because several days previously the northeastern trade winds had started to blow with full force. The sailing ship lay close-hauled before the wind.

Alonso de Arellano, commander of the "San Lucas," stood, compasses in hand, at his large cabin table spread with a map of the Pacific Ocean. Two days before he had sailed into an atoll on this map, which at night would have almost spelled doom for his ship. That morning he was amazed once again that he and his crew had even come that far. He was fairly sure that their position 7° north of the equator was correct. But he could only guess how far west of their starting point they had since come. If his clock had given the correct time, it would have been simple to determine the vessel's present position. However, hourglass clocks on board ship could only give a very rough estimate. And it was even worse regarding his ship's speed. He was only able to estimate it by a rule of thumb relating to the time it took the spray to be driven from the prow to the stern. Several coincidences needed to occur before the desired destination could be known; and the commander of the "San Lucas", even after so many years at sea, was not accustomed to being at the mercy of such coincidences.

While Alonso de Arellano was busy calculating the likely distance that they had covered since the discovery of that lonely atoll, agitation broke out on the upper deck. He listened. Above the roar of the northeasterly gale and the creaking of the rigging, he could hear voices through his cabin wall. He thought he could make out words like "the Philippines" and "Mindanao." "Impossible," he reasoned and dropped the compass on the map.

Alonso de Arellano climbed on deck, ran forward and stopped next to the first mate who had obviously been waiting for him. Without turning around, the officer pointed southwestwards with outstretched arm. He could make out some mountainous islands barely visible in the bluish haze. A few hours later they reached the outer reef of a gigantic atoll. The "San Lucas" had discovered Chuuk.

We do not know much about the history of the Micronesian islands. Before the 16th century no information exists at all, and before the 19th century it is very sparse. Spain had discovered the islands but over the centuries had only shown scant interest in them. This was to change suddenly at the beginning of the latter half of the 19th century. The value of an occupied country always seems to rise suddenly, whenever a second party starts to take note. This second party was Germany.

In 1885, a dispute arose over the Carolines. On August 26, the German gunship "Iltis" reached the island of Yap, and on October 13, the gunship "Albatros" anchored at Pohnpei. The Spanish were literally up in arms about this. Pope Leo XIII was asked to settle the dispute. His verdict reflected that of Solomon: Spain was to have the right of administering the Carolines, while Germany was allowed to carry on trading.

For Chuuk, the era under Spanish administration was of little or no consequence. One almost gets the impression that Madrid was ignoring it deliberately. Not even one government official was constantly in post. Thus the Spanish did not long remain lords of the Carolines. In 1898 the Spanish-American War broke out, and difficulties ensued. However, on the islands under Spanish rule the war remained unknown. The only event one could describe as an act of war took place on Guam.

One day, the American cruiser "Charleston" appeared in Apra Harbor on Guam and fired at the Spanish fortifications. In his optimism the Spanish governor mistook the booming guns for a salute; he quickly expressed his regret to the Americans that he could not reciprocate the salute because, unfortunately, his men had run out of gunpowder. Nobody had thought to inform him that war had broken out between the United States and Spain. Once the captain of the "Charleston" had explained the actual situation, the Spanish governor had no option but to surrender Guam to the Americans without a fight. Apart from a short interval during the Second World War, Guam has remained one of the American territories to this day.

After the war ended, Spain was in financial straits because it had to pay off war debts. In those days it was relatively simple to make money from the colonies. An objection on the part of the natives was not expected. It would probably not even have been noticed. So the Carolines and the Northern Marianas changed owners. On September 30, 1899, Germany paid twenty-five million pesetas for them. By today's values this would amount to about eight million U.S. dollars.

German rule lasted fifteen years without interruption. During this time the economy on Chuuk developed greatly. The Germans were interested in the trade of "colonial goods" such as copra, dried coconut kernel. Systematically, the natives were trained to cultivate coconut plantations. One major obstacle in this was the fact that individual villages and islands maintained sporadic or continuous hostilities towards each other. This problem, however, was dealt with simply and brutally.

In 1904, the German warship "Condor" visited the Chuuk Lagoon and collected guns and ammunition. People were paid for their pains, but anyone resisting the measure was simply deported without further ado. The people of Chuuk did not resist, and from that time on were, indeed, busier producing copra than quarreling with each other.

Certainly, under the German administration much more was accomplished for the economic development of the Micronesian islands than during all the previous three hundred years of Spanish presence and rule. Yet this period was too short for any long-lasting impact. In the case of Chuuk especially, the Germans were of lesser importance than, for example, for Pohnpei. With one exception: In 1907, the first German missionaries, Rudolph Mäder and Ernst Dönges of the Liebenzell Mission, came to Chuuk. The reason was as follows:

After the German Reich took over the administration of Micronesia, American missionaries, who had ministered on Chuuk and its circle of islands since the 1880s, were of the opinion that it was time to entrust their work to a German mission because they were unable to meet the requirement to teach German in their schools. The Americans were aware that a Christian organization had been established in the States by the name of "Christian Endeavor," abbreviated as CE. This association of committed Christians had a branch in Germany, called *"Jugendbund für entschiedenes Christentum"* (Youth Association for "Engaged" Christianity, abbreviated EC), which still exists today as Youth Alliance *"Entschieden für Christus"* (Committed or "Engaged" for Christ). Thus, the American mission turned to Dr. Wesley Clark, founder of the CE in America, with its concern. He, in turn, contacted Rev. Friedrich Blecher, then chairman of the *"Deutscher Verband der Jugendbünde für EC"* (German Alliance of Youth Associations for EC). The alliance was indeed decidedly mission-oriented, but had neither its own missiological training center nor any organization to send out and care for missionaries overseas.

Friedrich Blecher, who wanted missionary work to be done professionally, in turn passed this concern on to Rev. Heinrich Coerper, director of the Liebenzell Mission, who took this task on immediately, although his organization was only a few years old. In addition the government of the German Reich was interested in establishing German missionaries on all the islands within their sphere of influence.

Once the Caroline Islands (with the exception of Kosrae) had become the outreach area of the Liebenzell Mission, the first missionaries departed for Chuuk and Pohnpei in 1906.

A long time before the outbreak of World War One, another country had already started to cast an eye on the Micronesian islands, as they particularly suited its economic and demographic plans, namely Japan. It was not alone in this. Australia, likewise, was showing an interest. Both countries were biding their time.

In August of 1914, Japan, on the side of the Allies, declared war on Germany. It was inevitable that Japan would seize the Micronesian islands; the whole thing was rigged in advance. When Britain had occupied the German colony of New Guinea in September 1914 from their base in Australia, the Japanese also jumped at the chance – they beat the Australians only by a few days. They occupied the islands, beginning with the Marshall Islands in the east. Thirty years later they were to be driven out of the islands again from the same direction by the Americans. Germany itself could do nothing at the time to defend its sphere of influence in the Pacific Ocean against such overwhelming force.

Then, in 1918, something peculiar happened. A small Japanese contingent of troops landed in southern France, supposedly to support the Allies, although the Allies had no need of this reinforcement. The war had already ended. Japan was to be rewarded for this and other gestures. During the Paris Peace Conference at Versailles, England, France, and Russia decided in secret negotiations that they would give Japan a free hand if Japan wanted to declare the former German islands north of the equator as their own national territories. However, since Japan was a member of the League of Nations, the outcome was that this area was not to be annexed but granted to Japan as so-called mandated or trust territories. Its rights, therefore, were limited and, in a certain way, complemented by obligations. This meant especially that Japan was not under any circumstances allowed to consolidate and fortify its mandated territories for military purposes. The only goal that the League of Nations had in mind when it allocated mandates was the eventual independence of the trust territories.

Japan kept up its contractual obligations for years, to some extent. Even after it opted out of the League of Nations in 1935, it still submitted accurate reports about events on the Micronesian islands. But then news from these regions petered out. If beforehand these islands had hardly gained global publicity, they now disappeared from view completely. Japan had every reason to keep the area hermetically sealed off. What it had to hide was indeed outrageous. The Micronesian islands had been turned into fortresses bristling with weapons. On Chuuk, at times, almost the whole Japanese Naval Force lay at anchor, and the number of Japanese living in this part of the South Seas considerably exceeded the actual population of the islands.

During the time up to 1926, Liebenzell missionaries were either evicted or tolerated by the Japanese. After that date, a certain calm and continuity came over the ministry. And this was exactly the situation in which Wilhelm Friedrich Kärcher, by then thirty years old, found himself on Chuuk in 1937.

6

Beginnings in Chuuk

Off to Toon

So he had arrived: Friedrich Wilhelm Kärcher, missionary and carpenter. At the end of the pier Johannes Rattel (1901–1981), the field director in those days, was waiting for him in order to take him to the island of Toon, about 20 miles (30 km) away in the western part of the lagoon, where the main Liebenzell Mission station was located at that time.

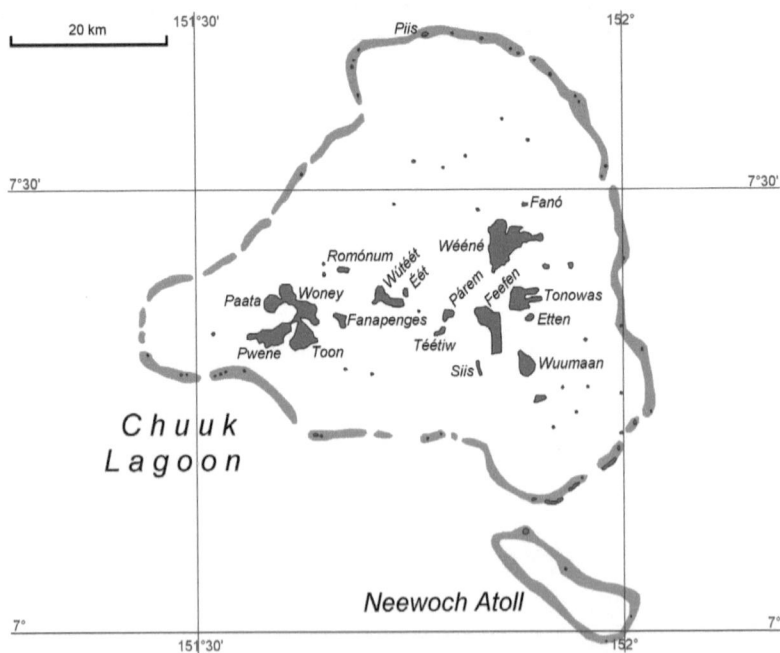

Chuuk Lagoon (after Hofmann 2014:107)

The first thing Johannes Rattel did, after the two of them had greeted each other, was to impress upon Wilhelm very strongly not to ask any questions about the islands or point in the direction of anything while crossing over to Toon, whenever Japanese ears would be listening. The

Japanese, he said, were suspicious to the point of hostility. They worried about espionage everywhere. Especially in the case of foreigners, they immediately smelled a rat because they could not understand what people were speaking about.

So neither one of them spoke a word during the whole trip to Toon, as long as they were on board ship.

Between the islands of Tonowas and Toon lies Wútéét, where the Liebenzell Mission maintained a girls' school with Elise Zuber as principal. Both of them briefly went ashore there. The students greeted them with the hymn "Now Thank We All Our God" – sung in harmony and in German.[20]

Work for the Carpenter

For the first three months Wilhelm lived with Johannes Rattel and his family in the village of Fóósón on Toon. At that time, the mission station was called "Pataaniyen" (Bethany, akin to the German name "Bethanien"). His most important task during those days was to learn the islanders' language. But there was also manual labor to be done. In the villages on Toon churches had to be repaired, their construction completed, or totally replanned and rebuilt.

Pataaniyen on Toon
On the left: Johannes Rattel, on the right: Wilhelm F. Kärcher

[20] *Nun danket alle Gott!*

During these weeks, the dealings between Wilhelm Kärcher and Elise Zuber at the mission conference in Bad Liebenzell in the fall of 1936 were being continued. Just a brief reminder: The missionary lady on home assignment had been with him on the podium, but had not exchanged one word with him, because she had been of the opinion that another missionary on Chuuk would be totally superfluous. One could, therefore, well do without the help of Wilhelm, thank you very much. In the meantime, however, the situation had completely changed, which eventually proved to be greatly to his advantage.

The girls' school on Wútéét was situated on a hill. Besides having their classes there, the girls also lived in the two-storey building, because many of them came from other islands and could not return to their families every evening. A typhoon, which had swept over the island shortly before the arrival of the new missionary, had "made the school crooked," as he himself expressed it. It had not fallen into disrepair, nor could it be left in this condition. The islanders had already tried to straighten things out again, but had not proceeded very far with it.

Elise Zuber knew very well what trade Wilhelm had trained for. But she hesitated to ask him to start with the necessary repairs. And no wonder, since she remembered what she had said about him a few months earlier in her rather derogatory remarks. So it took her a while to bring herself to ask the field leadership what they thought about the young missionary coming to Wútéét and showing his mettle....

The skilled carpenter didn't play hard to get; he looked for a few strong helpers; and the problem was soon solved. Elise Zuber was highly satisfied. Not only did she cook a big pot of *Spaetzle* for him (the Swabian noodle speciality)! – "From this moment on I was her man. Everything that had happened earlier on was forgotten." And when he also fulfilled her request to change a pillar obstructing the view in the classroom by putting a smaller supporting jack in its place, he was definitely in Elise Zuber's good books.

First Impressions of the Islanders

Until well into June he was busy with the construction of church buildings. He communicated with the islanders by sign language. Admittedly, he first had to get used to their way of working:

"Some among them are quite capable. Only, everything goes pretty slowly, and it is not that simple to get them out of their easy-going South Sea amble. They could even save some of this nonchalance for us Swabians! On the other hand, singing is definitely something they find easier than working."

The food, too, was at times something he had to get used to. On the day before the dedication of the new church building in one of the villages, the people served a juicy roast of dog meat.

Oh, the food! In this regard one needs to know that food has a somewhat different priority for the islanders than for foreigners. For the islanders just an ordinary meal has a much higher social significance than for us. Appreciation of a guest is expressed by offering him plenty of food, such that he cannot generally eat it at one sitting; he is allowed to take the leftovers home. Others will enjoy it there, too.

The service in the brightly decorated and overcrowded church on the following day lasted for almost three hours. In his welcome address the Japanese official said something Wilhelm found rather strange: his comments emphasized the good relations between Germany and Japan. These words did not really fit the impression of distrust and paranoia concerning espionage by foreigners that the field director had already warned Wilhelm about shortly before his arrival.

The drive and commitment Wilhelm Kärcher displayed in his work were enormous: for example, the fact that he had finished building the church in Chuukiyénú, a village on Toon, in a matter of only four days. Even though the building was relatively small and simple with about 20 by 30 feet (six by nine meters) of floor space, it still meant a considerable physical feat in those tropical climate conditions.

The Outer Islands

Around Chuuk, i.e. the lagoon that forms the actual center of the area, lies a ring of islands with a totally different character. In the islanders' language Chuuk means "mountains." These are elevations of volcanic origin with fertile soil. Crop failures and famine are rather seldom; and the islanders can escape to higher ground in case of flooding through typhoons or tsunamis (tidal waves triggered by submarine earthquakes). But not on the islands some distance away from Chuuk, i.e. on the Mortlock, Hall and the Western Islands around Pwolowót. The islanders call them Fánáápi, which means "Sand Islands." At the most, these are ten feet (three meters) above sea level. Consequently, their inhabitants are much more in danger whenever their islands are flooded by the ocean and their plantations swamped with saltwater. The soil will then remain infertile for about seven years. Moreover, when Wilhelm Kärcher came to Chuuk, the islanders were living in dire circumstances and in very great isolation.

The Mortlock Islands are situated in the southeast corner of Chuuk. Their name is derived from the captain who had discovered these islands. On Chuuk today, they are called Mwóchunók, or Mwochunong, or Mwochulok. Before colonial times the islanders called them Fánáápi Éér, which means "Southern Sand Islands."

On these, so the Mission's leadership intended, Wilhelm Kärcher was to be stationed to gather his first experiences as a missionary.

Almost at the southern end of the Mortlock group is a lagoon on whose ring-shaped coral reef there are two inhabited, flat islands: Lúkúnooch and Woneyopw.

In 1927, Liebenzell missionary Otto Joswig (1897–1967) and his wife Gretel (1896–1957) had taken up the work on Lúkúnooch Island, started by Karl Hausser in 1912, i.e. shortly before World War I had broken out. In 1916 Hausser, incidentally, had left his mission field, and eventually also the Liebenzell Mission, under circumstances that have never been totally cleared up.

When Otto and Gretel Joswig had returned to Germany in 1937, unable to depart again for the mission field after being home on furlough, their work on Lúkúnooch was to be continued by Wilhelm Kärcher.

Just like today's inhabitants, the people who lived there at that time were extremely friendly towards strangers, providing they behaved appropriately. For the Japanese officials working there, the islands were not, however, considered to be a preferred field of activity; those who had been transferred to the Mortlocks usually had been remiss in some duty or had "a skeleton in their closet," as the saying goes. When, after spending three months on Chuuk, Wilhelm Kärcher packed his few belongings to travel to Lúkúnooch, the islanders whispered behind his back, "Aha! He has already done something he shouldn't have. That's why they have sent him to the Mortlocks!"

He didn't feel especially worried about this. If someone is watching other people to understand their actions, it is only natural to presume they have the same motives as oneself. Islanders who watch Europeans do the same. Much more difficult for Wilhelm was the boat trip he had to undertake in order to get there.

Off to Lúkúnooch

With only the most necessary baggage he went on board the "May Maru." This was a sailing boat with an engine, about sixty feet (eighteen meters) long and twenty feet (six meters) wide. The engine room was also the passenger cabin. He was not on his own here; there was the engineer, black and oily like the engine he constantly had to repair on the way, because the thing, weak with age and badly maintained, kept stalling all the time. He was travelling together with a young Japanese family and a number of islanders. Even the captain and his brother camped in the same room, in which were also stowed the hand luggage, crates, and sacks filled with rice. One couldn't cook anything worthwhile here, only some coffee in a tin can. If Wilhelm had to learn that life in the South Seas was not exactly the life of Riley, he did so on this trip.

Having crawled into this engine-room / passenger-cabin on all fours, he didn't really find it attractive. How would he be able to stand this sticky atmosphere choked with the stench of diesel oil and exhaust fumes for two days and nights? He decided to look for a space on deck.

It wasn't much better up there. With difficulty he found a place in the crowded cluster of people where he could sit down. Even the helmsman only had standing room. The boat, which was fully loaded, if not overloaded, bobbed ceaselessly up and down in the swell of the open ocean. As it shot down into the trough of the waves and came up again like a drunken sailor, only to ride the next wave, Wilhelm had to hold on for dear life, in order not to go overboard, since the boat did not have a railing. He became terribly seasick and finally was so miserable and helpless that he imagined it being like the feeling one would have in hell. In his desperation he crawled back to the cabin, because there he could at least lie down. He would just have to put up with the overheated and sweltering air.

After some time, which seemed like an eternity, he arrived on Lúkúnooch. There he was welcomed by a fellow Swabian. They knew each other well, since both of them had entered the Liebenzell Mission Seminary in the same year, spending four years there together.

Richard Neumaier

He was born on May 30, 1907, in Oberkirneck, a small community by Lorch (Württemberg). After his school education, he had started in 1921 as an apprentice to a baker and confectioner in Stuttgart, and he continued as a skilled practitioner until he entered the Liebenzell Mission on May 1st, 1930.

He did his practical internship in 1934 and 1935 in Ulm, in the Fellowship of the "Southern German Association." Why he departed for Chuuk one and a half years earlier than Wilhelm Kärcher is no longer ascertainable.

In an autobiographical note (1989:102–112) he wrote that even as a child he had been searching for a gracious God, and as an adolescent he had attended the YMCA (at that time: Young Men's Christian Association) and the Christian Scouts. In 1924, he had his first contact with the Liebenzell Mission in Monbachtal in the northern Black Forest.

Richard Neumaier was an impressive personality. He had a distinct aptitude for linguistic phenomena of every kind and was, therefore, highly motivated. This explains the success he achieved between 1935 and 1947 – that is how long he was active on Chuuk – regarding the Chuukese language. In the years to come he also devoted himself fully, in many and various ways, to the islanders and particularly to their language.

What he bequeathed as a result of his research and literary evidence is all the more amazing as he had had no training in general linguistics whatsoever. He was an autodidact *par excellence*. None of his predecessors knew the Chuukese language as precisely as he did. Wilhelm Kärcher, incidentally, noticed very quickly how well Richard Neumaier had also mastered Japanese.

However, the fact that he was a layman in linguistics had obvious disadvantages. It made him vulnerable to attack. Because he did not have any related training, he was on the receiving end of criticism for his work from professional American linguists and ethnologists. Criticism also came especially from missionaries who arrived in Micronesia after World War II, pulling rank over their German colleagues, because by then the United States had taken over the administration of the islands. Their reproaches and rebukes stunned Wilhelm.

The German Liebenzell missionaries of that period were looked upon as representatives of a conquered nation. Later on Wilhelm Kärcher, too, had to deal with the issue. For Richard Neumaier the struggle began with his linguistic research and translation work, and he had to fight from the position of the underdog. This lasted several years, required his enormous patience, and at times drove him to despair.

The significant events and processes were closely interlinked with Wilhelm Kärcher and his life's work. Time and again he had to get involved in this battle. We will, therefore, treat these matters again in subsequent chapters. At this juncture it suffices to say briefly what Richard Neumaier accomplished for the "Evangelical Church of Chuuk" of today, for its theology, and for those of its community interested in linguistic and literary issues.

We owe the first clear and useful translation of the New Testament in the Chuukese language to Richard Neumaier himself.

A printed translation of this part of the Bible had existed as early as 1879. The American missionary Robert Logan (1843–1887) had worked on it on the island of Woneyopw and completed it in 1873. Under the circumstances, Logan's achievement was quite respectable. However, his knowledge of the language seems to have been rather modest. At the time it must have been hard to understand even for the people of Woneyopw: it had the further disadvantage of being written in the language particular to the Mortlock Islands, being understood only with some effort by the inhabitants of the other islands.

For these folk, especially those on Chuuk, where Logan's translation was also used for almost seventy years, three different facts emerged. Firstly, different dialects of the Chuukese language were spoken there, which made it difficult for people who had no experience in reading. Secondly – and this was more serious – Logan's version contained words which, without distasteful connotations on Woneyopw, would nevertheless sound vulgar elsewhere and which were therefore taboo. And thirdly, because of its geographical location, Chuuk had achieved a key position during the first half of the twentieth century. The region was governed from here, and a development had thus been started within the Chuukese language which increasingly elevated it to the status of a standard language similar to High German in Germany.

In addition, to do theological work with only this version available proved enormously difficult. Years later, Richard Neumaier characterized the problem in a letter of June 23, 1953, to Rev. Heinrich Hertel in vivid words: "Working with the Mortlock Testament is like mowing grass with an axe."

Under these circumstances of language diversity it seemed more sensible and important to write versions intended for all islanders in the Chuuk area in a form that would result in a happy compromise. Richard Neumaier set to work to achieve this through a completely new translation of the New Testament.

Since there was neither a language school for would-be missionaries nor a useful textbook with basic vocabulary and phonetics on Chuuk, he also started work on expanding a grammar book published by a German Capuchin missionary (Bollig 1927) a few years before his own arrival on the islands. He also included exercises to help the process of learning the language. As the years went by, this grew to a textbook with 99 lessons. It was never published but, in the sixties, the manuscript was transferred onto wax matrices and copied by Waltraud Rist, second oldest daughter of Wilhelm and Elisabeth Kärcher.

From a current standpoint this teaching material was problematic in that it presented the Chuukese language in the categories of Latin grammar. However, it would be unfair to reproach Richard Neumaier for this. He wanted to write a language textbook to facilitate practical learning. And indeed, this amateur linguist succeeded in doing so. Quite a number of the Liebenzell missionaries, including this author, active on Chuuk during the second half of the twentieth century used this textbook to acquire their knowledge of the language.

Moreover, Richard Neumaier and Wilhelm Kärcher very quickly realized the need to provide the islanders with reading material. Faith is linked with learning and, essentially, learning comes through reading. The missionaries discussed this topic at length, trying to clarify their ideas and deliberate on how to implement them.

From this emerged the first catechism in the islanders' language: a textbook of the Christian faith in the form of 289 questions and answers. Its title: *Anen manaw* – The Way to Life. Richard Neumaier simultaneously worked on a collection of 111 Bible stories, first published in the 1950s. The title: *Wuruwo mii pin* (lit. holy old stories).

Yet Richard Neumaier was not just someone with linguistic skills and allied interests. He also possessed a poetic vein and was very musical. There exists a whole series of songs he composed, singing joy and courage into his heart in hours of loneliness, as he once wrote later. Whenever he was alone for months in the solitude of the Outer Islands, he accompanied his singing "on a harmonium with a simple, autodidactically acquired technique of phrasing," writes his son and church musician Wilfried Neumaier, who published several of the best songs his father wrote "together with a new, stylistically adapted piano accompaniment" (1988).

For the island congregations this meant another gain. The songbook *Kkéénún namanam* (Hymns of Faith), which is still being used in all the islanders' church services and meetings today, contains more than one hundred texts that he either wrote or translated himself.

Richard Neumaier, who shared successes and defeats with Wilhelm Kärcher, (especially years of horror in detention during World War II), left Chuuk forever in 1947, spent several years (1948–1952) in the inland missionary services of the Lutheran State Church, and afterwards founded the Protestant Circle of Deaconesses (*Evangelischer Diakonissenring*). During this time, as well as his official activities, he was primarily concerned with the completion and printing of his revised translation of the New Testament into Chuukese. Later chapters will deal more extensively with related issues.

How Best to Learn the Islanders' Language

So then, the two "classmates," Wilhelm and Richard, were once again united on Lúkúnooch, among friendly people, but far removed from any civilization.

There was much that these two had in common. Not only were they both bachelors, they complemented each other almost perfectly. Put simply, Richard was the theoretician who busied himself with the language and thinking of the islanders; whereas Wilhelm was the practical one who knew how to translate theoretical concepts into practice. These two also differed in that Richard looked at the future of the islanders rather pessimistically, whereas Wilhelm regarded their future more optimistically.

The energy driving both of them was occasionally hampered by problems. Their attitude towards a society and culture alien to them shows that they still thought in very ethnocentric terms. That is, they observed and assessed the behavior of the islanders essentially from their own European point of view. This, in turn, led to a real lack of charity in the way these two young missionaries treated the islanders in daily life. However, with time, their treatment of others around them became more and more moderate.

For a while, Richard helped Wilhelm learn the islanders' language. Wilhelm did not find it easy, especially since his heavy burden of physical work did not leave him much time for studying. But by mid-August already he started to give brief devotions. This must certainly have been difficult, given his scant knowledge of the language, nevertheless it was important, for only those who acquire the ability to express themselves in another language can expect to win the people in their sphere of service and comprehend their way of thinking. Still, a person must have the courage, especially at the beginning of language learning, simply to "get cracking;" which also means risking making mistakes. The islanders are full of patience and honor such courage. Wilhelm definitely had it. Occasional bursts of laughter on the part of his listeners at the beginning of his language studies, whenever words he put together resulted in comic expressions – he learned to accept such moments calmly and did not allow himself to be put off.

Of course, beginners were not spared a certain amount of stress. One Sunday he happened to take only his New Testament to church; he had left behind on his desk at home the sermon he had prepared. He did not discover his mistake until the end of the first hymn, when he wanted to start to preach. What was he to do in this dilemma? Without hesitation he had the congregation sing a second hymn with a great many verses "to celebrate the day." While the congregation was busy singing, he was able to fetch the forgotten script.

Learning Through Teaching: School Classes

In this early phase of his own language studies Wilhelm especially liked to teach school classes. At any time missionaries might find themselves facing the need to be teachers. In those days, the school curriculum on the islands of Chuuk consisted of the essential skills, namely reading, writing, and arithmetic. In many villages, especially on the Outer Islands, no schools existed for children to learn these things.

Whoever wants to, or has to, read the Bible must learn to read systematically. The results of Bible reading on the islands were similar to those arising from Luther's Bible translation upon the development of German society. Knowledge and education no longer remained the privilege of the upper class; the majority of the population also had the opportunity of educating itself through reading. In the long run the schooling provided by missionaries, and the Bible versions they produced, helped the people on the South Sea islands (and also in other parts of the globe) access the advanced knowledge of Europe and America, including such important areas as medicine. Education in mission schools made the exchange of ideas possible and impacted the societies concerned. In Europe this had already started in the age of Enlightenment. When one considers the difficult circumstances under which school classes had to be taught, one can see clearly what great achievements the missionaries produced – even benefiting the secular world in which they worked.

The following will show the significance of this schooling. Even in the seventies, i.e. thirty years after Wilhelm Kärcher started his work on the islands around Chuuk, there was not a single delegate in the "Congress of Micronesia," the islanders' parliament, who had acquired his qualifications for political office elsewhere than at a mission school.

However, as positive as all this may sound, there is another side to the coin.

In societies such as could still be found on the islands of the South Seas at that time knowledge traditionally equates with maturity, and is possessed as a rule only by older people. With the younger generation accessing school education, this principle becomes obsolete within a short time. Authority structures, dictating the roles people play and the expectations that go along with them, then begin crumbling, producing tensions within society. The resultant gender and generational conflicts alter family structures: women and girls are given the opportunity to emancipate themselves and to gain access to academic education; but the men are largely upset.

School education may also lead to individuals renouncing a proper self-image. There are instances of people refusing to render traditional services to the chief, claiming as a reason that, after all, they could now read and write (Eggert 1970).

Another effect of the advancement of education at that time – which was not intended by the missions and, therefore, regretted – was the fact that students who had been painstakingly educated used their writing skills to compose love letters to fellow students of the opposite sex. But the fact that mission schools often had to wait a long time for the fruit of their labors (or even saw none at all) had an even more momentous impact. Their mostly well-educated graduates all too easily drifted off into secular institutions (and still do so today), which offered them far better positions than their own church organizations could afford.

Missionaries should certainly not use such disadvantages as an excuse not to offer school education. This was clear to Wilhelm Kärcher already from the beginning.

He taught school classes every day for two hours. The schoolhouse on Lúkúnooch was a wooden hut. He and Richard Neumaier had made desks and seats for the school from old church pews. With these furnishings their school was the height of luxury, compared to those maintained by the Japanese Mandate administration. In most schools, the children sat on the floor cross-legged and scribbled on their slates that, at best, consisted of a tile of slate with a wooden frame around it. But not so on Lúkúnooch. Still, conditions were very simple. When the boys came to school, they were mostly dressed only in a shirt, or something that had been a shirt at one time. Several among them came to the attention of their teacher because they were very attentive and worked carefully; their response encouraged him that schooling in this situation could accomplish a lot by promoting the future of people generally, but especially the work and growth of the churches.

One Extraordinary Trowel

During this time Wilhelm, together with Richard Neumaier, completed the church building started by Otto Joswig. In this, too, they complemented each other. Richard, the baker, knew something about cooking, which was very much appreciated by Wilhelm. The latter, as we know, was a construction worker. So Richard, who had no clue about building or carpentry, "apprenticed himself" to him, as he used to say.

The church building itself was a structure of solid concrete. It was planned not just as an assembly hall but also as a shelter to protect against typhoons. The walls had to be plastered.

Plastering was really not carpentry work. But on the islands no one can consider himself a specialist in certain jobs only. Somehow you must know something about everything. Sometimes somebody has to accomplish a task without much notion of what they are attempting; often what is needed is bold initiative: somebody just has to do it. So a carpenter-missionary also had to be able to plaster! The fact that the job turned out less than professional didn't matter much to the islanders. And yet, Wilhelm ensured with his keen and watchful eye that all construction work was done meticulously – vertically as well as horizontally: plumb line and spirit level had to be respected! The islanders took note. When something was finished, especially a concrete wall, the impression was perfection. The *samwoon*, i.e. the chief, who watched him at times, attributed this fact to the trowel Wilhelm used.

It was a tool from Germany, surely a miraculous tool, charged with *manaman*. For the islanders this implied some sort of magic power. At the time, power like this was much in demand, because a very important event was to take place on the islands: The Japanese governor of Chuuk had announced his visit.

For this reason, as instructed by the police, they not only had to get the church ready but also the house that was to serve as meeting place for political decision-making, the "council house" where the *samwoon* was to function as mayor. Small wonder, then, that the *samwoon* asked whether he could use the trowel. His request was granted. Despite this, against all expectations, the results were rather modest.

After the church building on Lúkúnooch had been completed the two young missionaries decided to implement an idea they had discussed and thought through many times.

New Ideas

North of Chuuk are the so-called Hall Islands. The group is called Pááfeng by the islanders. Until then, and according to the wishes of the so-called Western Islands of Pwolowót, Sowuk, and Pwúlúsuk, no European or Western missionary had ever lived and worked there permanently until the late thirties. The islanders had put in a request for a missionary to a delegation of German colonial officials, who had come on an inspection trip to the Hall Islands back in 1899, after Chuuk had come under the jurisdiction of the German Reich (Müller 1979:21).

Richard Neumaier, together with Johannes Rattel the field director at the time, had visited the island area a short while before and got to know it. The two young missionaries thought that now was a good time to start a work there. They saw this as their task. To begin with, however, they would need money.

Just how difficult it must have been to raise funds for such an undertaking is best seen by the fact that at the time the Liebenzell Mission was only able to provide their mission workers with the bare minimum for subsistence, plus five Reich marks for maintaining the individual stations. From this, they could neither pay for the building of churches nor for longer sea voyages. If the two young men wanted to buy building materials, they could only do so with the support provided by missionary friends from Germany and Switzerland. This support had apparently materialized, and both of them had pooled their finances. The project could start.

That evening, when they decided to put their plans into action, they both came across a statement by the apostle Paul in his letter to the Colossians (4:2–3): "Devote yourselves to prayer, being watchful and thankful. And pray for us, too, that God may open a door for our message, so that we may proclaim the mystery of Christ ..." That was what they wanted.

One Sunday, it was September 12, 1937, the two of them embarked for Chuuk. The sea crossing was alarmingly eventful. The captain was so drunk that he could barely stand on his feet and had to be carried on board. The prospects were not reassuring, considering the responsibility a captain has to exercise in negotiating the countless reefs, cliffs, shallows, and sudden depths lurking everywhere in Micronesian waters. It really takes the greatest concentration to steer a boat through all these obstacles. The two missionaries were full of misgivings once they had boarded the boat.

The cabin, in which they were cooped up, was indeed nine feet by nine feet large (2.5 by 2.5 meters), but only about four feet high (little more than a meter). Besides themselves, they also had to stow away their luggage and all kinds of Japanese household stuff. For sleeping, they had just enough room for their upper bodies to be in the cabin, but their legs stuck out on board ship, wherever they could find a gap between the oil barrels stowed there. Their feet lay there, constantly washed over by the waves. The fact that space on the boat was so extremely limited almost proved fatal for one of the islanders during the second night. He was sleeping in a sitting position, and so close to the edge of the boat, that he fell into the sea. Fortunately for him, this was noticed right away and he was found and fished out of the water after a brief search. Once the boat almost capsized because it was built too narrow for a voyage over the open sea and tended to list easily.

Despite these times of danger, they both arrived safely in the Chuuk Lagoon. They bought their building material. Originally, these were priced at 1,000 yen. But because they paid in cash, they got a discount of 100 yen. In addition, the trading company offered to load the material and ship it to the Hall Islands for free, since the boat had to pick up copra (dried coconut meat) from there anyway.

Two Hotheads

Neither of them had any idea that they had made a big mistake with their undertaking in their youthful fervor. The project had been planned and started by them without consulting others. Such unilateral actions do indeed afford the opportunity of putting well-intentioned new ideas into practice quickly and vigorously. But, unfortunately, one can easily snub others in doing so, who will then react by being upset, especially if they carry superior responsibility. This was the case here. Richard and Wilhelm had neither informed their field director nor the other missionaries, not to mention consulting them as to their opinions or advice. And worse still: They had confronted them with a *fait accompli* by buying those building materials. These young whippersnappers!

In the meantime it had dawned on them that they had really blundered, so they decided not to leave for the North but to turn around and go to Wútéét again, in order to take leave of their superior and older coworkers.

As one can imagine, they met with stern reproaches: Official process! Mission leadership! Matters are to be decided on in due process! Unlawful assumption of authority! How could they?!

Discussions went back and forth. Both of them admitted that it was not right to simply pass over older fellow workers in such a manner. But they also stated that Rev. Ernst Buddeberg, i.e. the mission director himself, had told them before their departure that they should be concerned about the unreached islands.

The argument they used to defend themselves against the accusation of having acted on their own was partly valid. Negotiating prescribed channels would simply have taken too much time; and where many have a say-so, young people find their initiative easily squashed by too many words and the steam goes out of their motivation. Wilhelm Busch (1832–1908), the famous German author of "Max and Moritz" (tales of two naughty boys and their pranks) and other books, once described this effect sarcastically and at the same time with a touch of genius, "The greatest oomph will soon be gone if spent clashing with another one." That's how these two young missionaries had thought about the matter. If the plan had been presented to the leadership of the Mission, they would have had to wait a long time for permission to put it into action.

In those days, a letter to Germany took two months. Allow a further month before the appropriate committee meeting. If no decision were made on that occasion, the matter would be postponed to the next meeting. And until the letter with the permission arrived back, another half year could have passed. Besides, the two had to reckon with the possibility that the letter would inform them that their plan had been rejected. The appropriate mottos seemed to be: "Better to let sleeping dogs lie" and: "Ignorance (on the part of the leaders on the field and at mission headquarters) is bliss."

The concern of the leadership on the field was, naturally, that Richard and Wilhelm had set a precedent by acting on their own authority. This could then serve other younger fellow-workers as a pretext to proceed likewise in future.

The two, however, did not give up. They asserted themselves. They did not need to fear a mission inspector who would have held them accountable; it would have been too much trouble for anyone to undertake a trip for that reason. And, as they said, "We felt like free missionaries, just like free architects. Those who ask a lot of questions get many answers." Besides, they had the impression that there were already enough missionaries on Chuuk itself; it was time to start something new.

Off to Nómwiin

The remaining missionaries certainly raised considerable objections against these two younger ones' plans, but finally they let them have their way. So the young men went ahead.

Having stowed their building material and baggage on the boat and got on board, they discovered that the ship's captain taking them to the Hall Islands about forty miles (sixty km) away, had appeared on deck completely drunk.

82   6. BEGINNINGS IN CHUUK

They, nonetheless, thoroughly enjoyed the night voyage to Nómwiin on
a calm sea under a starry sky. On the island of Fanaanú they experienced
first-hand how islanders reacted in those days when they met strangers. In
sheer panic the women fled into the bush when they saw them.

On Nómwiin the captain urged them on. He demanded that things
were unloaded as quickly as possible. There was a reason.

As a rule, South Sea islands are surrounded by a ring of coral reefs.
Boats can, therefore, only get to the beaches during high tide or via certain inlets. This, again, is only possible during daytime when there is
good visibility.

The ship lay at anchor in shallow waters some distance from the
beach. The captain was determined to reach the open sea again before
darkness fell. So he was in a hurry. He did give the two missionaries sufficient time to get cement bags and tin sheets on land by boat. But all
other materials which could not sink, like boards and other lumber as well
as metal barrels, had to be thrown overboard and transported by floating
them ashore. This gave the young people from Nómwiin a great time.
With great commotion the naked fellows jumped into the water, grabbed
the things floating around and towed them to land.

The appearance of the two Germans caused quite a stir among the islanders. Both were constantly surrounded and gazed at: "*Ree wóón*! Foreigners! Germans!" What a sensation and diversion in the otherwise une-
ventful life of the islands! Over the coming days they were followed by a
troop of kids at every turn. The grownups, too, whenever they didn't have
work to do, watched all they did.

Weeks later, Wilhelm was still on the receiving end of queries from
women wanting to feel his stockings, even inquiring how far they reached
up the legs of his pants …

The first night on Nómwiin must have been a special experience. Both
of them arranged themselves as best they could in the so-called *wuut*, a
house bigger than average, where the islanders met in order to discuss
matters of import to all island dwellers, where the big outrigger canoes
were kept, and where the men in those days stayed overnight before going on longer voyages or for deep-sea fishing. In those days, these *wuut*
were also the place where ancestral spirits were worshiped and consulted
through mediums.

There was no possibility to have a shower or even to wash. After a
strenuous day in the tropics one is usually soaked with sweat, really longing for a bath. In this place, that was an unattainable luxury. Covered in
dirt as they were, they set up their camp beds. They could not withdraw

to private quarters, either. The whole male community had decided to spend the night with them! These two were, in fact, the first foreigners to ever stay overnight on Nómwiin. That was a sight not to be missed for anything by the thirty or so male islanders. For Richard and Wilhelm this meant stress. But since they were dead tired, they finally fell asleep.

For the islanders it is normal even nowadays not to have privacy; almost everything takes place in the constant presence of others. Europeans can only stand this for a short time before becoming grouchy and irritable. Sometimes even the two missionaries found it too much, probably because there was no semblance of any comfort in the hut; huge cockroaches and rats scurried back and forth, and the roof was leaking.

So the next day they asked to be allowed to sleep in another house. They wanted to be left alone at least at night. And, indeed, a little house was found for them. It was more of a hut and so small they could hardly fit in; and it had no walls on the gable ends. Here, too, they could be observed at all times. When it rained, they should really have slept under rather than in the beds, in order not to get wet, because the roof of the little house leaked so much. Here they lived and cooked – always in plain view of the islanders. Early in the morning, before the locals woke up, the two men went to wash in the ocean, so at least they would not be constantly eyeballed doing so. They only endured this kind of life because they were looking forward to moving soon into the house they were building for themselves and that they intended naming "Elim."

Even at that time there was some property on Nómwiin that belonged to the Mission. Decades earlier, the American missionary Alfred Snelling (1855–1905) had visited the island and bought a piece of land. Unfortunately, his visit had a tragic ending. During a sea voyage, he and his companions encountered a typhoon. Their boat, an outrigger canoe, was carried off several hundred miles towards Éwúripiik, west of the Central Carolines. Four men died of thirst or exposure on the way. Snelling himself was still able to reach the island, but died a short time later of exhaustion on the island of Weneya. Klaus W. Müller had an old man from Éwúripiik tell him the story of this tragedy himself, recounting it afterwards in a gripping book (1975) about his experiences.

For Wilhelm Kärcher and Richard Neumaier, however, this piece of land, bought by Alfred Snelling, was to be the beginning of a success story.

Nómwiin Hears the Gospel

The property first had to be cleared of tree roots. Then the islanders brought sand and gravel. In return for their assistance, when the men could neither work in their taro gardens nor go fishing, the missionaries had to provide food for their families. So they gave them rice from their stores. House "Elim" was taking shape.

The islanders apparently noticed after a while that Wilhelm did much more physical work than Richard, who openly admitted, "They only talk about you."

He must surely have said this without jealousy. But it did seem that he, Richard Neumaier, changed his original plans as a result; for he informed a surprised Wilhelm of the fact that he wanted to return to the Mortlock Islands. He wanted to look after the churches there and then return after a year, once the house was finished. No sooner said than done.

In the course of all this work Wilhelm, now alone, rounded off his knowledge of the language not only by seeking contact with the islanders but also by starting to preach and give school lessons; he would use a piece of tin, sketching with chalk whatever he happened to be talking about. He tried to communicate vividly through visual aids. This has always been an important principle in missionary work. We cannot just keep on talking to people who can neither read nor write things down; they must be presented visually with whatever they are to learn and remember.

Wilhelm's talent for explaining things in a simple but vivid way and enlivening them with stories helped him to overcome the remaining gaps in his language knowledge. His listeners were indeed fascinated by him.

Exactly how attentive the islanders listened to him was brought home to him a few weeks later, when he was explaining the events surrounding the capture of the city of Jericho (Joshua 6). Wilhelm Kärcher was able to recount a story like this in glowing colors and with bold gestures; his arms and hands drew things and events in the air so that his listeners couldn't help picture the scenes that in reality they could only make out in words. Thus while he was marching the Israelites around Jericho with their trumpets and making the walls crash down, a boat was approaching the island. Normally, everybody on the Outer Islands would run on to the beach whenever they heard a motor chugging. But this time they remained seated, spellbound, to hear the end of the thrilling story.

On the boat – to everyone's surprise – was Richard Neumaier. It is no longer possible to explain today, why he had left the Mortlocks again after such a short time and returned to the Hall Islands. In any case, he was amazed that nobody had come to the beach, and he feared that something must have happened to the inhabitants during a typhoon, as he knew that one had devastated the Hall Islands some time ago. What had actually happened?

For days, a severe storm had raged over the Hall Islands. Lightning had flashed from low-hanging clouds, and mighty thunderbolts had frightened people and animals. When, finally, the storm increased to a typhoon, the gusting gales whipped into the rows of palm trees on the long side of the island, where the newly set-up mission station stood. Wilhelm bolted windows and doors. The men of Nómwiin ran shouting through the pouring rain with their machetes and tried to secure their houses with the help of ropes made of coconut fibers by tying them to the trees so that the wind would not tear them away.

The corrugated tin roof of the missionary house groaned under the violence of the oncoming mass of air. Rain, seawater, sand, and coral gravel beat against the walls of the house. Under the force of the typhoon the trunks of the coconut trees, which usually gracefully swayed in the wind, began to break, splinter, and fall over. That was bad news for the islanders, since the coconut palm is a basic staple underpinning their existence.

Suddenly the winds changed direction. The gale now came from the east, hitting the breadfruit trees with their big leaves with full force. In the roar that now arose people could no longer hear their own words. Branches were ripped off and carried away by the wind. The hurricane tore huge trees out by their roots and crashed them to the ground. That, too, was bad for the islanders. Breadfruit is a food containing starch. It is especially appreciated because breadfruit wood provides the people with important building material, including for their outrigger boats.

Close to the mission station there was a house where a sick old man and his family lived. When one of the heavy branches of a breadfruit tree broke off, it crashed through the palm-frond roof. This happened just as the missionary was looking on. He ran over to see if anyone was injured, and found the people of the house frightened but uninjured cowering in a corner. Since the house threatened to collapse, they had to leave it.

The foaming ocean waters surged over the island, snatching everything along in their path that was not nailed or screwed down. The roaring of the water and the storm, the splintering and crushing of the falling tree trunks, and the screams of the islanders running to and fro produced together a spine-chilling noise. They tried to reach higher, more secure parts of the island as they passed the missionary's house. Some tried to find shelter under the projecting roof and asked Wilhelm to pray that the storm would stop. They were wondering why he kept so calm in it all.

The typhoon raged for two hours. Finally, the greatest danger was past. And after the storm had subsided, it was discovered that the mission station had not suffered any damage.

A Lamp Against the Spirits

Wilhelm owned a gas lamp that operated on compressed air. Its brightness far outshone the dingy oil lamps familiar on Nómwiin. Every time he turned it up to full burning power, he would arouse enthusiasm. The islanders were convinced that this kind of lamp was effective at warding off evil spirits especially well.

According to their imagination, which can sometimes be found even in today's thinking, there are not only benevolent spirits living around us as humans do, but also a whole lot of malevolent spirits whose only purpose is to attack people, bite them, make them sick or devour them, in order to kill them any way they can. To their way of thinking these evil spirits have a whole range of attributes. Among other things they fear light. So they are a kind of spirit riff-raff averse to light. From this idea came the conviction that evil spirits can be kept at bay by burning a light or at least a fire. Even today, many islanders can only sleep peacefully when there is a light on in the room.

But what the islanders on Nómwiin could not fathom at all was their observation that Wilhelm never had the lamp on at night when he slept.

How could he neglect such a fantastic means of protection against evil spirits? Time and again they asked him whether he wasn't afraid. His answer was always the same: "No, I am not afraid, because my God protects me."

One day, he tried to give a rational explanation to a pastor: "With the spirits it is just like with a dog protective of her puppies. If you fear it, behave stupidly, or even approach it with a stick, it will get angry, attack and bite you. But if you behave in a normal way, without thoughts of fighting and without fear, the dog will remain calm."

Shoals of Fish!

During these weeks, something happened that established his position as a missionary in an extraordinary way. As a result, he was able to do his work more and more efficiently.

One day the islanders seemed to be especially busy. They explained to him that they absolutely had to get out on the ocean. The shoals of fish that during certain seasons of the year regularly came close to the Hall Islands had been staying away altogether, for a number of years; but now they had returned.

For a European or Westernized scientist it would presumably have been easy to explain why the fish had turned up again at this particular season. He might mention a natural cause and emphasize a likely effect. The islanders explained the event totally differently. They, of course, also knew about the principle of cause and effect. In their understanding, however, the cause of the event was not a natural but a supernatural one. They attributed the unusual reappearance of the fish shoals to the presence of the missionary – which was likewise unusual. There seemed to emanate from him a mysterious, unexplainable, extraordinary effect that had caused this natural phenomenon. Now they had first-hand and very clear evidence that he was *iiman*, that he possessed *manaman*, that supernatural ability, which the chief of Lúkúnooch had already attributed to Wilhelm's trowel a few months ago: "Your God has sent us these fish." From this the inhabitants of Nómwiin could only deduce that they absolutely had to become Christians if they wanted to continue receiving such blessings. Remarkably, they did not blame the missionary for the damage from the typhoon. At least not yet.

The biblical God sometimes uses strange ways to grant people access to himself. This can be seen in many examples from the Old and New Testaments. The islanders of Nómwiin came to this understanding via a logical but wrong conclusion by linking two events causally that did not match reality.

Anyway, it was clear to the islanders that the God of whom Wilhelm spoke had kept him safe in the typhoon and sent them the shoals of fish himself.

Such simple connections, which are not really authentic, can also lure the missionary into a difficult situation that calls for an explanation he can't give. Islanders regard sickness not only as malevolence on the part of evil spirits, but also as punishment for wrong behavior and for sin. Ancestral spirits send a sickness or allow some other misfortune to come over them or their families when they do something wrong. If the missionary gets sick they are quick to ask, "What kind of a God is this who is said to be almighty? Surely he cannot strike his servant with sickness! Maybe he sinned? Is he indeed *iiman*, or do our spirits possess more of it that they are able to make him sick?"

Overall, in those days the missionaries succeeded within a short time in winning the inhabitants of the Hall Islands over to Christianity. Only thirty years later several lively Christian churches had been established. Recognition of this achievement was not long in coming either. The missionary fellowship on Chuuk as well as the mission leadership acknowledged that the two young men's initiative had had been focused in the right direction.

Going Separate Ways

Of course, Richard Neumaier and Wilhelm Kärcher did not limit their presence merely to Nómwiin but also visited the remote islands of Ruwó, Fanaanú and Mwirilé. On one of these "mission trips" they seem to have discussed between them how their work might develop in the near future, and what goals they should set for themselves. As a result they came to the conclusion that Richard should continue the work on the Hall Islands by himself, while Wilhelm would return to the Mortlock Islands. Reasons for this decision cannot be found in their letters nor in other sources. Perhaps Richard intended to work in a "pioneer situation" like the apostle Paul, i.e. where no one else had been active before him? We simply don't know. In any case, the Mission leadership apparently agreed to this plan as well.

At this juncture it became obvious that they had very different personality characteristics that could not simply be summarized by describing Richard Neumaier as a "theoretician" and Wilhelm as a "practical man." Above all, each had his own way of regarding the islanders and dealing with them. Richard Neumaier was more direct in his approach to people, being convinced that he knew what was necessary and right for them. His tendency to pessimism when viewing their future as Christians may have been the reason why he was less willing to compromise, less lenient, and had a more demanding attitude towards them, albeit without wanting to be harsh.

Wilhelm Kärcher's disposition was different. He was not especially optimistic in his assessment of the people he had to do with on the islands, but he was certainly more optimistic than his fellow worker. His special strength lay in the congenial warmth emanating from his personality. He spread an atmosphere of compassion that made him not hesitate, if necessary, to enter into another person's suffering. As a consequence he occasionally complained about the fact that Richard Neumaier accused him of being too soft, even urging him to react more harshly in order to reach an objective.

This, too, pointed to another significant difference between the two missionary personalities. Richard Neumaier was less inclined to shy away from conflict situations than Wilhelm Kärcher (who was more inclined to seek harmony) and this gave him problems. Richard Neumaier, by the way, was aware of this, at least by the time he had left Chuuk. In one of his letters he admitted that he had "become more gracious these days."

Back on Lúkúnooch

Apparently Wilhelm had celebrated Christmas of 1937 while still on Nómwiin. In January 1938, he again boarded a boat that took him back to the Mortlock Islands. Richard Neumaier seems to have insisted on this, because Wilhelm would have preferred to stay on the Hall Islands.

Back on Lúkúnooch, he happened to set eyes on a pepper bush for the first time in his life. As he looked at the red pods he was reminded of how his mother used to sigh "I wish you'd go where the pepper grows!" whenever he and his siblings got on her nerves. At that moment he had the feeling that her wish had been fulfilled as far as he was concerned.

Altogether, about 1500 evangelical Christians lived on the eight islands of the Mortlock area. They formed, so to speak, a parish – his diocese. This was also the first time he had to fend for himself; and loneliness was to be the determining factor in the next stage of his life.

His daily schedule started with the so-called *felikis*, morning chapel, which took place in the church every day at sunrise. Then he would have school classes for a few hours, and in the afternoon he would practice playing the guitar with the islanders. Several young women had gone to school on Wútéét, where they had learned a number of hymns. Now that new people were joining, they had a reason to learn them thoroughly to be able to sing them in church as soon as possible.

All these activities, school included, took place in the church hall, the biggest room on the island with a roof. So there were many days when the church was full of people from sunrise to sunset. When darkness fell, everyone returned to their huts. There was no electric light.

His language knowledge had improved considerably over recent weeks under the instruction of Richard Neumaier. It was indispensable for Wilhelm to start getting to know the ideas and mindset the islanders adopted for leading their lives and succeeding.

It occurred to him more and more at this time how little he knew about their way of thinking, and how little his colleagues in the Mission had thus far been concerned about getting acquainted with the islanders' language and world-view. Was this, perhaps, the reason why their lives as Christians still exhibited so many occult elements that, by his reckoning, they should really have shaken off after so long? It was taken for granted that primitive religious elements, incompatible with Christian ones, existed alongside. Why was everybody so indifferent? Should there not rather be some soul searching in himself and the islanders about the reasons for this?

Older missionaries than he had not seen the necessity for this. Rudolph Mäder (1880–1940) openly was of the view that it would be better not to ask too many questions. It was assumed that such questioning would only give the islanders the idea that it wasn't all that wrong to bring their deceased chiefs some food offering to ward off a typhoon, or to try and heal sicknesses by means of magic.

From today's point of view, not to ask questions was an error with dire consequences. If you want to change something, you have to be thoroughly familiar with it.

Likewise, Wilhelm found it strange that people were excluded from the Lord's Supper for being wayward in their married life or sexual behaviour, or for smoking, but not if they practiced occult rituals or communicated to the dead and brought them flowers – even in church. Wilhelm wanted to reverse these priorities, but it wasn't easy to get the message across to the islanders.

The reason the Christians on the islands continued to practice ancestor worship was because the social hierarchy on the islands included a person whose function combined a political and religious role – the so-called *itang*. He was some kind of religious chief, a political priest. Something like it had once existed in Europe in the office of prince-bishops and prince-abbots, highly placed clerics in the Roman Catholic Church, possessing seats and votes in the Imperial Diet. The *itang* was, of course, only approximately comparable to that of a prince-bishop.

The importance and effectiveness of a man like this were based on the fact that people were attributing *manaman* to him and his words: energies, charisma, and authority that could work the extraordinary. So in the islanders' expectation, he was endowed not only with political power but also with magical prowess. Those enjoying his favor were fortunate; they were taken care of. But anyone who fell out of favor had nothing to laugh about. Since the *itang* was feared, it was often easy for him to abuse his power.

When an *itang* became a Christian he did not lose his office or give it up. Chiefs were indispensable for law and order; public order required them to continue in office. But having magic powers in addition, they were problem figures in a society that had embraced Christianity or was at least showing interest, for their power base was their supposed connection to the deceased *itang*[21]. It was from them that people expected help and blessing in their daily lives, and this could only be mediated – so the islanders believed – by the living *itang*.

Incidentally, even today, church structures on Chuuk show clear traces reminiscent of the office of *itang*. The *wuwáánpóron*, a pastor in elevated position, may often hold a political office as well, or his family group will urge him to aspire to one; for it offers power and financial benefits for those concerned.

A Throne and Its Great Power

Pili was an *itang*. In English his name would presumably have been Billy. Throughout the Mortlock Islands he was seen as an important *sowuroong*, a powerful magician. But at the same time he was a church elder, clearly somebody with great authority and prestige. This was due to the fact that he presided over a powerful and highly regarded clan. In church his exalted position was evident from his being seated on a kind of throne, especially made for him.

Wilhelm was really disturbed by Pili's obvious special position. It just was not right and proper for a Christian, he thought. Pili's affected display of power was a virtual affront to him. One day, therefore, he simply had Pili's seat removed from the church. This proved to be a big mistake.

His action was by no means unjustified or without reason, but it was wrong because Wilhelm, in his inexperience, had acted too rashly and

---

[21] *itang* has no plural form in Chuukese.

without thinking it through. He just did not appreciate at the time that a younger man must not cause an esteemed older man to lose face and shamed so abruptly; moreover the disgrace to himself was inevitable. Likewise, he did not understand that his risky action would insult Pili's entire clan. He had caused immediate outrage. The people of Lúkúnooch worked themselves into a fury. Suddenly Wilhelm had everyone against him.

Mission workers' ignorance about social relations and the disastrous effects resulting from insensitivity to such issues until that time caused Richard Neumaier in particular to delve into the matter, by questioning the islanders and recording his investigations.

The Missionary as *Itang*

It so happened that a severe typhoon then swept across the Mortlocks. To start with, Wilhelm merely found this natural phenomenon interesting: the howling gale, the swelling waves on the lagoon, and the torrential downpour from the low-hanging clouds. The islanders, on the other hand, were afraid. They begged him to pray: "*Kepwe iyóótek!*" To him, the situation did not seem that threatening, for as yet he did not know that during a typhoon the waves could mount so high as to totally flood the flat islands. When the land floods, the saltwater inundates the taro gardens and causes the soil to be infertile for the next seven years.

Such an event had led to a severe famine in 1907. Without prior warning a typhoon had come over the islands, flooding everything and sweeping many people into the sea. The German colonial government was then forced to evacuate many Mortlock islanders to Sokehs on Pohnpei. There, the Roman Catholic Mission workers had taken care of the people, and many had become Catholics. When they returned to the Mortlock Islands years later they were accompanied by a priest. From then on, Protestant as well as Roman Catholic Christians lived on the Mortlocks, resulting in a lot of relational conflict. For Wilhelm Kärcher in this typhoon, a totally different issue was to the fore.

He responded to the request made of him and prayed for protection in the storm. Soon after, when it became evident that, unlike 1907, there were no disastrous consequences from the typhoon, the islanders were firmly convinced that the missionary's prayers had brought this about. It proved to them that he possessed an enormous amount of *manaman*, which usually was only available to the *itang*.

He was unaware that he might also have got himself into a difficult situation through the typhoon. According to the islanders' logic, two unusual events in succession must be causally connected. Wilhelm had experienced this already on Nómwiin, where his presence was seen as the explanation for the fish shoals appearing again. The fact that the typhoon had occurred after the arrival of the white missionary could also have been interpreted by the islanders as happening because of him. For that they would use the word *seringngaw*, which means something like "unfortunate coincidence."

Now, however, the comparative harmlessness of the typhoon was to them a good omen. Wilhelm himself took it as a sign that God wanted to clear the way for him, to grant him quicker access to the islanders. This impression was reinforced in a spectacular manner when, shortly afterward, great shoals of fish that the islanders had been longing for reappeared here too, after several years of absence. They were those flatfish that periodically appear in the Carolines in great numbers and that are highly prized as a delicacy. Now the people could again catch plenty of them, delighting the people; they ascribed this effectively to the missionary: "His God has sent us fish again!"

Nothing Can be Managed Without a Wife

There was, however, another factor he was not yet conscious of. Had he known this, he would surely not have treated Pili so harshly.

In the islanders' society young men possess only a lowly status, i.e. they do not yet count for much. They meet with little respect, especially when they are still unmarried and have no children. The islanders consider that a young man simply does not really know what life is all about and thus cannot have a say in matters.

Wilhelm almost perfectly fulfilled the condition for having no authority in the island society. Over the two whole years which he spent alone on the Mortlocks he neither had wife nor children. This drawback was somewhat mitigated by the fact that he was a *ree wóón*, i.e. a foreigner, that he could read and write, that he knew much more than the islanders, and possessed books, not to mention his ability to influence the typhoon through his prayers, as had been witnessed.

The phenomenon of the lonely European among islanders with their totally different mentality sometimes affected him quite badly. In the end, it was to be two years – two long years – during which he could neither speak to nor see his fiancée. He missed her in every way.

Wilhelm really did not "live" in a house, he simply "set up camp" there. He did his laundry and cooked his food himself. But that was obviously not so easy: "Today I noticed in my garden that I have some beautiful green beans I planted a month ago. I could then make some bean salad – if I only knew how. Maybe, I should just look in my cookbook, perhaps I'll find an entry under bean salad. I also have Munich beer radishes. But they are still small."

Takuwo, a younger fellow who occasionally lent him a hand, would from time to time express what he thought of Wilhelm's culinary skills: "That certainly is a special kind of food you are cooking there." Wilhelm told him he was quite right and admitted that he sometimes found eating harder than cooking. "I almost bit off more than I could chew, but I persisted bravely."

What he really missed was bread (the German kind). One day he found some flour in a tin container in his kitchen, left over by his predecessors, the Joswigs. That gave him the idea of trying to bake bread. His problem was, he had no yeast. But he thought, in the tropical warmth of a South Sea island dough, properly mixed, would surely rise even without yeast.

What he then mixed together seemed a bit runny to him and was more like a pancake mixture than bread dough. The baking pan he wanted to use was extremely rusty and full of holes. He would have to be careful not to let the dough leak out of it. His mother had taught him that dough needed time to rise before baking. So he let it rise in hopes that it would thicken as well. But after two hours, the dough still did not show any signs of rising. Even during the afternoon it remained passive. Wilhelm patiently tried to coax it into rising by lifting it in different places with his fingers. Not a chance! Finally, he had enough. If he waited any longer, he assumed the dough would start to ferment and form bubbles. Perhaps that would result in some kind of sourdough? He didn't hold out much hope. So he took a shovel, dug a hole in the ground behind the house and dropped the dough including the pan into it for good; never again did he try baking bread.

No Money!

After the National Socialists (Nazis) had come to power in Germany, a political situation begann to develop in Europe, which was to lead to the catastrophe of the Second World War several years later. It meant a lot of hardship also for the Liebenzell Mission workers on Chuuk. Wilhelm Kärcher soon felt the first signs of it.

One of his most pressing problems was the fact that, in the meantime, the National Socialist authorities were no longer allowing Germans to transfer monies to foreign countries. The finances for the upkeep of the mission station suddenly stopped. A short while later so did Wilhelm's money that he badly needed; he still had to pay off certain debts incurred in Japan after purchasing part of his equipment for life on the islands. He had even been strongly encouraged to get properly equipped there, so he had followed the advice given, assuming that the Mission would cover the cost. He was wrong!

As early as the 1920s, the Japanese Mission that had been charged with the responsibility for the work on Chuuk, had introduced some kind of salary for the pastors: 10 yen per month, for fostering and maintaining the indigenous church. Chiefs, however, only received 5 yen per month from the government. And as the pastors also had mission property at their disposal, not only living quarters but also an allotment, they were among the best provided-for members of society at that time, on Chuuk in general and on the Mortlocks in particular.

Since Wilhelm was not receiving income any more, it was impossible for him to pay the 10 yen pastors' allowance due for their work and that they, of course, expected. His predecessor, Otto Joswig, who had worked on Lúkúnooch uninterruptedly for ten years, had managed to fulfil this obligation regularly; and Richard Neumaier, who had been stationed here for a short time in the beginning of 1937, had had no problems with it. Incidentally, for fifty years these two were regarded as legends for that reason. People never forgot it. It was a good example of islanders liking to talk about "the good old days." And here came Wilhelm Kärcher, a young man lacking experience and status; and one of the first topics the pastors had to broach with him was being the stopping of payments.

For sure, he could have paid one of the pastors by giving him his tithe, but he could not have managed eight! And if he had only given money to one pastor, the others would have accused him of favoritism; an awkward situation. Explaining to the island churches that from now on they had to pay their pastors themselves was almost impossible.

For his station and boat travel expenses he had so far been remunerated 5 yen per month. Included in this was also an amount for the needy, for orphans and semi-orphans. Now he had to inform them, too, that he could no longer get funds for them.

He got into big trouble because he no longer corresponded to the picture the islanders had of a missionary. They even started doubting whether he had really been sent by the Liebenzell Mission.

A further difficulty arose because his predecessor had had an impressive boat, with sails, named "Immanuel." The Roman Catholic priest also had a boat. But he had nothing. That, too, diminished his status in the eyes of the islanders. A boat-owner possessed status and prestige, akin to someone in those days in Germany having a car on the driveway. To the islanders' way of thinking it was obvious that with this young missionary a new and strange era must have started.

In the following years, the shape of things was to become even more drastic. In Otto and Gretel Joswig's household several young islanders had been employed: a cook, a children's nurse, a woman to do the laundry, one to iron it, someone to cook rice for the employees, and someone to see to the firewood. All this, however, was not a luxury, considering how strenuous life can be and how much energy Europeans expended living in the tropics, where almost everything had to be accomplished without machines and electricity. Besides, it was an opportunity for local people to earn money.

Wilhelm Kärcher could no longer afford such assistance. Even later, there was only one maid lending a hand to Elisabeth Kärcher, for half-days only.

The young missionary had no other choice than to travel by outrigger canoe. That was unheard of among the islanders; *they* would travel like that, but never a *ree wóón*. For a foreigner to travel by canoe would be tantamount to someone in Germany driving to the supermarket by horse and cart.

But the church elders did not leave him in the lurch. Since he had no more money, they finally took him from island to island for free whenever he had to visit the churches there.

Success Stories

Working with the students in the mornings, he soon noticed how well the boys and girls remembered what they had learned. There was a simple reason for this. Island culture is oral, not literate: information is basically exchanged by word of mouth, and the knowledge needed for coping with life is passed on to the younger generation orally and not in written form such as books.

On Lúkúnooch, the Christians met once a week to pray together. Wilhelm had actually expected this meeting to be suitable for adults only. Instead, he now experienced the children present also starting to pray earnestly. He had the impression that they really believed in what they had learned.

He himself recounted another success story like this:

"It was a special joy to me when, at the close of a Sunday morning service, the *chóón ánisi*, the "assistant" – as the indigenous catechumens were called then – gave an invitation and quite a number of men and women stood up to witness publicly to the fact that they now wished to break with the paganism that had held them in its grip and in the fear of death until now. What's more, they also all stayed behind afterwards to talk things out confidentially. Their awareness of sin may not yet be very deep, but we want to continue to hope for them and believe that they will be brought into the freedom of the children of God."

One day, an old chief impressed him, telling him after a severe typhoon that he had earnestly prayed to the God of the Christians during the storm, and not one of the many fallen trees had crashed on his house.

One evening, Wilhelm was sitting on the beach at dusk enjoying the atmosphere over the landscape. Suddenly a young man appeared out of the bushes, sat down next to him and asked him to forgive him for not having kept his word so far. Some days previously he had promised Wilhelm that he would come to the services. Wilhelm now had the opportunity to talk to the young man about his personal salvation. From then on, this fellow came to almost all the meetings even though he had a comparatively long way to walk.

Wrong Decisions and Their Consequences

Wilhelm did not find it hard to win the islanders for the gospel. He had the impression that they were "tired" of paganism, as he said. But: "We preached without having researched the old culture. That made things lopsided from the start."

By saying "we," he did not just mean himself but all missionaries of all mission organizations who had so far worked on Chuuk. Even in this comparatively short period of time he had noticed that people with the thought patterns of South Sea islanders inevitably find it extremely difficult to try and understand the contents of the New Testament without knowing the Old Testament. Statements of basic theological significance like "In the beginning was the Word" (John 1:1) or "The Word became flesh" (John 1:14) were on such an unfamiliar level of comprehension that there was virtually no dimension to the islanders' thinking that would have allowed them to make a connection and grasp the statements' meaning. This process was being aggravated by the fact that the Mission workers at that time simply were not aware of the strong influence of their German mother tongue on their preaching, distorting it to such an extent that it could hardly be expected that the islanders should make an attempt to understand it.

The fact that the gospel would be introducing something new into a target culture, and that missionaries first had to create the conditions for its acceptance, was certainly not foremost in their thinking.

Cultures and thinking patterns work like a grid or filter, through which the Bible teachings pass and, in doing so give them a characteristic form. Many things of importance thus become meaningless, e.g. Jesus as the Lamb of God – a picture that will not be understood because there is no animal on the islands that would have a similar function for the islanders as sheep and lambs would have had for the Jewish society in the time of Jesus. Other matters, by way of contrast, become inappropriately weightier, such as baptism and the Lord's Supper, as they are understood by the islanders as rituals activating magic powers of protection against catastrophes.

The older missionaries were of the opinion that the gospel merely had to be introduced into a "heathen" culture, and in the course of time everything heathen would disappear from it and the rest would remain. But this is not the case. For, on the one hand, there is no guarantee that whatever is heathen would indeed disappear, as experience has taught us, and, on the other hand, everything in a heathen culture remains heathen or, at least, so tied in with it or integral to it that it can only be separated with difficulty.

The evidence of this was obvious. The islanders' Christianity, as the missionaries found it, was a mixture of the pagan and the Christian.

Wilhelm Kärcher grasped this fact intuitively early on, though not its actual extent; quite without the resources that have come to light through linguistic research since then. In any case, it did not take him long to be convinced that among these "people of nature" – as he characterized the islanders – he should not start with the New Testament but with the story of creation. In this way he aimed "to bring them, step by step, close to this great God, whose existence they all sense."

Mistakes in transmitting knowledge about the content of the faith arising through attitudes that were Euro-centric (the term used for the behaviour of foreigners convinced that their worldview is uniquely true and self-evident) were one thing; much more serious in their consequences were wrong decisions justified from a European and Western standpoint, but quite without justification from the islanders' standpoint.

Before Wilhelm arrived, there lived on the island of Lúkúnooch a man by the name of Riing. He was the son of a chief, held the office of an *itang*, and was thus a key figure on the island, especially concerning the future of the church. He wanted to marry. The young woman he loved was one of his cousins. This met with the solid disapproval of the two missionaries who were stationed on the island prior to Wilhelm Kärcher.

Now, a cousin is indeed a comparatively close relative and, in European and Western societies, it would not be easy to marry a cousin; the fear is that children produced in this marriage would evidence traits of degeneration and handicaps. Among the relatives of such a pair there would be those who would at least frown upon the thought of marriage; certainly others would discuss whether such a union was desirable or should be ruled out. Legally, however, there would be nothing against such a marriage.

The so-called "rule of exogamy" – so named, though unspoken, because of the assumption that a marriage partner should not be chosen from within one's closer circle of relations, but that one should instead "marry outside" – exists in all human societies that we know. The islanders on Chuuk likewise adhere to this rule. However, the rule of exogamy is far from being universally uniform. What constitutes a relative biologically can only be defined imperfectly. Relatives are always defined by a given culture also, and foreign societies define many things differently from Europeans or Americans.

Thus, the islanders – similarly to the Turks and other ethnic groups that have meanwhile settled among us – know the difference between a parallel cousin and a cross cousin. If I described this in detail, I would have to go a long way back, too far for this biography. Suffice to say the following:

Parallel cousins come under the prohibition of incest almost all over the world, which means they are too closely related to be considered as marriage partners. For cross cousins, by contrast, this prohibition of incest is not given. In fact, the opposite is true. Often they are looked upon as preferred marriage partners; although, here too, further details would be excessive.

The young woman, on whom Riing had cast his eye, and who was herself willing to marry him, was his cross cousin.

It is no longer clearly discernible whether the missionary due to marry the couple was knowledgeable about the totally different way of looking at relationships or not. It should really have been obvious to him to get acquainted with it, because without this kind of knowledge Bible relationships cannot be explained to the islanders. In any case, the missionary did not want to permit the marriage, as he considered it problematic by his own Euro-centristic thinking. He did not, in fact, make this decision on his own, but asked the advice of the mission leadership in what was, for him, a difficult situation. But the leaders, too, expressed their Eurocentristic views and, with it, their rejection: Incest should not be condoned.

The rather dramatic consequences were as follows: The priest did not have such scruples, so Riing converted to Roman Catholicism; and since an islander cannot take such a step alone, especially not if he is of high rank, Riing's whole clan likewise became Roman Catholic. This important family group was thus lost to the Protestant church and had, in a certain way, become opponents. Wilhelm Kärcher clearly came to appreciate the consequences, and to this day they have not quite been overcome. He commented on this wrong decision in these words: "We wanted to remodel them according to our German custom. Here we had the leading man of the Mortlock Islands in our church, we drove him out and thought how wonderfully well we had handled things."

Christmas, but No Mail from Anywhere

Life on the Outer Islands had always been more difficult than on Chuuk itself. There, every four weeks a boat would arrive with mail and people had some sort of connection to their homeland and relatives. On the Outer Islands this was only rarely the case.

Almost a year had passed since he had first lived and worked alone on the Mortlock Islands. The end of 1937 was in sight.

On December 24, he was awakened early in the morning by the muffled hooting of the conch shell echoing over the island. Shortly after he could hear shouting. The reason: Several men who had gone to Chuuk weeks earlier to sell their copra, had now returned and were just then being greeted with shouts of joy. He had asked them to bring back the mail that would presumably be kept for him at field headquarters. But they had to disappoint him. There had been no mail for him, they said.

It had already been three months since he had last received mail. "Here, in isolation, far removed from the hustle and bustle of the world, a person just doesn't know what is going on in civilization any more."

Firstly, he did not celebrate Christmas 1937 alone. About 40 children larked around on the porch of his house. He told them the Christmas story, sang with them, and in the evening the children were even given presents. The boys got fishing hooks, the girls loincloths. A lighted storm lantern substituted for the missing Christmas tree.

How he managed to do all this without money has not been passed on. We only know that he crafted many of the gifts himself. For the chiefs he had even made wooden footstools so they could sit more comfortably in church.

Late at night, he celebrated by himself. He recounted that he read the Christmas story to himself, sang German Christmas songs, and thanked God for allowing him to be there so he could "bring the glad and blessed Christmas message to these foreign folk."

Late on New Year's Eve, the islanders made an "unholy din" as they went screaming and hollering around, drumming on old tin cans; amid the noise one could hear the monotonous blowing of conch shells. "They presented me with an extra rendition of their New Year hymn."

Experiences in the Church Work on the Islands

The Christmas mail, so longingly awaited, finally arrived the following June. Since at the time he was in a hurry to leave for one of the first more far-flung round trips, he could not open it. So he packed the letters and packages on to the outrigger canoe that was to take him first of all to the island of Mwóóch.

Mwóóch belongs to a lagoon whose main island is Satawan. As a new missionary, Wilhelm was downright besieged and gazed at, just as he had been on the Hall Islands. Since the *samwoollap*, the head chief, had gone to Chuuk for a few weeks, all work, fishing trips, turtle hunting and dance celebrations – which he usually ordered at this season – had been cancelled. So it was especially the men who had plenty of time to listen to the new missionary. During this stay many sick people also came to him to get medication. It was a matter of course for the islanders to suppose that the missionary would also be knowledgeable about medical matters. In their eyes, religion and medicine were connected with each other. Their own "medical experts," too, the *sowuroong* and *sowusáfey*, combined both functions for religious and medical matters in one person. Unlike the missionary, these healers, of course, did not work on European and Western medical principles but according to their own animistic ones.

From Mwóóch Island, Wilhelm traveled on to Téé. There, Luuwis was the chief, one of the most powerful *sowuroong* on the Mortlock Islands, who was also feared as *itang*. Since on his island he also functioned as a medium through whom the family ancestral spirits were thought to speak, his power ruled over people's lives. He inquired of the dead why someone had become sick. Under his leadership on Téé people still offered sacrifices to the spirits publicly. Wilhelm's brief commentary was: "Things still looked very dark." The reason was that, at the same time, Luuwis was something like a pastor of the church on Téé. One can imagine what this meant for the young missionary. He had enormous difficulties explaining to people that there could be no compromise between ancestor worship and the Christian faith. Because of it he had many strange experiences.

One night, he woke up. It was around midnight. Outside he could hear noises and shouting. On investigating he discovered that people were busily working in their cooking huts. The women had been boiling taro roots and were now in the process of energetically mashing them into some kind of puree using stone pestles. That had caused the noise. When he asked why they were cooking food at this time of night, he only got evasive answers. To his surprise, the women gave him a sizeable amount of mashed taro, obviously to stop him from asking any more questions. They were afraid of this, for they could not tell him the true reason for their cooking frenzy in the middle of the night without exposing their actions to him. That would have been the equivalent of confessing a sin. They were engaged in presenting a food offering to one of their high-ranking *énú*, i.e. one of their ancestral spirits, in order to placate his supposed wrath. They were afraid that he, the missionary, would be opposed to this. Then they would have to be ashamed, since they regarded him as a higher-ranking person who would criticize them. His criticism, they feared, would mean a curse intended to bring disaster on them. Therefore, they gave him part of the food so he would not criticize them; because for them, someone receiving a gift could not complain. If he did, he himself would lose face.

The sexual life of the islanders also caused a serious problem. To be sure, there were societal norms, even quite strict ones, governing it. But these were only a sham. There was a kind of double moral standard. Anybody ensuring his public conduct appeared to conform to the norm was looked upon as morally upright. But behind this façade many things were possible. There were plenty of extramarital contacts.

This situation arose because marriages were not made on the basis of mutual love but were contracted by family groups negotiating with each other. Marriage partners frequently had other sexual partners.

Another factor was added to this. Women could hardly deny men's advances. They were simply afraid to do so. If they did refuse to submit, they had to take into account that the rejected man would cast an evil spell that might bring disaster on the women, their children, and even their whole family clan. The pressure on the women not to risk such a thing was enormous. They almost always gave in.

The consequences on Téé were severe. Although there was still no AIDS around, there were plenty of other sexually transmitted diseases. Wilhelm spoke of an epidemic.

Téé and the neighboring island of Satawan are situated on a coral reef. These two islands are only separated by a narrow strip of very shallow water. One can wade the two hundred yards. Thus Wilhelm was able to reach Satawan. His luggage was delivered to him by canoe following him.

His daily schedule on Satawan was like normal: two church services, school classes, on some days a meeting with church elders, and visiting the sick. One day the following happened:

A man had asked him to visit a sick child, one of his relatives. In the hut where the child lay, Wilhelm right away noticed a bundle of magic medicine hanging down from a beam over the child's sleeping mat. In a corner of the house cowered a woman, a female *sowuroong*. She had hung up the medicine bundle in order to drive away the spirit she thought was the cause of the sickness. On inquiring about it all, he received the evasive answer that it was totally insignificant. So, without a word, he grabbed the "stuff," prayed with the child instead and noted that after a few days he was healthy again.

In this situation it is clearly evident that the inexperienced young missionary tended to persist in his European mindset and imposed his own ideas about sicknesses, their causes and possible treatment against the ideas of the islanders. He assumed that, at the time, they were still acting with evil intent whenever they used magic.

Yet, as a rule, this was not the case. But to the young missionary it was simply not evident that the islanders knew of no other medical remedies to start with and, secondly, could not acquire any. He also did not consider that knowledge gained during childhood becomes so entrenched and plausible in a person's mind that he or she won't even question it as an adult as to whether it could be wrong, or something else might be better. People all over the world act on the premise of knowledge, no matter whether it is proven to be correct or whether it is bogus. That goes for islanders as well as Europeans. And when people have existential needs they always do what seems natural and self-evident to them. This had been the case with the woman who had sat with the sick child and hung up the magic medicine.

The fact that she replied evasively regarding its significance, is – as seen from our present standpoint – quite understandable: magic-medical knowledge could not be passed on to strangers without further ado. In the first place, it meant power and influence; secondly, people were paid for it; and thirdly, such knowledge was not the individual possession of the woman but belonged to the whole family group. If she had explained why she had hung up the medicine bundle and what it was supposed to cure, she would have been informing a potential rival: Wilhelm could then – so she might have assumed – have used the process himself to heal others. This, in any case, might have been her fear. Furthermore, she must have had panicked, thinking that he would disgrace her in the eyes of others by declaring publicly that he, the *ree wóón*, did not think her work to be of any use.

Wilhelm's description of the scene reveals that he really did not yet recognize the thinking patterns determining this woman's actions, and the emotions that may have motivated her here. In the coming years he learned to see it differently. At the time he was still intent on tackling matters outright, unilaterally from his point of view. Even his choice of words failed to show the grace that a missionary needs even towards those who cannot yet manage to distinguish properly between "Christianity" and "paganism" in their lives, because they are unable to do so for a variety of reasons. This is especially true of people who are first-generation Christians.

That he himself had not yet internalized how these matters were inter-related (leading him sometimes to treat people harshly) is shown by the fact that he did not refer to the women through whom sexual diseases were transmitted or who practiced magic medicine as *"Frauen"* but as *"Weiber"* (a derogatory term).

He decided to address the issue in a sermon. For this he chose Matthew 13:45–46, the parable of the "pearl of great value." In it he emphasized that one had "to give up everything," including magic stones and magic herbs, in order to gain this pearl. He had brought the medicine bundle; as he spoke he placed it on the table in front of him for all to see. Immediately there was a great stir among his listeners. His *chóón ánisi*, the "helper" or catechumen who was assisting him, finally grabbed "the stuff" and suggested that, in future, no one should have anything more to do with it, not even in times of sickness.

For the woman who had been the target of the sermon this whole thing was a rather difficult experience. The missionary had made her *sááw*, publicly disgraced, something hardly bearable for any islander. Moreover, she had to listen to the other women accusing her of being remiss in disclosing such matters to him: "You have been very stupid, you should have hidden everything before the missionary came into the hut." She defended herself fiercely, but without success, pointing out that she had not betrayed any secrets: the missionary had found out by himself.

In this experience Wilhelm Kärcher acknowledged he had in human terms responded too harshly, though not in error. Sickness entails much more anxiety and terror for islanders than for a European who can always get medication and, if need be, treatment at the hospital in Chuuk. This much was brought home to him a few weeks later on the island of Nómwuluuk. Many islanders there suffered from "consumption," i.e. they had tuberculosis. The sight of these "sick people with their tired eyes" moved him terribly, and he began to understand why the islanders still relied on magic and occult means when they were ill.

When he returned to Lúkúnooch he was called out to help because two women struggling to give birth lay dying. What should he do? He felt powerless. "When I was home again and stared out into the night, I really felt very inadequate. In such a situation you are reminded of the words: 'LORD, if you had been here, my brother would not have died' (John 11:21)."

There were also totally different, positive experiences. One day he was present when a sick child's mother had started the lament for the dead, as was usual on the islands in those days: she thought her child had already died. But Wilhelm, who had seen that the child was still alive, gave him some medication and prayed for him, and a few days later the child was well again. "Again and again, God gives us also joyful experiences," he commented.

One day in October, he and some of his students rowed over to Woneyopw, the island in the west of the lagoon, opposite Lúkúnooch. In those days, Anna Dederer, a missionary from the Liebenzell Mission, was stationed there. He saw that church services were well attended here, and he got to know a young man, "who was really engaged; one could see that he was serious about following Christ."

Altogether, his numerous experiences during those two years on the Mortlock Islands opened his eyes to the syncretism, the pot-pourri of mystical notions, by which the islanders tried to make sense of their lives. This hotchpotch of Christian, animistic, and occult teachings made him highly apprehensive and caused him to look for ways to get out of this situation.

The "Jewel of the House"

But, meanwhile, he was also busy with other matters. When Christmas 1938 approached, his time of solitude was at an end. His fiancée Elisabeth Wagner was due to arrive on Chuuk within a few weeks. That was an event to prepare for: "These past days, I have been very busy repairing and painting the house I live in, with the help of several others. Now everything looks in fine shape again, but the real jewel of the house is still missing."

The letters he wrote to his relatives during the Christmas season of 1938 were peppered with humorous – even boisterous – comments, showing he was full of anticipation and optimism for the future.

He wished his future brothers-in-law, Fritz and Karl Wagner, "just such a stormy trip on a little boat across the open sea as I had last month." That must have been a severe one, because he commented on his experience with a line from "Nis Randers," a poem by Otto Ernst: "Boat up on top, boat down below – a hellish dance."

He indulged in reminiscences of the Christmas celebration they had just had on the island of Lúkúnooch, and imagined what it would be like, "once Elisabeth accompanies us on the harmonium she'll bring along from Japan."

He started his letter of December 26 with the words, "Today it is two years since I first came to Waltenhofen. In 35 days I will be able to pick up Elisabeth, and I am looking forward to that day mightily."

She had sent him a telegram a few days before, on December 23, which he described as his nicest Christmas gift. In it, she had announced her imminent arrival and suggested that he should perpare for their wedding – "the immediate wedding," as she phrased it in the telegram.

This remark really astonished him. It was customary for the future wife of a missionary to first get acquainted with the conditions in her new sphere of service through an experienced missionary couple, and then get used to the work. He assumed that the Mission leaders had changed their plans, because they had let him know some time ago that they should hold off getting married for three months.

What he could not know was that Elisabeth herself had seen to it that this rule would be passed over in their case. But how this came about we won't hear for a chapter or so. We now go back in the next chapter to Europe, two years before, to follow what was happening with Elisabeth Wagner, what she had been experiencing, and what it meant for her to be preparing for a life as a missionary wife, while Wilhelm was working alone on the Mortlock Islands, waiting for her.

7

Elisabeth Wagner's Journey to the South Seas

New Orientation

After Wilhelm had left Bad Liebenzell on January 2, 1937, time for Elisabeth seemed rather slow-moving. From now on she saw herself as something of an outsider in the Mission House. She knew she would not become a "sister" but the wife of a missionary. Since that was not yet the case, she felt out of place. On the other hand, she sensed an extraordinary motivation because of her new life situation. She followed the classes at the seminary with great interest, especially English language, taught by Susie F. Thompson. But despite her being highly motivated she did not achieve as much in English as she would have liked.

Her mother was now writing to her more often. Her letters showed that she had not just acquiesced to the life plans her daughter was making, but that she was now happy with them.

These weeks saw Elisabeth going through the most variable emotions. On February 7, she received her first letter from Wilhelm. He had mailed it in Port Said on the Suez Canal. A week later, another letter followed, bearing a postal stamp of Colombo, Sri Lanka (at that time still called Ceylon).

It was planned that Elisabeth – different from her fiancé – should spend some time in language study in England, starting in April. But at the beginning of the month she contracted flu and became so seriously ill that her trip to England had to be postponed.

On April 23 – she was doing much better health-wise – she found five of Wilhelm's letters together in her mail; two of these he had written during his voyage, the other three earlier on Chuuk. In her journal she compared her joy over them with what is written in Psalm 119:162 (NASB), "I rejoice at your word, as one who finds great spoil."

She was also able to rejoice again and again about the money that kept arriving, regularly but unexpectedly, from her "Klub" in Berlin. Not only was Wilhelm at that time on the Mortlocks living with the constant weight of having to make do with very little money, but so was his fiancée. In her diary she constantly mentions her worries at the prospect of not being able to pay her medical insurance premiums on time. But there are also regular expressions of gratitude to God, sometimes downright jubilant, for providing the necessary funds at the last moment.

Off to England

It seems there had been plans for Elisabeth to first go to Hagen (Westphalia, Germany) in order to start nurse's training. But nothing, apparently, came of it, for by the end of August her journal shows a first entry written in Hoglake, a place in England.

On August 1, 1937, she had left Bad Liebenzell at the crack of dawn to go to Waltenhofen. Saying good-bye to the Mission House was not easy for her. She found it strange being sent off not as a sister but as a bride. In her home village she noticed that she didn't know the children quite as well as she used to, and that she did not have a proper relationship with the adults anymore.

Her trip to England led her from Waltenhofen via Ostend in Belgium to Dover. While crossing the English Channel she became seasick, which prompted her remark that it certainly did not bode well for the South Seas. In this she was to be proved right.

The formalities for entering the country were surprisingly simple for her. The English doctor due to examine her was lying on the couch when she entered his office. He was friendly but abrupt, and only asked, "Are you in good health?" When she confirmed this he said, "Well, then you may go."

At customs, too, there were no problems. She did not need to open her suitcase at all, and the customs official even helped her to board the train that was about to leave.

In London she had to find out the train to Liverpool and realized that she was getting on quite well with the English she had learned so far. But this impression only lasted a short while. In the home of the Watts family where she stayed while in England it became evident very quickly that the early phase of learning a language can be fraught with problems.

At Liverpool station she was picked up by Mrs. Watts. In her family there were only sons, five of them, and the little guys were obviously a lively bunch. Occasionally, Mrs. Watts seemed to be absent from home, even overnight. Elisabeth then had to make breakfast for the five children – English breakfast!

Flowers or Rather Cauliflower?

Doing her housework once, Elisabeth asked for a wet cloth. To her amazement Mrs. Watts handed her floor polish instead. It seems she did not use the correct word.

After a meeting at the church one day, Mrs. Watts asked her to go home and put the cauliflower in water so that it could be cooked when they got home. Since Elisabeth did not know that cauliflower was not some kind of "cut flower," she looked everywhere in the house for a bunch of flowers so she could put them in a vase.

On another occasion she wanted to talk about when she had warmed herself at an open fireplace, causing amusement when she declared, "I was sitting on (instead of at!) the fire." Whereupon the other person replied that, seeing she had sat on the fire, she really did not look very burned.

Money!

In England, too, she was plagued by financial worries. She had to be unusually thrifty with her budget. One day, a lady asked Elisabeth whether she would like to teach her German. At first, she thought it would be too much for her, but after all she did not find the work too difficult. She was very surprised when the lady offered to pay her for the lessons. She had really wanted to do it as a favor. Now, however, she was able to earn some pocket money.

Success Stories

She had plenty of opportunities to speak English because in the Watts family they regularly had what they called "drawing-room meetings" or a "cell group" in modern parlance.

By the end of November – she had now been in England for about three months – her knowledge of the language had reached a remarkable level. In her diary, she included longish English quotations from the books she happened to be reading. In otherwise exclusively German sentences she now occasionally used English words as well: *"Wir tranken tea zusammen"* (We drank tea together). On and off, whenever she was angry with England, she would express it as "I was cross with England."

Her handwriting began to change. She had started out recording her notes strictly in Gothic script (Sütterlin). In England the letters became more and more Latinized, as written in English. But only later in life did she write fully in Latin script. She kept to her Sütterlin (Gothic) script at least until 1951, when she stopped recording things in her journal.

Her attitude towards her own thinking had also experienced a broadening. Under the influence of the English way of thinking and the difference in values connected she came to realize her own limitations, including the way she understood and lived her life as a Christian. One remarkable statement from her diary entries for November 1937 reads: "So often I have such falsely pious thoughts, instead of being totally natural."

Such self-knowledge, or at least the capacity for it, is one of the most important character traits a person needs if he or she wants to live in a completely different order of society and not fail. Elisabeth Wagner quite clearly had this gift. She allowed her very German mindset to be changed by the different cultural environment in England. She did not close herself off against it, even though the considerable adaptation she had to undergo in her personality could be very painful, forcing her to take a critical look at her own individuality. This was an important preparation for her future life with the South Sea islanders.

Also, in other respects she now seemed to have been rather well-integrated into the English way of life. She evidently had less time for her diary than at the beginning of her language studies.

Nursing Patients and Infants

Shortly before Christmas 1937 she learned that she was expected to return to Germany by the end of February 1938. There she was to be trained as a nurse at a gynecological clinic in Detmold.

Leaving England was not easy for her as she had put down roots there. This time crossing the English Channel didn't bring on seasickness.

In Detmold she needed to readapt. As a nurse, it was right for her to wear a bonnet again, which she found a bit strange .

Preparations for Departure

After a tonsil operation she began her farewell visits to relatives, acquaintances, churches, and Fellowships. She traveled to Berlin, Nuremberg, Munich and, of course, also to Waltenhofen. During this time she learned that it would probably be November by the time she could leave for the mission field. However, she definitely counted on celebrating Christmas in the South Seas.

During the last weeks of early summer in her parental home she trecked up the 7,300 feet (2,224 meters) high Nebelhorn mountain near Oberstdorf.

In July she once again spent time in Tübingen at the "DIfäM," the German Institute for Medical Missions, called "Paul Lechler Hospital" today. There she attended a course in Tropical Medicine. She apparently also had contact with people from other mission organizations who did not share her views on the Christian life. This, too, must have bothered her considerably because she said, "Unfortunately, these are often missionary people of a different inner persuasion, and I am quite sad about it. And yet, God can straighten them out."

After that, she spent some time in the Mission House again and also in Mühlhausen. A long time of waiting had begun, since her departure date was still unclear. She also met Otto Joswig, the missionary, during that time. She was able to discuss many issues with him about her future sphere of work, including questions about life on Lúkúnooch Island.

Again and again she found herself in financial straits. She had to purchase her equipment bit by bit, but had no money. But then, time after time, the money came in when she needed it and in exactly the right amounts. Thus, she once received 10 Reich marks as "down payment" for a sum of 100 Reich marks, expected to be paid out to her later, which someone had promised her; and when she went shopping, the receipt came to exactly 110 Reich marks, in other words, neither more nor less than the amount she needed but did not have before she went to the shops. One day, when she wanted to get herself a clock that would withstand the tropical climate, she was amazed when the store owner refused to take the money she wanted to pay for it.

At the commissioning service in Bad Liebenzell she was given the verse Philippians 1:27, "Conduct yourselves in a manner worthy of the gospel of Christ. Then, whether I come and see you or only hear about you in my absence, I will know that you stand firm in one spirit, contending as one man for the faith of the gospel."

"China's Millions," one of the information bulletins of the Liebenzell Mission, records her testimony (year 39, no. 10, Oct. 1938). It reads as follows:

"'Praise the LORD, O my soul; all my inmost being, praise his holy name. Praise the LORD, O my soul, and forget not all his benefits' (Psalm 103:1–2).

"This word keeps ringing in my soul as I look back on all the wonderful ways the Lord has been guiding me in my life.

"I experienced a sunny childhood and youth in my beloved Allgäu Mountains, cared for by faithful parents who did their best. When I came to Berlin as a 16-year old, I still did not know that the Lord had led me there. It was later that I understood the words of Psalm 18:19, 'He brought me out into a spacious place; he rescued me because he delighted in me.' Though I was a devout churchgoer, I still had not encountered Jesus. In Berlin God led me to a circle of dear, young believers, and it was there that I was able to find the Lover of my soul – Jesus Christ! Soon after, the Lord awakened in me a love and an interest for foreign missions; but I never thought that I would one day go out myself. It happened at a missionary lecture that I felt very clearly: The Lord also wants you in His service abroad. But alas! My defiant heart asserted itself again. I was unwilling, and for half a year I struggled against it. Gone was my peace of heart. Then, once again, God spoke to me very insistently on one of the mission Sundays when Miss von Redern used to speak. I asked myself the question posed in a little poem:

Can I live here as a Christian
In my faith so free and glad,
While abroad so many people
Live in heathen darkness sad?
No, I must obey God's mandate,
Risk my life in word and deed;
In the Name of Christ the Savior
Meeting people's deepest need.

"But when I asked my parents for permission, I received a definite 'No.' This was understandable because I am the only daughter among three brothers. So I just had to wait until God chose to make the way clear. I waited for five years. During this time of waiting God gave me the word from Isaiah 66:19, 'I will send some of those who survive to the nations ... and to the distant islands.' Then I knew: My course is set for the South Seas. I surprised myself saying to our sorority mother in such a forthright tone, 'I have come to register for Liebenzell; and when I am accepted, I will eventually go to the South Seas.' And that's exactly how it happened!

"In the fall of 1936 I entered our beloved Mission House. After getting over the initial problems I experienced wonderfully blessed times there, for which I want to thank everyone who contributed to them from the bottom of my heart.

"However, things worked out differently from what I expected. Our faithful Lord guided the vessel of my life on to another course, so that now I am on my way to the South Seas as a bride. Indeed, 'Your ways, O God, are holy' (Psalm 77:13).

"After a time at the Mission House, I went to England for half a year, and then for another time to the women's home at the clinic in Detmold. And now, by God's grace, I may leave for the mission field in the late fall.

"Amen, Lord, You will fulfill it,
What Your faithful mouth has spoken;
My expectant heart, You still it,
Not one promise shall be broken.
As You live, forever true,
Yea and Amen are in You!"

After that, she again held farewell meetings in various Fellowships and churches.

A Special Dispensation

The last days in Bad Liebenzell must have been very strenuous for Elisabeth Wagner. She met many people who wanted to talk to her one more time. One event, which seems to have drained her of most of her strength, she only confided to her journal when she was aboard ship.

The statutes of the China Inland Mission, of which the Liebenzell Mission formed the German branch at that time, stipulated that the future wife of a missionary would have to spend two years on her designated mission field, counting from the date of her arrival, before she was allowed to be married. This statute was still in power at the time when Elisabeth and Wilhelm got engaged. But since Elisabeth's departure was not going to take place until two years after that, they both would have to wait four years in all before marrying. This, she felt, would be too much to ask of herself as well as her future husband.

It is true that the Liebenzell Mission leaders had meanwhile softened this rule, such that a future missionary wife needed only to spend six months at her posting until her wedding. But even that was unacceptable to Elisabeth. And, wonder of wonders, she found support from the director's wife. Frau Buddeberg ably persuaded her husband that he should have no fear of creating a precedent by granting an exception in this case.

Just how Elisabeth reacted to all this and how she then achieved her objectives, she describes in the following words:

"Even though I had been willing to submit thus far, try as I might, I simply could not do so on this occasion, just on grounds of reason. After a hard struggle it was acknowledged that I was right, and I received my permission in writing."

She really did need this exemption in written form, because the field leaders on Chuuk would probably not have accepted a simple oral communication.

Elisabeth Wagner's personal initiative was nonetheless something of a revolt against the leadership of the Mission.

Farewell from Europe

At the beginning of November 1938 she traveled via Milan and San Remo to Genoa. Her farewell from Bad Liebenzell she described as "one of the most decisive hours in my life." On the boat, a steamer named "Scharnhorst," she was not alone, nor the only stranger. She found a sister from the Basel Mission who had attended the course on Tropical Medicine in Tübingen with her, and her cabin companions were two young English ladies with whom she got along very well.

The route took her past the volcanic island of Stromboli, where she witnessed a lava stream flowing down the mountain. In the Suez Canal she was impressed by the seemingly endless stretches of desert on both sides; and when the ship was in the Red Sea she became aware of what the Israelites must have experienced on their way from Egypt to the Promised Land, when Moses parted the waters as a means of escape for his people from their pursuers.

In the Gulf of Aden a feeling of trepidation crept over her when she stood on deck and saw a small island in the ocean passing by. The thought that in future she would have to live in such an environment made her say to herself, "If I didn't know that this was God's will, I would rather turn around and go back."

Toward the end of November, the "Scharnhorst" lay at anchor in the port of Colombo on Sri Lanka. One of Elisabeth's cabin mates went ashore here. She decided with those remaining to go sightseeing in the city. In a flash they were surrounded – as happened to Wilhelm two years earlier – by a horde of rickshaw drivers, all keen on earning some money. In a shopwindow she discovered a Christmas tree with its candles all bent over by the heat.

In Singapore all fellow travelers that had so far accompanied her left the boat to proceed to their areas of work from there. In the city itself she encountered much squalor, and she compared the people's living conditions with those in Germany: *"Deutschland, Deutschland über alles!"* (Germany, Germany above everything!) she wrote in her diary.

On November 28, she celebrated her birthday, lying seasick all day long in her deckchair: "Never before had I felt less like having a birthday. No mail, no birthday table of gifts." When she was feeling better at night and came to sit down at her table for dinner, she was greatly surprised to find her place specially arranged: the head steward had decorated it with red carnations.

A Mix-Up

A few days later she encountered a rather amusing situation:

"On Sunday, the head steward came to my cabin and said that a man from the first-class deck would like to see me. When I was introduced to him, he told me that in Berlin he had been informed that I was sailing with the "Scharnhorst" to Yokohama in order to get married there to one of his friends. Apparently he was attached to the German consulate. When I explained to him that everything was correct except the last part, he was visibly embarrassed. Wouldn't that be hilarious! In the end, they'll pair me off with someone in Japan and I won't get the right husband at all."

In the Far East

Hong Kong was the next port the "Scharnhorst" called at. Again she suffered from seasickness because the trough of a typhoon was just then sweeping across the South China Sea: "I am glad that none of my brothers is in the Navy. They certainly would have nothing to laugh about."

In Shanghai news reached her that she would probably have to stay in Japan for another month. So then, Christmas in the South Seas, which she had anticipated and prepared herself for, would be out of the question.

On December 13, 1938, the "Scharnhorst" entered the harbor of Yokohama. First, her eighteen suitcases had to pass a strict customs control, and then she herself had to submit to an even stricter passport control. But then she was also welcomed by friendly people whom she knew. These were missionary Karl Nothacker (1899–1983) and his wife Rosa (1903–1998).

She felt very well taken care of by them. Together they celebrated Christmas – with a real Christmas tree. In Tokyo there was a German butcher, and the menu in his restaurant offered black pudding (blood sausage) and liver sausage with sauerkraut: "Wonderful!"

It was unfortunate for Elisabeth that the boat to Chuuk, which she really wanted to catch, was leaving Yokohama the same day as she docked. She was told that she would have to wait for the next one on January 15, 1939.

The following weeks were spent getting the necessary papers to enter Micronesia. At the so-called Nanyo-office, the authority responsible for the Japanese Trust Territory of Micronesia, she was faced with a passport official who was obviously totally overburdened by his task. He did actually ask her where on earth Chuuk was situated, whether that might just be in South Africa. Other officials hassled her: "I have rarely encountered such rudeness as from those 'gentlemen' there! Whatever happened to Japanese decorum? It looks as though they don't really want us out there; we are only tolerated." It was a foretaste of everything the Kärchers and other Liebenzell missionaries were to experience on Chuuk during the coming war years.

Finally, on January 5, 1939, she had her entry papers in her hand. And now she grew very aware of the fact that she had given up life in Europe for a long time. It is true, she was looking forward to see her fiancé again, but she was also recalling Psalm 77:5, "I thought about the former days, the years of long ago."

The Last Leg of the Voyage

The Japanese ship "Palao Maru," which she boarded on January 15, bore no comparison to the "Scharnhorst." But at least she was traveling in a first-class cabin all by herself. She thought her situation rather strange. Among the few passengers she was the only European: "At mealtimes I was seated alone at a table. A young Japanese steward stood constantly behind me and waited for my infrequent orders. Just terrible!"

When she compared the boat to the "Scharnhorst," she came to the conclusion that the food in the second class of the German ship tasted better by far than on the "Palao Maru" in the first class. But she did not lose her humor. In the meantime, she had learned to eat with chopsticks, which to her was *"knorke"* – an expression she had learned in Berlin, meaning "awesome." But otherwise she was rather bored, as not much was happening.

The situation changed slightly, though not profoundly, when an American came aboard in Kobe: "At least it was another face." From then on, she had frequent conversations with him. Of the four Catholic nuns who boarded ship in the port of the Mariana Island of Saipan, only one spoke a little English. But talking with her was as strenuous as with a Japanese who only managed a bit of German and tried to draw her into chat whenever he could.

Saipan is one of the most northerly islands of the Marianas. At the passport control she had another foretaste of what she would have to put up with in the coming years. The official checking her papers expressed his suspicion, totally out of the blue, that she must be a Communist spy.

From Saipan it was only three more days until her landing on Chuuk. This thought really inspired her: "Only three more days and I will be able to see him again, the man who will become my life partner."

Between Saipan and Chuuk the waters seemed to be somehow rest-less. She was amazed that she did not get seasick. As a precaution, how-ever, she lay down on her deck chair for hours. That diminished the ef-fects of the swaying noticeably.

A Japanese chemist, who for days had been wandering around her at some distance, seemed to want to talk to her but did not come out with it. When he finally plucked up enough courage to do so, it was evident that he spoke German surprisingly well, having learned it in Berlin and Dres-den. "You can well imagine how happy I was to finally find someone who could speak German. Otherwise, everything has to be in English only. But I am grateful that I no longer have difficulty speaking it. With-out English it is simply impossible to manage."

Tonowas Island

On January 28, 1939, almost exactly at 3:00 p.m., the steamer docked at the island of Tonowas. Elisabeth knew that Wilhelm had been waiting for her for almost two weeks already. She had written him a number of weeks beforehand that she would arrive on Chuuk on January 30. Small wonder that he, consequently, had decided to go to Chuuk "in order to pick up the letter writer personally."

This had not been all that easy. Wilhelm had asked some islanders to take his luggage to the boat that was to convey him from Lúkúnooch to Tonowas. But they had brought it back again: "The captain said there's no more room for you, you are supposed to try again several weeks later." But Wilhelm insisted resolutely to be taken along. He firmly refused to leave the boat until he had arrived on Chuuk two days later, on January 16.

There he found a telegram from Elisabeth stating, "Arrive 28th." That was two days earlier than originally announced. Well, all the better! He sent her a telegram also, which reached her on January 20 on the "Palao Maru": "Arrived tonight on Truk. Received telegram. Expecting you. Wilhelm."

On board ship he was then able to "welcome a fresh-looking German girl whom I hadn't seen for two years. But I still knew her."

Well, what do you know!

8

Their Years Together on the Mortlock Islands (1939–1943)

A Japanese Stickler for Red Tape

The reader has perhaps noticed that, so far, the unfolding events have been conveyed in the past tense. From now on, since Wilhelm and Elisabeth are going to share their lives together, their story will continue in the language of the present, so we can participate in it at close range.

In spite of all the joy of seeing Wilhelm again, this first meeting strikes Elisabeth as rather strange. The weather conditions, too, are less inviting, for Chuuk is blanketed in pouring rain. Neither she nor her luggage can get ashore. So she stays in her cabin on the boat overnight.

Their first walk together takes them to the immigration office. There, she encounters a grotesque scene of Japanese bureaucracy. First of all, the official wants to know how tall she is. Since she doesn't know it exactly, they measure her. Then she has to answer the question as to how many gold teeth she has: "Please to make exact statements relating to upper and lower!" The official even wants to know the names of the people in Germany "who love Elisabeth." Since it is customary in Japan to mention the family name and then what we call the first or Christian name, he cannot understand at all why Elisabeth Wagner's father Michael is not also called Elisabeth.

After the questioning – with all the signs of an interrogation – ends, their civil marriage takes place, to the satisfaction of the Japanese Colonial Administration. It is being sealed, not only with their signature but also with their fingerprints. For this, both of them have to press their thumbs deep into red ink.

In later years, Wilhelm loved to tell what the Japanese used to do to their names. Not only the Chinese, but also the Japanese are known to have problems with the pronunciation of the consonants "r" and "l," a problem giving rise to many a joke. Both of the sounds occur several times in the names Wilhelm Friedrich and Elisabeth Kärcher, née Wagner. Moreover, in Japanese and, by the way, also in Chuukese, the rule requires that a vowel must be followed by a consonant; and Japanese words very frequently end in a vowel. These peculiarities make it hard for those whose native tongue is Japanese to pronounce the names of German missionaries correctly. In Japanese pronunciation Wilhelm thus sounds something like "Wiruherumu," Elisabeth sounds like "Erisabeto," and the Kärcher family name sounds like "Kerukeru." Hilarious to our ears!

Less hilarious seems a sentence added by the young husband to a letter written by his wife to her parents on February 1, 1939. He still addresses them with German formality (similar to calling them Mr. and Mrs. Wagner in English). Apparently in those days that was still required of a son-in-law who had only been married at the registry office, for "the wedding will not be until tomorrow!" By this they meant their church ceremony.

Wedding on the Island of Toon

The following day, they both go to Wútéét. No sooner have they arrived on shore than they are greeted by girl students singing a song in German.

On the following day they arrive on Toon. The Pataaniyen Mission Station is spick and span. The female students being educated here have polished everything like a mirror to ensure Wilhelm and Elisabeth get a sparkling welcome. On February 3, 1939 they celebrate their church wedding.

The day before, almost all inhabitants of the Mortlock Islands who were present on the Chuuk Lagoon at this point in time, had come to Toon. At five o'clock in the morning, the islanders start their great sing-song they always perform when they want to express affection for somebody. The wedding is postponed until two in the afternoon, because on Chuuk events do not take place at the time scheduled, but only when all those who want to participate are present – and not until the rain stops.

At the wedding a Japanese missionary is the first to give a message, then comes Johannes Rattel, who also administers the vows. Their wedding text is taken from John 2:5, "His mother said to the servants, 'Do whatever he tells you.'" After that they all celebrate and sing until late into the night. Several days later, Elisabeth writes in her journal, that it was as merry an occasion as it must have been at the wedding of Isaac und Rebecca in Genesis 24.

The First Official Trip Together

This trip is also their honeymoon and leads them to Lúkúnooch where Wilhelm has been stationed now for two years. For the trip out there he buys a Japanese sleeping mat for his wife – expressly meant as a wedding gift. He himself intends sleeping on the floorboards. She does accept the present but tells him that she is now also a missionary. If he has to sleep on the floor, she will do likewise.

The *"Dämpferle"* (little steamboat), as she calls the boat, is a bit much to take. The so-called aft cabin, scarcely more than a yard high, with a floor area of about six and a half by ten feet (two by three meters), is more like a dog kennel. Here they live and sleep together with three Japanese and one islander among the luggage bags belonging to each. The men smoke like chimneys, and the air can be cut with a knife. Already after the first night Elisabeth gives up her resolve to sleep on the floor boards like her husband. When they arrive on Lúkúnooch she thanks him almost profusely for the sleeping mat. Even though she slept on it the whole second night, she can feel all her bones aching. She feels, if she had lain on the bare boards, she would surely be bruised all over.

The First Boat Trips in the Mortlocks

The following Sunday, Wilhelm introduces his wife to the congregation during the service and translates her first message. The coming weeks are filled with converting the missionary living quarters into a comfortable home. She learns the first language phrases in order to be able to have simple chats with the nationals, and in doing so she begins to appreciate the people for whom she has come here.

It is not quite clear what she means when she writes, "It is really amusing – my husband sometimes forgets that he is married!" Presumably, on occasions, he meddles in household affairs that he had to see to on his own until now; though he should not continue to do so because by now his wife regards them as her department.

Missionary work in the area of the Mortlocks makes boat trips unavoidable. Since the Mission does not have a modern motorboat at the moment, Wilhelm and his wife have to make the trips in an outrigger canoe, as is customary in Oceania.

These boats are very narrow and have interesting sailing equipment. The so-called outrigger, without which the boat would not be stable, is connected to the main hull of the boat
by poles and struts, whose surface forms a
platform with room for paraphernalia and fellow travelers.

One day, Elisabeth is sat between boxes on
just such an outrigger platform. They are on
their way to Woneyopw at the west end of the
lagoon of Lúkúnooch, about 7.5 miles (12 km) away. Sister Anna Dederer is stationed there. The trip takes about two and a half hours. On the
way, Elisabeth gets seasick as never before. But obviously she disdains
succumbing to self-pity. In her journal she makes the comment about her
constant need to throw up: she is just feeding the fish – as you do in such
situations. She even thinks of the sharks: "This time I just can't help feeding all the predators."

She recognises that those moments when the sail has to be shifted
from one end of the boat to the other are especially dangerous. The technology of the outrigger canoe makes this necessary, as it cannot tack
against the wind. The process is a balancing act, and a boat can easily
capsize in the process.

However, she soon recovers and is able to give a short message in
church. The return trip is undertaken in a bigger sailing canoe. This time
she does not sit on the outrigger platform as the boat sails along, but under the roof of a small cabin situated on the leeward side. She won't get
seasick there because she can lie down.

Communication Problems

During these first months Elisabeth is getting acquainted with the totally different orientation of the islanders' personality. This is especially
evident among the students.

One day, a boy comes to her to get a slate pencil. After receiving it, he
doesn't go back to school as he really should, but lingers. For a time he
wanders around. Finally, she has to send him back to school in no uncertain terms. He obeys and disappears like lightning. Her husband then
informs her that this particular boy had ripped his trousers and was
ashamed to be seen from behind. The rip that would reveal his bottom
was, of course, an embarrassment for him.

She notices that another student is missing in the Sunday service. Her husband knows that he is not coming to church because he has no trousers at all.

Elisabeth finds herself in an unpleasant linguistic quandary. Her modest knowledge of the language gives her the greatest trouble when visitors come who only speak Japanese, such as the police officer's wife or the Japanese merchants who administer the "warehouse" on Lúkúnooch. Whenever she has to talk to them she speaks in German, her husband translates her words into the language of the Mortlock Islands, and a local person finally translates that into Japanese. Such conversations are strenuous and cumbersome. Another eventful activity for her is to go shopping. Without a knowledge of Chuukese she is dependent on her husband and finds herself more or less confined to the house because of it. In her diary she complains about the slow progress she is making, in spite of regular efforts every night to tackle the language. Her husband is genuinely striving to introduce her to the secrets of grammar; and she herself admits that he really has problems with her in this, especially when it is as hot as it has been for weeks already.

She is amazed that she can communicate with the chief on Kútú in German. He had learned to speak it during the German colonial era.

School Classes

It is a well-known fact that one always learns and retains the most when one has to teach a subject. A language, too, is learned much more quickly when it is used in teaching. You just must not be afraid to "murder" it at the beginning.

Elisabeth is very determined to make use of this opportunity. One morning, when her husband cannot start his class on time, because he has to go to some government office, she goes over to the school building, summons all her courage and teaches the class herself. Her experience is an immediate success: "It went better than I thought it would!" The feeling of certainty is even stronger the next day, as she stands in front of the class again. Now she knows that, at the least, she can act as his substitute.

Event-Orientation versus Time-Orientation

She still has her problems with the islanders' behavior – they are event-oriented and not time-oriented like Europeans. Someone can just happen to appear at the door shortly before midnight to bring her some fish. It is as well to know in this regard that the islanders catch some fish more easily by night than by day. And since there are no fridges, the fish spoils unless it is eaten as soon as possible. "So you get out of bed, accept the fish, and start cleaning and scaling!"

Everything Is Always Half Broken

At the end of February, a boat brings the boxes containing Elisabeth's equipment. The first surprise comes while unpacking them: The sewing machine is damaged, broken pieces fall out of the box with the best china, and the beautiful white shade of the floor lamp has a huge dent.

The boxes also contain a gramophone. It is operated by a steel spring – at that time the state of the art in music technology. That, too, is half broken. The narrow part of the acoustic horn is bent all out of shape. The real damage, though, is not discovered until later at the festive meal that the islanders have put together to commemorate the Kärchers' wedding. At the appointed time Wilhelm winds up the wondrous box with a key and sets the steel needle on the shellac disc. Everybody is in suspenseful anticipation. The contraption is starting to move, but after a few turns it begins to croak and stops. Fortunately, the damage can be repaired and it is working again.

The worst is that the cans of meat have not survived the transport well at all. Nearly all of them have been totally flattened and most of them have burst open; and the rising odour can be imagined only too well.

They have barely unpacked when the stove in the kitchen collapses. Bricks have fallen out and Wilhelm has to get busy building a new fireplace.

And yet, she feels very much at home in the house. Her husband arranges and makes everything exactly as she wants it. "You surely cannot find any more attentive husband than mine," she writes.

In her dreams she sometimes sees herself carried away to Germany, "and that is always so pleasant." Still, she emphatically reassures her relatives, "But you must not think that I am homesick because of it. We are otherwise doing fine."

What Swabians Eat in the South Seas

One day, Elisabeth opens one of those cans that remained undamaged on the trip from Europe. She assumes that it contains beans. To her amazement it turns out to be meat. Wilhelm is overjoyed and at once wishes his wife would make more "skillful mistakes" of this kind. When she adds sauerkraut to it, his happiness is complete. He feels *kinamwmwe*, as the islanders would say, and cannot praise his new German relatives from Waltenhofen highly enough "to the skies;" they have packed such unexpected and noble delicacies into the boxes, as Elisabeth later writes in a letter.

She seems also to be very successful at making *Spaetzle* (the Swabian noodle speciality), for which he has been waiting for six weeks by now. However, there are also failures that do not please him at all: "My last bread was not a success because I tried out some different yeast." His comment was that they would soon be able to open up a brick factory!

Once in a while the islanders bring her breadfruit. These can be used like potatoes for cooking, frying, or deep-frying. One can even make something out of it tasting remarkably like Swabian potato salad, and even surpassing it greatly in quality.

In the meantime, the two of them have planted a kitchen garden, from which they can pick something every morning. Among other things, they are growing papayas and lemons there. Only vegetables refuse to grow properly.

Missionary Experiences

In June 1939, we see them busy in various ways, collecting mutual experiences in dealing with the islanders. They have two to three meetings a day visiting one of the islands in the Mortlock region; they also teach school classes and give singing lessons as well as dispensing medical aid. There are always many sick people in the villages, especially people with skin rashes. Wilhelm is primarily busy with dental care, commenting: "Even pulling teeth is a joy for me, though not so much for the patients. Afterwards, though, they are grateful to me."

They find it hard to get used to funerals and lamenting for the dead. This is a ritualistic behavior, which Europeans find very oppressive. Elisabeth and Wilhelm do too, especially when it lasts all night long. Those who are hearing these laments for the dead for the first time will think it eerie. The ritual involves a number of customs that really cannot be condoned by Christians: The dead are presented with food and other offerings on their graves. Furthermore, a light must be kept burning there. For Wilhelm and Elisabeth such customs are a cause for concern.

In one of the houses Wilhelm one day discovered things hanging down from a rafter. They turned out to be so-called magic for making things less heavy. The islanders believe that it will give an outrigger canoe better buoyancy and will not let it sink so easily.

What should a missionary do in such a situation? Does he have the right to intervene in the practice of religious rituals that are alien to him? Should he even be allowed at all to meddle in the affairs of foreign societies? There are certainly many more islanders who are not Christians and want to keep their animistic thought patterns. But what of those who profess to be Christians and still continue to make use of magic whenever something needs to be accomplished? Should the missionary ignore the matter, or should he rather condemn such things?

First of all, Wilhelm asks for these magic objects to be taken down. No one moves. Is this for fear of the consequences, of punishment by the spirits that supposedly govern these magic powers? When nothing happens, he himself takes hold of the objects and throws them into the ocean. A younger man helps him to do so.

Such action is risky at that time, because it makes people angry. Missionaries can endanger the success of their work in this manner or even hinder it completely. Wilhelm is aware of this. Again and again he asks himself these questions and addresses the fact that the islanders still have not totally broken with such things. He also makes an effort to remain patient.

On one occasion things get difficult when they have to travel on a boat belonging to the Japanese Administration, whose crew is dead drunk while at sea. One day they nearly have a severe accident. The captain and the engineer can barely avoid crashing their boat at full steam into the pier superstructure.

On Mwóóch, a small island in the neighboring lagoon of Satawan, the two missionaries experience their first wedding between local people. Just the following day the young husband has to leave the island. The reason: he has been drafted into service on Angaur, an island in the Palau region, where the Japanese Administration is mining for minerals. He will have to work there, and because of the long distance he won't see his wife for a long time. Wilhelm and Elisabeth bear witness to a heartbreaking leave-taking.

Sometimes the islanders perceive strangers and their conduct in a strangely distorted way. One day, the chief wants to know why Wilhelm happened to marry such an old woman, since he himself is still so young. The reason why the chief was wondering about this is that Elisabeth wears glasses, and for him that is a sign of advanced age.

Life on the Mortlocks can be very strenuous. During a trip to Ettaal, an atoll northwest of Lúkúnooch, Elisabeth is very seasick for two hours. Her husband carries her the last stretch to the beach through the water. Once they arrive there, they first have to make their lodgings somewhat livable. They hammer nails into the wall so that their clothes and utensils are not just left at the mercy of the rats on the floor but can be hung up.

Elisabeth describes her physical exhaustion in the words, "I lay down and slept and dozed and dozed and slept."

Her husband seems to be of a more robust nature. He is constantly full of energy. Often he holds an impromptu devotional with the people who have come to the beach to welcome the missionary couple. In doing so he saves them the trouble of having to come a long way again to a later church service, especially on far flung islands like Téé.

The kindnesses shown them by the islanders have a style of their own. After an afternoon meeting, an elderly woman comes toward them, pulls a fish out of her skirt and hands it to them as a *niffang* (a present), which leads Elisabeth to make the remark, "She had kept the fish there for the whole meeting; hence it was pre-heated. Enjoy your meal!"

In those days, a guest invited by the islanders to a meal has to reckon with surprises. To them nothing is known at that time about E. coli bacteria and their effect. Long drawn-out intestinal infections and parasite attacks are, therefore, almost unavoidable.

On one occasion, Elisabeth is preparing a fish for lunch. She throws the head out to the chickens. A dog, noticing it, grabs the fish head and runs off with it. A few minutes later a man comes to her house, bringing her the fish head on a leaf with the remark that the dog must have stolen it from her.

She is, though, for ever mindful of her actual concern "that God would work through his Holy Spirit and that his word would not return to him void. You stand there all powerless and totally dependent on him."

Everyday Life on Lúkúnooch

Those who live and work close to the equator know that in these latitudes there is only sunlight for about twelve hours; it has to be fully used. Working in the evening by the light of an oil lamp is barely feasible.

While Wilhelm is teaching school classes, Elisabeth takes care of the household. At noon, the hottest time of the day, all islanders as well as missionaries hold their *aséésé*, that is to say their siesta. Late in the afternoon, about five o'clock, there is another chapel service at the church before sundown at six o'clock.

By now, Elisabeth has been on Lúkúnooch for six weeks. Time is just flying by. The fact that she has to get up at five o'clock in the morning doesn't please her very much. But otherwise she enjoys life. Shortly before six a.m. it's time to go to church where Wilhelm leads the devotional. Then the people come for the dispensing of medicine. There are eye infections among the adults, and many children are suffering from ringworm. In those days, she had nothing to combat this sickness except injections of arsphenamine (under the trade name of Salvarsan).

She has one problem with this: "If I could only speak the language!" She still has to call her husband in to help her when she cannot understand the people. They are, however, very patient. Often she finds it quite amusing how her patients try to help her with her broken Chuukese, even understanding what she says, no matter how incorrectly she expresses herself.

Wilhelm and Elisabeth experience how fateful some sicknesses, even seemingly simple ones, can be for the islanders. If someone in Germany, for example, gets appendicitis, he can, as a rule, quickly find a doctor or a hospital. On a South Sea island this diagnosis often means the sick person's death sentence; which is especially tragic for a young person like Krimentine.

She is fifteen years old and suffers from tuberculosis. Wilhelm and Elisabeth take care of her and endeavor to keep the sickness in check with the modest means and antibiotics at their disposal. One day, Leonora, Krimentine's mother appears and begs them to come to her hut. There they find the girl lying down and weeping.

"Why are you crying?"

"Because I am bound to die!"

Wilhelm reminds her of Psalm 23, well known to Krimentine. They pray it through together.

After that, the girl is carried into the *wuut*, the clan's assembly hall. All her relatives gather around her. They sit there and start with the lamentation for the dead. Wilhelm sits down beside her, when Krimentine suddenly says:

"*Éwusapw kkechiw!* You are not to cry!"

And after a while:

"*Raa etto! Wúwaa pwaapwa!* They are coming! I am happy!"

At that moment, the lament stops. No one is crying anymore, nor through the whole night.

They put a cross of breadfruit wood on her grave. On it, a heart is engraved with the inscription: "Blessed are the dead who die in the Lord." Even at the funeral no one is crying.

They never have found out what Krimentine had really seen and who had come. In a narrative entitled "Through Crashing Waves" Wilhelm dedicated a chapter to her (1965:33–35).

Being on Her Own

Wilhelm Kärcher takes his responsibilities seriously for the churches in his care and visits them regularly and conscientiously. His wife cannot always accompany him. Nor must the work on Lúkúnooch be left undone. This means that she is often on her own.

In May 1939 Wilhelm sets off to visit Nómwuluuk island for a week. At his departure she doesn't feel well. She is afraid she is getting a kidney infection. But in spite of it she agrees to let him go.

She confides to her journal how depressed she feels:

"In the evening, when things quieten down on the mission field, loneliness creeps up like a grey spectre. One longs for beloved company. It is then that my harmonium becomes my refuge and in playing I forget everything around me. It is a blessing that music helps us get through lonely hours; how grateful I am for it. Since I do not yet know the language sufficiently, I have no real opportunity of conversing with anybody. Fourteen days then seem like an eternity."

In such a mood, little incidents act like balm. A little boy comes, accompanied by others, and brings her three coconuts ready-to-drink from. She doesn't quite know why he wants to give them to her. The boy makes no move to go home again but seems determined to stay. Finally he comes out with it: "I have a birthday." Of course, persistent as any child can be, he is expecting to get a present. Once she gives him a handkerchief, he is happy to leave.

Those who work in missions and have to live in a remote area know that everyone is constantly expecting to get a letter, or rather many letters, with the next boat that arrives. On Chuuk, people are always dependent on someone who will take care that the letters written get to the post office on Wééné, and that incoming mail will be picked up from there as well. This is especially difficult on the Mortlock Islands, since letters have to be left with an islander or a boatman going to Chuuk, and one never knows for sure whether the couriers will really be dependable. Sometimes there will be unpleasant surprises because of their unreliability.

One day, Johannes Rattel is traveling on a boat in the Chuuk lagoon that is also going to the Mortlock Islands. By chance, he looks over the shoulder of the captain steering the boat, and cannot believe his eyes: he sees letters written by Anna Dederer and the Kärchers that long since should have been on their way to Germany but which, out of pure negligence and sloppiness, have been making the rounds of the islands. Learning of this, Elisabeth writes to her relatives: "From now on I will number our letters so that you will know whether one has been lost."

She is suffering from the immense heat dominating the weather for weeks now, and she witnesses the jetty being ripped away one night during a storm.

To find some diversion in her loneliness she occasionally takes some of the boys to row her over to Woneyopw and visit Anna Dederer.

In this situation Iinas, her domestic help, gets embroiled in a scandal. She is involved in a very complex adulterous affair and has to go to jail. For Elisabeth this is terribly embarrassing.

From time to time she has to listen to some hostile statements. One of the church elders bluntly announces during a service that it is not appropriate to give missionaries anything since they obviously have plenty of everything. Taking into account how little the islanders have, this assertion certainly has some truth to it. Still, Elisabeth feels somehow personally attacked.

Sometimes Roman Catholic children try to insult her by calling her a *Pirositan mii ttipis*, which means something like a "sin Protestant."

This remark is a sign that the relationship between the Catholic and the Protestant population is somewhat strained; the effects are also felt by Elisabeth. Of course, she does not treat Catholic patients asking her for medication any differently from Protestant ones. However, she is open to the risk of being misunderstood.

One day, a woman comes to the mission station with her sick child. Elisabeth notices right away how serious the condition of the little patient is. She has no expectation of the child getting well again. If, in this situation, she gave some medicine to the child and it should die, she could possibly be accused of purposely having caused his death. But she also can't very well refuse to help. So what does she do? She prays fervently, gives the child the medication and hears soon after that he is doing much better.

Situations where it is a matter of a person's life and death – and where she alone has to decide what medical measures to take are very burdensome to her. In a letter dated September 19, 1939, to her "Klub" in Berlin, she describes having been called in to help with the difficult birth of a daughter of a young Christian. Her name is Kilaata. During her training in Germany Elisabeth had twice witnessed the death of a woman during childbirth. What would happen if the same situation were repeated here, with no doctor and no possibility of an operation?

The work she has to accomplish, especially before noon, when the crowd needing medication is the largest, also has its good side. She has to get along with the language on her own and is frequently forced to "defend herself vigorously, organizing the threatening chaos," and this preoccupies her very much. The language learning progress she makes through this is enormous. By now, she can speak fluently.

At last she feels she can tackle the demands placed upon her by a women's club. Several girls are coming to her for sewing. They are working for an exhibition of handicraft, organized by the Japanese Administration. A few boys are even joining them because they want to learn how to sew and crochet. She gives them some pictures to draw instead.

Premonitions

In September 1939, letters from Germany are starting to contain more and more disturbing news. War has broken out. Elisabeth is asking about her brothers who have been conscripted, and she asks for newspaper reports.

On the islands, too, signs are increasingly pointing towards war. In July already there had been a rumor that a lighthouse was to be built on Satawan. How unusual when one day, even in the remoteness of the Mortlock Islands, a plane is spotted.

During these weeks, Rev. Heinrich Hertel, Mission inspector responsible for the South Seas, is being expected to arrive on Chuuk. The missionaries think he is already on Palau, but in reality he is being detained in Japan. The Japanese military government refuses him admission to Micronesia, and give no reasons. Nobody knows what they are afraid of. This does not augur well.

Life Is Getting More Difficult

In October, Wilhelm and Elisabeth go to Chuuk. They have to run a few errands. As they say good-bye, the islanders of Lúkúnooch are quite concerned; they are afraid the missionaries will not return because of the war happening in Europe.

On Tonowas they live with their Japanese missionary colleagues on what used to be the German mission station. Two rooms are still reserved for them there. One of the hotels where they want to eat refuses them entry. They are told the place is full. The reason is that a big Japanese steamship has arrived a few days earlier, bringing many passengers.

Elisabeth is celebrating her twenty-seventh birthday on Toon. She invites a few islanders to it. They are having rice and fish from a can, served on banana leaves – very practical eating dishes that do not need to be washed or dried afterwards.

Their return trip to Lúkúnooch is filled with obstacles. They have hardly got out on the open sea when they have to turn around because the engines are not functioning properly. Because of this a whole Sunday is frittered away. The waters remain fairly calm until they reach Loosópw, But then a storm breaks loose. They will take five days for a trip that under favorable weather conditions only takes two days. The boat is creaking at all its joints; and even though they keep the windows shut, water leaks in. The storm persists, so that they cannot dock in Lúkúnooch. The boat has to return to Woneyopw in order to wait out the end of the bad weather there. In a letter to her relatives Elisabeth is of the opinion that a trip like that would surely not be to their liking, seeing that even the Swabian Railway is too much for them![22] However, she includes some pictures of their home and expresses the wish that her relatives would come to visit them some time, knowing full well that they will be unable to take up her invitation for the next while.

Anis

Anis – the equivalent of the German name "Hans" – is the *samwoollap* on Woneyopw, which means head chief. He has been living as a Christian for a long time already and is a dependable member of his congregation. But his health is not the best.

Shortly after her return from Chuuk to Lúkúnooch she receives news that Anis has died. Wilhelm holds the funeral. The church on Woneyopw is filled to overflowing. The Japanese district official is present as well and gives a remarkable eulogy. Wilhelm reports on this in a letter dated November 25, 1939, as follows:

"I was happy with the way an educated Japanese bore witness to one of our Christians. Among other things he said, 'Your chief Anis was a Christian, as you all know. But he wasn't a Christian in name only; rather, we all saw it in his words and, above all, in his work. He always had the welfare of the whole island at heart, helping everybody. Today, you can see this especially in all the new kitchen huts that have been built very neatly according to one single type. Then, too, his being a Christian was evidenced by the fact that he never drank any alcohol offered to him and that he never smoked.'"

---

[22] The Germans have a humorous song about it in the Swabian dialect.

Sayiriiniwus

Before Anis' funeral Wilhelm has to bury the daughter of church elder Sayiriiniwus, whose conduct in life shows that his Christianity, at least in his thinking, is still strongly influenced by animistic elements. He erects a hut over his daughter's grave and places his mat in it to sleep on. For a long time he doesn't even want to leave the place during the day. His fear is that an *énú*, a malevolent spirit being, will steal the body of his daughter and eat it.

Wilhelm is constantly being confronted with such behavior. One day, he preaches about God the Creator and the power He also has over the sea and the wind. That is one topic the islanders constantly think about. In answer to his question who, in their opinion, rules over the wind and waves, a man on one of the back benches says to his neighbor, "*Énúún Mwárisi.*" By this is meant the spirit of the rainbow, a seafaring spirit that is feared and must be placated by anyone out on the ocean.

Wilhelm experiences constant agreement in one-to-one conversations whenever he argues against such attitudes; but in his absence, people always act in accordance with their old understanding. That is a bitter pill for him to swallow.

Karel

Karel – the equivalent of the German name "Karl" – is a *sowupeták* on Woneyopw, which means he holds the office of island pastor. His house is located right next to the mission station. Anna Dederer, who is stationed there, has thought for some time already that Karel is not really suited for his duties. She wants another man to replace him, thinking he would be more competent. As Wilhelm explains later, he allows himself to be influenced by her opinion; he removes Karel from office. This is a great risk for the congregation on Woneyopw. In those days, it is not a rare thing for islanders to take revenge for such actions on the part of the Mission by simply converting to Roman Catholicism, taking the whole congregation with them. That does not happen in this case. However, there is a sort of protest against Karel's dismissal.

The man favored by Anna Dederer does not take over Karel's spiritual role as expected, but only the office of head chief, which had been held by the deceased Anis. Wilhelm soon recognizes that his initiative had been totally wrong. He apologizes to Karel and is "only too glad that he wasn't in a huff and came back." After this, the groups on Woneyopw that had been considerably stirred up, slowly but surely calm down.

Etuwarit

Etuwarit – the equivalent of the German name "Eduard" – is church elder on the island of Nómwuluuk. He also does the preaching as best he can. One day, when Wilhelm cannot come to the island until after dark, he learns that one of Etuwarit's children has fallen ill with dysentery and is about to die. The child dies during the night. At the funeral the father laments the fact that this was already his fifth child he had to bury. What can one say to comfort a family faced with such grief?

Kiristiyaan

Kiristiyaan – the equivalent of the German name "Christian" [pronounced Kriss'-tiyawn] – is an especially zealous student and churchgoer. He is poor and has nothing suitable to wear. But he would very much like to come to the church meetings. So he gets an idea; either he comes dressed in father's old jacket, reaching almost down to his toes, or in big brother's wedding garment. Whether it fits him or not, makes no difference to him. In any case, he comes to church "dressed nicely."

Dissatisfied with the Conditions

One day, two strapping young men of the church on Lúkúnooch come back from Nómwuluuk, where they have been teaching their peers the art of wrestling, a sport taken up by the young islanders with great enthusiasm. Overjoyed, the two of them talk about the warm hospitality they experienced. They each bring back not only a pig ready for slaughter, but also report that during their ten-day stay five pigs had been slaughtered in their honor. Wilhelm, who rarely sees such generous behavior, is rather more disappointed and comments, "If a missionary nowadays wants to eat chicken, he usually has to pay for it or give a present of approximately the same value for it."

Christmas 1939 comes and goes without news from home. The last mail had arrived at the end of November. Since then the government boat has failed to appear. But this also has its advantages. There won't be any of the usual drunken orgies around Christmas among the men on the islands, because as long as the government boat stays away no beer and liquor get delivered.

Holidays like Christmas and the Japanese New Year always bring great temptations for the Christians, especially for the young men among them. Rice liquor plays a big part in this. The Japanese officials even promote alcohol abuse by openly encouraging the islanders to drink.

Those who refuse are publicly denounced as sissies. The storekeepers try to persuade the men especially that liquor and cigarettes contain substances that will make them *péchékkún*, that is to say "strong." It takes a good deal of effort for Wilhelm and Elisabeth to dissuade the responsible state official from forcing the Christians to join in drinking alcohol and smoking. To their surprise, he agrees and even prevents a shipment of liquor from getting ashore which the government boat, finally arriving in mid-January, wants to deliver.

After a few weeks, Anna Dederer returns from Chuuk and recounts a terrible event. She and Elise Zuber have survived a boat accident, during which eleven adults and five girls attending the Mission School on Wútéét, drowned. As happens so often, the boat was overloaded.

Light

During this time an event takes place on Woneyopw, which causes Wilhelm to write a detailed report in "China's Millions" (6.40:43–44). Esirom, the old head chief, has died.

Esirom had faithfully discharged his responsibilities for decades. Wilhelm describes him as an islander with a vision, who used every opportunity offered him, not only widening his own knowledge but also ensuring that the Mortlock Islands' population would have the opportunity to do so. Esirom was the only bearer of a title who supported the Japanese Administration in establishing a school on his island. He himself could neither read nor write. But every Sunday he had Selem, a catechumen, read to him from the Bible in order "to know more" as he emphasized again and again. For Esirom, the Bible had assumed the same significance as Martin Luther's translation for the broader population of Germany in the early modern era.

Preaching from the Sermon on the Mount, Wilhelm uses every opportunity to remind the islanders how valuable Esirom had been to them. He appeals to his listeners to preserve the legacy of their former chief and to open themselves to the light that has come to their islands because of it.

This statement contains a comparison frequently used by Wilhelm in later years whenever he came to talk about his work as a missionary on the islands around Chuuk: the imagery of the light. Again and again he says that more light had come because Christianity had replaced the old animistic religion of the islands.

This statement is true. Looking only at the tense relationships that prevailed among the islands at the beginning of the German colonial rule over Micronesia at the turn of the 19th to the 20th century, even somebody skeptical about mission work must admit that things had brightened up. At that time there were constant conflicts among the individual chieftainships, leading to violent clashes. The fighting was so devastating that the German colonial government, as already mentioned in chapter five, saw itself forced to send a gunboat to Chuuk in order to collect all the firearms from the islands. However, that had only brought a little light into the darkness of the political realm.

Darkness ruled the people in altogether different areas as well, as their aggressiveness did not only vent itself in armed violence. It often happened that a personal dispute led to someone going to the *sowuroong*, the sorcerer, to have him mix a magic potion of "medicine" that would make those who were disliked sick and eventually kill them. Darkness also covered the minds of the people when they tried in vain to conquer their fear of demonic influences in their lives through their cult of the dead. Here, too, more light was needed.

Hannah's Lament (1 Samuel 1:1–8)

In Elisabeth's diary and in her letters towards the end of 1939, evidence is mounting that she is suffering increasingly from being alone, as her husband has to be absent on visits to the churches on the Mortlocks. Among these writings one can occasionally also find expressions of regret over the fact that they still don't have a child. Thus she writes on September 13, 1939, to her relatives in Berlin, "Our 'next in line' seems to be a long time in coming." (By this she meant, of course, a "son and heir.") At the same time, though, she lets it be known how privileged she feels. In her diary we find the remark, "In Germany the women have to give up their husbands for the war, so in this respect I have much to be grateful for."

On February 3, 1940, she has her first wedding anniversary on Lúkúnooch, without Wilhelm. The political situation is getting grim. A Japanese warship has entered the lagoon. This causes great excitement. For the young islanders this event means a diversion from the uneventfulness of their existence; they gather at the beach with torches and are happy when the Japanese respond with light signals and fire off rocket flares.

Elisabeth takes a certain comfort from the experiences she has with children. There is Lutuwik, German "Ludwig," a little boy she is treating against ringworm. Out of gratitude he gives her a small piglet.

One of the Japanese officials has a little daughter. Since he fears that she would "run wild" among the island boys and girls, he asks Elisabeth to teach her reading and writing.

When, on February 18, her husband still has not returned from his trip, her journal entry becomes a lament: "I am still alone. No husband and no boat is coming. This almost is more than I can bear so that I constantly have to fight off my tears. Tears are often my only supper, and sleep is a sweet potion of oblivion." This is followed by the remarkable sentence: "If only I had at least one in my loneliness. But no husband and no child – O Lord, how long!!"

Indeed, she ends this with two exclamation marks. She must have felt like Hannah, second wife of Elkana of Ramathim Zuphim from the hill country of Ephraim: "O LORD Almighty, if you will only look upon your servant's misery and remember me, and not forget your servant but give her a son…" (1 Samuel 1:11).

At the end of February, her husband finally returns. Because of contrary wind conditions he had not been able to travel. On March 25, 1940, he writes a letter to the Mission leaders. Its contents appear in "China's Millions" and was to be the last report of the work of Liebenzell Mission on Chuuk for the next six years.

At the end of May, Elisabeth is alone again. Her health is not the best. She loses weight, weighing a mere 105 pounds. She mourns the "dead" Christians: "It is a hot southern land, but where are the fountains of water?" She is especially concerned about the conduct of two young women, Ruut and Katuura, who once attended school on Wútéét but have since become guilty of various sexual transgressions. Ankela also worries her. She is sitting in the *kanapwus*, under arrest.

Shortly after midnight one day, at the end of June, she hears the put-put of the boat coming from Chuuk. Her husband is not among the passengers. She lies down and is almost asleep again when she is called to attend a childbirth. She is afraid of this because the young woman, whom she is supposed to help, is very weak. The child comes into the world a healthy girl.

She is restless. Her husband, whom she knows to be on Nómwuluuk, has been gone for so long and she fears that his supplies are all used up. What to do? Without further delay she decides to travel to Nómwuluuk herself, as soon as an opportunity opens up. There she finds her husband in good health and unscathed. He is overjoyed at her unexpected arrival and explains why he could not get back to Lúkúnooch yet, even though he had found a crew that was willing to take him back home. Here is his account:

"I was cooking the last of my rice for the people. At first, everything went briskly and the warm rice put them in a good mood. We had a day's journey before us, but they kept on gathering around the food and dug in with good appetites. Suddenly the wind changed and the captain explained to me that he could not get to Lúkúnooch with wind like this. So we turned around and docked at an island located in front of Nómwuluuk, went ashore – and again they dug into the food. Then they wanted to wait on the island for a favorable wind. But I suggested that we simply return to Nómwuluuk. Shortly before dark I moved back into my quarters, and the family of nine pigs under the floor of the house grunted happily at this foreigner living upstairs again. On such trips one gets much better acquainted with the missionary journeys of the apostle Paul."

The house they live in is "a relatively decent wooden shack," even though the rain comes in during stormy weather. A table and two chairs comprise all the furniture. They sleep on the floor, and a small kerosene lamp serves as a light. They can only wash with great difficulty: the place is swarming with flies and mosquitoes.

This is Elisabeth's first visit to the island. That makes her interesting to the locals there: "One cannot go anywhere without being followed."

One day on Nómwuluuk they discover a very big old tree, standing there totally useless, and its wood is so rotten it is only good for burning. The little coconut palm trees around it cannot grow properly. At first, they do not get a proper answer to their question about the tree's purpose. Some students finally come up with the information: The tree is *fel*, taboo, and serves as protection. In earlier times, it was a receptacle for spears needed for warfare. In those days, it was even looked upon as an oracle. When the wind was strong and the spears moved, it was supposed to be a sign that they could successfully go to war against the inhabitants of other islands.

This was again proof of how strongly animistic thought patterns still influenced the life of the island Christians. Wilhelm and Elisabeth are reminded of 2 Kings 14:3–4, the record of Amaziah, then king of Judah. It is said that he did "what was right in the eyes of the LORD," but not in total commitment, for "the high places … were not removed…"

The return trip to Lúkúnooch starts in a dramatic way. They have westerly winds. Such weather conditions make it difficult to reach Nómwuluuk. The Japanese trading company's motorboat is waiting outside on the reef. Wilhelm and Elisabeth can only reach it with the help of an outrigger canoe. She settles down on it as best she can. They have to leave most of their luggage behind on the island. The trick is to wait for a favorable moment when the boat can push through the breakers and be rowed out to the motorboat. A few young men undertake a first trial run with their canoe. A high surging wave breaks it apart. Shortly after, the canoe on which Elisabeth is sitting succeeds in venturing out to deeper waters.

But now the problem is how to get from the canoe, dancing up and down, onto the motorboat. "At that moment, when our canoe was lifted up by a wave, two strong islanders gripped my wife by the hands, and in one swing she was aboard the boat." With these words Wilhelm ended his detailed report that he published in a small collection of stories about his work (1965:18).

After they have both safely boarded the motorboat, they find long awaited mail from Germany. Indeed, the mailbag is full to bursting. And, as it happens when one has not heard from home for a long time, they want to know as quickly as possible what news the letters contain. Elisabeth is reading with great enthusiasm. But her pleasure does not last long. Both of them get seasick as never before. In other respects, too, many things go wrong during this voyage. Twice the motor stalls and has to be repaired. They take ten hours for only forty-five sea miles. Situations like this make their hearts long for what it says in Revelation 21:1, "… and there was no longer any sea."

Missionaries have a lot of trouble with bad weather conditions when the trade winds blow between November and May. They have to endure many things when traveling in these small boats. Out on the ocean it is especially difficult to prepare food, so Wilhelm constructs a so-called "cooking box" to store all the utensils needed so one doesn't have to go hungry in primitive surroundings. The lid is screwed shut so that the contents of this box will not get lost when the waves are pounding. Sometimes the box is also used for other things than cooking. Whenever during a storm a breaker splashes so much water into the boat that it has to be baled out quickly, Wilhelm hastily unscrews his box so the cooking pot can be used as a ladle.

Back at Lúkúnooch, they cannot dock at the pier and have to return to Woneyopw. Things don't look good there. In their absence a storm has been raging. The brick shoreline wall has a gaping hole. Many papaya trees have fallen over.

Guitars and a Cow

The girls on Lukúnooch are learning to play the guitar. But Wilhelm and Elisabeth are not satisfied with that because the girls are not singing; they are only "strumming along" as they call it. Besides, the Japanese are forcing the girls that can play the guitar to perform during their drunken orgies. This soon leads both missionaries to lose interest in continuing the guitar lessons. Wilhelm sells the guitars belonging to the Mission to a Japanese dealer on Chuuk for 60 yen and, by doing so, can accomplish another unpleasant business. He has been asked to sell a cow for the missionary ladies on Wútéét. For this he demands 400 yen. The Japanese dealer does not want to buy the cow for that price, but since he is very interested in the guitars, he takes the cow anyway and gives Wilhelm the price he has asked.

The War Gets Closer

At the beginning of July, Elisabeth expresses joy "at the victories our troops are experiencing," but she is also worried about the fate of her brothers who are in the front lines. By the end of August her own situation has become bleaker: "The boat is not coming. The flour is running out and with it our bread. No news either from home. I wonder if the war is over by now? To be in such seclusion here! Several ships are said to be anchored on Chuuk and we have already seen planes."

After this entry, Elisabeth's journal contains a big gap. Until well into November she and Wilhelm are staying on Chuuk, where they are restricted because the boats are no longer running regularly. Elisabeth does not feel well; her body weight is going up and down.

Christmas 1940 has passed. Since October they have had no more news from Germany. She is afraid that the Japanese intelligence service is intercepting her mail and checking it. Her suspicions are well founded. The letters still reaching their addressees show signs of having been opened and read both by the Gestapo (the German secret state police during the Nazi regime) and the Japanese counter intelligence.

The beginning of 1941 puts both missionaries under increasing pressure. Wilhelm, however, still describes their situation with a twinkle in his eye: "One would think we were sitting on a branch that has been sawed into."

In April, a new Japanese official is starting his duty on Lúkúnooch. "The old one has drunk himself into a stupor," is the laconic comment made by Elisabeth. But the new one confiscates their camera. The reason he gives is that they could, after all, take spy photos of military operations on the Mortlock Islands. They never see it again. Some time later it is burned in an air attack on the administrative office where it had been seized.

There is still enough to eat. A pig can be fattened very nicely with coconuts. They can smoke the meat and by doing so conserve it awhile. But the situation is critical and in the meantime they have concluded that the war will also reach the islands. They can still do their work undisturbed but they feel that it has become harder and will be even more difficult in the future.

In this situation, Johannes Rattel, the field director, sends an inquiry by wiring the Mission's headquarters in Bad Liebenzell. He would like to know what is to be done with the missionaries under the present conditions of war. The reply states that he and his family should return to Germany, but the others should stay, "no matter what the circumstances." In April 1941, he and his family start on their way home. They are the last of the missionaries to be able to leave Chuuk.

Wilhelm and Elisabeth are also given to understand – by the Japanese – that they are free to leave for Germany if they want but they cannot think of ever coming back. These are dismal prospects for the future work on the islands. Meanwhile, they are no longer permitted to travel. They can only visit the neighbouring island of Woneyopw.

In June, a warship is sighted. Rumour has it that a high-ranking Japanese officer is expected to arrive. This is Admiral Yamamoto, the commander-in-chief of the Japanese Naval Forces. From now on, he will be planning and executing the military operations in Melanesia, New Guinea, and on the Solomon Islands, but above all the Battle of the Coral Sea. A little while later, he starts his last flight from the Mortlock Islands, never to return again.

There is no longer any news getting through to Chuuk from Germany, not for almost nine months by now.

Meanwhile Elisabeth, still writing her diary regularly, comments on these events with great apprehension. But something quite important has happened, and yet during all this time she makes no mention of it, not one word: She is pregnant.

Hannah's Joy (1 Samuel 1:20)

In the last days of July, we suddenly find the statement in the middle of her records: "Every day now we expect our 'next in line' (the 'son and heir'). This is a real test of patience."

On August 10, 1941, at nine o'clock in the morning – two weeks overdue – Hannelore is born.

So the expected "next in line" is not a "son and heir" – it is a girl. For German purposes she is not really considered to be "next in line" at all, as it has to be a "son and heir." For the islanders, however, she is indeed the "daughter and heiress." They trace their descent principally not via the father's genealogy but the mother's. Women are also the ones who inherit land and pass it on. Women thus have a prominent position in family history. The arrival of Hannelore is, therefore, a significant event for the islanders. But not only for them!

Her father is able to send a telegram of the birth of his daughter to Germany. What he does not know is that it was to be the last sign of life from the South Seas to their relatives. The postcard he sends two days after Hannelore's birth to her uncle and future godfather Karl Wagner in Waltenhofen will take all of five years to reach its intended addressee.

Getting Supplies Becomes More Difficult

The German Reich has meanwhile attacked the Soviet Union. In Europe they have what Joseph Goebbels calls "total war." From now on and for a long time to come there would be no more news from relatives in Germany.

Since boat traffic between Chuuk and the Mortlock Islands functions only sporadically, getting supplies of vitally important food for the family becomes problematic. Flour and salt have run out by now. Elisabeth has to salt her cooking with seawater.

Life also quickly becomes more difficult for little Hannelore. For a time there is still canned milk for her. Then this runs out as well. In this situation the islanders start bringing *áchi* to the young mother. This is juice as sweet as honey, produced from developing coconut buds by nipping them at the top and letting the resulting liquid drip into a receptacle.

One problem with this are the many insects attracted by the sweet juice as they fall into the vessel and drown. They have to be filtered out and the rest has to be cooked in order to sterilize it. But not all problems are solved in this way. Certain insects leave behind some chemicals that can cause bladder cramps. Whenever Elisabeth gives her little daughter the bottle, she often sits and prays that "the junk in there" will not do her any damage.

Obstacles

The Japanese officials and military try more and more to restrict the freedom of the missionaries to work. They are considered spies – probably because of their knowledge of English, even though Germany and Japan are supposed to be allies. As of that moment, they are not allowed to leave Lúkúnooch. Even the neighbouring island of Woneyopw is now out of bounds for them.

One day, Elisabeth wants to buy a few things for an exhibition of islanders' handicraft. As she is purchasing them she is ordered to leave the shop by a Japanese official.

But there are Japanese whose attitude remains friendly towards them, for example a man by the name of Mori San. Occasionally he even supplies them with flour and other vital things that the military have.

Meanwhile, their mail does not just seem to be censored; indications are mounting that their letters are being retained. Likewise, they are no longer receiving any news about the other Liebenzell Mission workers on Chuuk; and if the missionaries want to tell Wilhelm how they are doing, they always have to add an accompanying letter in Japanese to comply with the harassing regulations.

At the end of 1941, Japan executes a surprise attack against the American naval fleet in Pearl Harbor on Hawaii. America responds by entering the Second World War – a decision that from now on is to devastate the islands of the Pacific Ocean also. This date is a significant and incisive moment in the lives of the Kärcher family.

There is no more milk for Hannelore. The boat that until now, at increasing intervals, used to come from Chuuk, simply does not come any more. Sometimes Elisabeth awakes with a start and thinks she can hear it. But it is only the roaring of the breakers and the howling of the wind. She has given up waiting for mail from home. Now she is just waiting for food.

Her journal entries show signs of desperation. It has not been raining for quite a while. That means a shortage of water on the islands. She can no longer wash diapers properly, and the soap ran out five months ago. "Hold on!" She is now ending her evening entries in the journal more frequently with such exhortations.

Missing

Meanwhile in Germany, too, people are more than worried. On July 15, 1942, Elisabeth's mother sends the following letter to the Japanese embassy in Berlin. Here is the exact wording:

Since 1939, my only daughter Lisl has been married to missionary Wilhelm Kärcher of the Liebenzell Mission in Mortlock-Lukunotre on the Coral Islands (via Truk-Harbor Nanyo). As of the beginning of the war with Soviet Russia I have been without news from my daughter, and as of Japan's entry into the war with England and the U.S.A., my son-in-law and his wife had to move into Japanese Imperial territory. Her present whereabouts are, however, unknown to me, since my daughter has not been able to communicate with me, her last letter dating from June 25, 1941. On September 9, 1941, however, I received a telegram about the birth of a child, and since that time I have not heard anything more from my daughter.

It is now my request that my daughter be given some brief information regarding the welfare of her father and mother and the well-being of her three brothers on the battlefield, i.e. in an officially authorized way, perhaps by wireless telegraphy (radio message). I would gladly pay the expenses for this.

I am leaving the possible timing and the way in which the communication can be carried out completely at your discretion. I am just grateful if, in this time of war, you can provide me with the possibility of sending my daughter a sign of life from us.

I am looking forward to receiving your reply to my request at your earliest convenience. Included please find the return postage.

With best regards and thanks for your efforts,

Heil Hitler!
sgd. Marie Wagner

The statement "... *had to move into Japanese Imperial territory...*" seems to indicate that in Germany it was assumed that Wilhelm, Elisabeth, and Hannelore had been interned in Japan.

The diplomatic representatives of Japan in Berlin did reply a few days later on July 22, 1942, with the following letter:

The Japanese Embassy acknowledges receipt of your letter of the 20th of this month and regrets to inform you that inquiries regarding your daughter unfortunately cannot be made. We would, however, recommend you contact the Foreign Office (Auswärtiges Amt) in Berlin W 8, Wilhelmstrasse No. 75 in this matter, who will then give you further information.

p.p.
T. Sogi, embassy attaché

Marie Wagner then contacts the German Foreign Office in Berlin on August 4, 1942:

In the enclosed please allow me to present an application to the Foreign Office concerning transmission of news to my daughter Lisl Kärcher, née Wagner.

I have already sent this application to the Japanese Embassy in Berlin which informed me that you would be responsible in this matter and gave me your address.

I kindly request that you fulfill my wish, if at all possible, and I express my gratitude for your efforts.

I have included the return postage for your notification to me.

Heil Hitler!
sgd. Marie Wagner

It seems there was never a reply from the German Foreign Office.

On Lúkúnooch no one has the least inkling of these happenings. Wilhelm and Elisabeth appear to be somewhat paralyzed. She realizes that she has rather neglected her diary in the last days.

In September, Anna Dederer is able to get news from Chuuk through to them that mail has arrived from Germany. It takes another three full months, however, before it gets to Lúkúnooch.

During these weeks of growing desperation and frustrated waiting another important and happy event occurs.

Waltraud

She enters the world on September 12, 1942. At first, the little girl is doing well. But after a few weeks the situation regarding her diet becomes life threatening. She has problems digesting. No medication seems to help.

It is hard to imagine the missionary family's situation by this time. One day, Japanese soldiers lose some barley while transporting food. Wilhelm gathers what barley has been spilled. Of course, the barley is not clean, being mixed with sand and dirt. She cooks it anyway to sterilize it, and Waltraud can drink the liquid from her little bottle.

She gets so sick that it seems she is destined to die. It doesn't get that far, but she remains a sickly child. She only learns to walk at the age of two; for a girl this is very delayed.

For the islanders this is all very confusing. They expect that their missionaries are so automatically under the blessing and protection of God that things could never be so bad financially and physically as at present.

At this juncture we need to point out something that would only happen about twenty-five years later. In the sixties, Waltraud Kärcher is going to transfer the textbook of the Chuukese language, put together by Richard Neumaier, on to wax stencils to enable the book to be published.

Shortly before Christmas a boat arrives from Chuuk, bringing six tins of evaporated milk. What a valuable delivery! The tins must last for two months at least. They also butcher a goat. In the meantime, Waltraud is doing fine. But not so Elisabeth: "I look like an emaciated consumptive woman. Sometimes I am scared to look at myself." There is no mail from Germany on the boat.

For the Christmas celebration of 1942 they still have a little Christmas tree but no real candles anymore. Elisabeth remembers that she still has her "doll candles" somewhere. These quickly burn down; instead of candles the Christmas tree in the church is hung with a few oil lamps.

The stress that weighs heavily, not only on the missionary family but also on the Japanese officials and even on the islanders themselves, shows itself in the increase in alcohol abuse, so that even the Christmas celebrations are disturbed by numerous drunk people.

Years of Horror Are Knocking on the Door

A new official allows Wilhelm at least to travel to Woneyopw, but other harassment increases. Islanders who have not swept their property clean enough are being punished unusually hard. Elisabeth intervenes with a Japanese official for a woman whom he forced to stand in the sun for hours because of some petty offence.

Milk, rice, and sugar have run out again, and *áchi*, the sweet juice from coconut buds, is not available at the time. Elisabeth begs the Japanese soldiers for milk for her two children. They refuse, saying she should feed them with coconut milk. She is deeply disappointed: "German soldiers would not have acted that way."

In March 1943, she bakes bread for the last time. After that, the flour has also gone. Now there is only taro, their tubers growing in swampy areas on the islands. By now, Waltraud is six months old but only weighs about 13 pounds. Her mother is rather desperate: "I can only pray during these times that we will keep the faith and not forget to be thankful. This is hard. I am often afraid I can't stand anymore."

Suddenly one day, Lúkúnooch is teeming with soldiers. A troop transporter has brought them from Chuuk. The population is given orders to leave the island. It is needed for the construction of a big airport base for the war on the Solomon Islands and in New Guinea. The eviction notice also goes for the Kärcher family.

On April 26, only one incomplete sentence is written in Elisabeth's journal: "Booming artillery the day before." An American submarine, they are informed, had shot at the islands of Satawan and Lúkúnooch but did not hit its targets.

They are sitting on packed suitcases and waiting uncertainly for things to come. Wilhelm starts building a shelter in case they should come under fire again.

In this situation a small ray of hope, though a deceptive one, appears at the end of May. A boat comes in from Chuuk, bringing milk and soap again, but also the unmistakable command to come to Chuuk immediately, together with the Roman Catholic priest. Elisabeth is overjoyed: "Well, if this isn't a step on our way home!" She hopes that Hannelore and Waltraud will recuperate somewhat on Chuuk. But she is to be disappointed.

Wilhelm prepares for the journey. For the two children he builds two little wooden boxes, in which they will be able to lie safely and quietly during rough seas. His thoughts while working on these are rather grim. He asks himself whether the boxes will be their little beds or rather their coffins. With apprehension he thinks of the American submarine that he assumes to be still somewhere near the island.

On May 28, they leave Lúkúnooch early morning at seven o'clock. They find it hard saying farewell to the Christians there, and the islanders are also unhappy. Many are crying. The cabin in which they travel is really far too small because they also have to cook and wash as well as dry their laundry in it. There is no standing room. The windows are barricaded from the outside by cages filled with chickens and pigs. Hannelore gets terribly seasick, but manages only to bring up bile. Waltraud, on the other hand, is lying peacefully in her little box. Two young island girls are helping Elisabeth. Until Loosópw the sea is calm. But storm and rain are starting.

Shortly before reaching Chuuk's outer reef they are terrified to discover the American submarine very close by. For a time it follows them, but then turns away.

The people on board ascribe this fact to the *mana*, the magic power emanating from the missionary family and the priest.

9

Times of Horror on Tonowas and Wútéét

(1943–1946)

Internment

The island of Tonowas is, at that time, the seat of the Japanese colonial government and also the military headquarters of the islands around Chuuk.

Chuuk itself is of greatest strategic importance to the Japanese. Its long barrier reef, extending more than 125 miles (200 km), makes the lagoon an ideal harbour for greater units of ships and aircraft carriers. No wonder, then, that Admiral Yamamoto, the commander-in-chief of the Japanese Naval Forces, had moved his headquarters to Chuuk.

It is very strange, however, that Germans who, after all, belong to a nation politically allied to Japan, are being interned by the Japanese military authorities. The Japanese are, indeed, very suspicious of all foreigners, without exception, especially if these have knowledge of the English language. The existence of the "Berlin-Tokyo Axis," then, wasn't really of much use.

Because of Japanese suspicion of spying it seemed advisable to Wilhelm to destroy letters and records he had collected in the past years, when officials started searching through the houses on Lúkúnooch. The writings would have endangered him. Elisabeth, by contrast, continues to keep and cherish the letters from her relatives and continues writing in her diary. Her husband only finds out this years later; in a few months this was to put Elisabeth into a dangerous situation.

History has shown that the Japanese did not shrink from committing acts of cruelty against Liebenzell missionaries elsewhere. In the course of the Battle of the Coral Sea, missionary families Doepke and Gareis, as well as Maria Molnar, who had worked on Manus, a Melanesian island about 600 miles (1000 km) south of the Carolines, were rounded up and taken to a Japanese warship, where they were murdered by machine gunfire and their bodies thrown overboard into the ocean. This tragedy only came to light years later.

After their arrival on Tonowas, the Kärcher family had to wait rather a long time for the responsible official. Once he finally arrived, he dealt with them in a brusque manner. They were told that the hotel where they wanted to live had no room. They should contact their Japanese fellow missionary Yamaguchi.

Nan'yo Dendo Dan

When, after World War I, the League of Nations decided to give the islands of Micronesia to Japan as Mandated Territories, it caused apprehension about what would happen to the Micronesian Christians if they were forced under Japanese rule to accept Shintoism, which is the state religion of Japan. The responsible officials of the League of Nations feared that freedom of conscience and religion could be endangered under Japanese supremacy. In order to dispel such misgivings on the part of the League of Nations, Japan decided in 1919, especially through Jomosaburo Kato, the Japanese minister of naval affairs at that time, to allow Micronesia to keep its Christian orientation and even permit Japanese Christian missionaries to work on Chuuk, after the German missionaries, Roman Catholic and Protestant alike, had been exiled from Micronesia for a short period as hostile foreigners. Consequently, the *Nan'yo Dendo Dan* ("South Sea Mission") came into being, sponsored by churches in Japan oriented along Congregationalist lines.

Until about 1943, Liebenzell Mission workers operated, so to speak, as guests of the Japanese mission organization, i.e. they had no autonomous standing. This Mission was at that time represented on Chuuk by three missionaries and their wives: Kanhan Teruya, Naosaburo Kawashima, and Shokichi Yamaguchi.

The latter one is this Yamaguchi, to whom that gruff official now sends the Kärcher family that has just arrived. He lives with his wife in the Kuchuwa settlement on the north side of the island of Tonowas.

Elisabeth asks the official to at least take her and the two children there by motorbike. This he doesn't refuse to do. The Yamaguchis are not especially happy about having to share living quarters. They have just freshly painted their house. Hannelore knows that she should not touch anything, but it does happen – to the annoyance of the house owner.

The following day Elisabeth goes to see the Japanese doctor in the nearby hospital because she is still losing more weight. He thinks she may have contracted tuberculosis in her lungs. After a thorough second examination several days later he arrives at the reassuring diagnosis:

"Kein Befund" (results negative), he says in German and gives her a can of meat.

During these few days they have other happy experiences, too. Because there are no real kitchen facilities in their quarters, they want to go and eat in a restaurant. But it is closed for the day. A Japanese who happens to meet them invites them to a meal on the spur of the moment. This is remarkable, for by now food is rationed. One can only get it with food stamps.

The Japanese civil population by and large treats them kindly, and the islanders do so anyway. Only the police officers behave in a strange manner and treat them harshly wherever they can. Thus they demand that, whenever they are outside their house, they only move about on Tonowas accompanied by a translator.

No Home on Tonowas

They get the impression that they cannot remain on Tonowas and decide to go to Toon. The house they move into there is in a dilapidated condition. It takes a lot of work to fix it up and make it livable. But they are doing much better here than lately on Lúkúnooch. They have a cow, whose milk helps especially Waltraud, who is going to be one year old soon, to get her health back.

Elisabeth also is doing much better. Within a short time she puts on 10 pounds. "To us it is almost as if on our wanderings through the desert we have come to the land of Canaan."

News from Germany

On September 26, 1943, that is over a year after Elisabeth's mother had tried to get a sign of life from her daughter through the Foreign Ministry in Berlin, Elisabeth receives an anxious, and at the same time worrying, telegram – but it is from Mühlhausen rather than from Waltenhofen:

"Parents and siblings still well; Ernst fallen in mid-September. He was badly wounded. Please send sign of life right away."

What a tragedy! Ernst refers, not to Elisabeth's brother, but to Wilhelm's youngest brother. And the telegram, arriving in September 1943, bears the date of November 16, 1942, which means it had been sent off half a year earlier. Ernst Kärcher had been dead for many months before Wilhelm hears of it.

The situation the Kärcher family is in at the moment makes it totally impossible for them to answer the request and send a sign of life. They are interned in "preventive detention," as it is being called now in Germany. The Japanese military does not allow any news to get out. Conditions are critical. Any day now an American attack can be expected.

Fear and Harassment

A few days later, Wilhelm and Elisabeth are awakened by a noise that sounds like artillery thunder. In the harbor of the naval base a tanker has exploded and caused three other ships to explode as well. There are many casualties.

The roar of the explosion is so loud that the islanders on Toon, about twenty miles (30 km) away, are filled with fear and trembling. They start to flee into the bush, believing that the attack by the Americans has begun.

On Toon there is a Japanese trader who is still kind towards the Kärcher family, even letting them know when another delivery of useful household goods has arrived, things like matches and canned food. One evening, Wilhelm sends a young boy to the trader to pick up the things. But the Japanese teacher, who happens to be there at the same time doing his shopping, forbids the storekeeper to hand over the required goods. Pure harassment!

But the worst is something that puts the Japanese military under a heavy burden of guilt during the Second World, and not just here on Chuuk. They start by listing all unmarried young women and then forcing them into prostitution in their army bordellos. This causes considerable unrest among the islanders. Many women threatened by such a fate try to get out of it by marrying – too hastily, of course. There is no other way of escape for them. They are totally at the mercy of the Japanese tyranny.

These young women, who were euphemistically described as "comfort women," suffered terrible anguish through this abduction into forced prostitution in the Japanese sphere of control at that time, and this is well documented (further reading see Schibel-Yang 1996).

On November 22, 1943, her thirty-first birthday, Elisabeth gets a cheering surprise. On her table with the birthday gifts lies a telegram from Waltenhofen. It states briefly that her relatives are doing well. She is almost beside herself, even though the news is quite old. The telegram has been sent over a year ago. Her diary is full of jubilation, in total misjudgment of what is to come: "Perhaps the new year will even take us home!"

At the end of November, a Japanese officer appears at their house and informs them that they will have to leave the station on Toon by December 10 and move back to Tonowas. This not only involves the Kärcher family but also the remaining Liebenzell missionaries. Elisabeth is afraid that they will not stay on Tonowas for long: "Now they will slowly choke us, and the next posting will probably be called Japan."

It seems they all are purposely left in the dark about their future. In response to their inquiries they receive no clear-cut answers. Officials sent to them are changing constantly and they usually cannot take decisions nor fulfill their requests.

Although the eviction order was dated for December 10, a boat appears three days ahead of schedule to pick them up and take them to Tonowas. Elisabeth, of course, is not finished with the packing. But the official, a representative of the secret police, a rather vicious type who obviously by now has taken on the task of supervising them, forces them in no uncertain terms to hurry up and leave. Because of the children, he does allow them one more overnight stay on Toon, but only permits them to take the bare necessities with them. Their neighbours in the village of Fóósón promise to look after the things they have to leave behind.

A short while later, they are again living with Shokichi and Isoneku Yamaguchi on Tonowas. They are now interned and as such not permitted to leave the property. They make an exception with Wilhelm. He is forced again and again to help build fortifications and trenches. Since all of them have to live in one single room, they cook and eat on the porch. Wilhelm tries everything possible to obtain permission from the authorities for them to leave Chuuk and travel, if not to Germany, at least to Japan. He is put off from one week to the next. In reality, the authorities do nothing at all for the family's safety.

Between the Frontlines

Christmas 1943 is overshadowed by air-raid warnings occurring at shorter and shorter intervals. All of Christmas Eve they spend in a little church together with the islanders from the Mortlocks who are also living on Tonowas. Elisabeth's journal tells of a wonderful and quiet experience.

The food they have to eat at this time doesn't agree with them. Everyday one or the other in the family has a stomach ache and diarrhea. Hannelore is feeling quite miserable. There is no more rice. If the islanders did not occasionally bring them fish and taro, they would starve.

"You have to take one day at a time from God's hand."

At the end of January 1944, they are living alone in the Mission House. The Yamaguchis flew back to Japan in haste, fleeing from the threatening war. But the authorities simply won't allow them to live alone in the house for long. So Wilhelm tries to build simple accommodation for his family. But they refuse to give him the land or the wood necessary to do so, not to mention the workers.

Some scoundrel, or perhaps someone who is even poorer than they are, steals Wilhelm's shoes and the children's bedsheets.

On February 3, Wilhelm and Elisabeth's fifth wedding anniversary, everybody is sick: "Our intestines will probably never again function properly here." Elisabeth urgently implores a doctor to give them milk and oatmeal. But he is no longer in a position to help them either.

The Battle for Chuuk is Starting

Four days later, on February 7, 1944, the whole family is at the hospital early in the morning for an examination. Suddenly the sirens are wailing everywhere. The long awaited attack by the American naval and air forces has started.

They somehow manage to hasten back to Kuchuwa. In the meantime, Richard Neumaier, who had been forced to leave Wútéét, has also arrived.

In the next air raid warning things get serious. While the first bombs are falling and the anti-aircraft guns are beginning to fire, people stampede into the shelters. Elisabeth has Waltraud in her arms, slips on the wet ground and falls flat on her face. On the hill directly above them there is a gun emplacement, and its earsplitting thunder is almost unbearable. The crashing of exploding bombs and the ack-ack of the machine guns add to the chaos of their immediate surroundings. The attacking planes fly so low that they can see the pilots in the cockpits and the bombs falling out of their bays. This continues all day long.

The attackers have an easy game of it. The Japanese garrison commander has given orders to do maintenance on their own aircrafts. The defenders have nothing but anti-aircraft guns with which to counter the American attack starting from an aircraft carrier outside the outer reef. What the Japanese ships, now fleeing in all directions, need is an umbrella of fighter planes to prevent the attacking American planes having a totally free field of fire. Gruesome scenes are played out. Right at the start of the attack, a ship with about five hundred civilians – almost all of them women – receives a direct hit and immediately begins to sink.

All this is witnessed by the missionaries at close range. They cook and eat during the few breaks between attacks in whatever way they can. Hardly anybody feels like eating. Whenever there are no planes nearby the two men repair the shelter that is constantly being damaged by grenade and bomb splinters flying around.

At the end of this day, Tonowas presents a terrible sight. Almost all airports in the Chuuk lagoon are useless; about forty ships have sunk to the bottom, among them numerous battleships. That is almost the complete war fleet the Japanese Empire owned a little time ago. In reality, on this day the Japanese experienced on Chuuk what they did to the Americans several years before in a surprise attack on Pearl Harbor.

The following night is quiet, but hardly anyone can sleep properly.

After midnight, around one o'clock, they are torn from sleep by loud noises. A Japanese officer orders them brusquely to pack their belongings. They are to be transported. Where to, nobody is told.

In haste they grab a few things. Both children are stuck into a laundry basket and then they start out into the night with a two-wheeled cart. Other refugees are joining them. It is a sad company, stumbling ahead there in the darkness.

After a little over a mile (c. 2 km) they find shelter in the church of Rééré, where they await the morning. Light has hardly come when the airplanes attack again. There is loud crashing like all hell breaking loose. Splinters cut through the church roof and smash through the windows. A huge oil tank on the beach gets hit, explodes with a deafening racket and keeps burning for three days. They try to calm themselves by reading Psalm 91: "He who dwells in the shelter of the Most High…"

Around nightfall, the church is occupied by foot soldiers. The missionaries have to get out and into a little house nearby. There they spend the following night.

During the next day, more and more soldiers arrive in Rééré and dig their trenches. At night, the family and Richard Neumaier have to go back to Kuchuwa. The Yamaguchi home they still find there looks a bit worse for wear but the roof is still intact.

The village of Kuchuwa lies in a bay called Amara. Opposite is the village of Enin. From their house they can see that troops are being assembled there also. More and more they get the terrible impression that they have been placed in the midst of the battle area.

"If only we could get to Wútéét!"

In Kuchuwa, many islanders have lost their lives. The corpses from the sunken ships are also strewn among the ruins and debris of the flotsam.

Transported

The battle for Chuuk rages on through February. In the vicinity of Toon, as they find out later, a tanker has been torpedoed. The discharging oil starts burning, reaches the beach, and sets the Catholic mission station, not far from the Protestant one, on fire. The American pilot who led the attack, is shot down, jumps out with his parachute, and falls into the hands of furious Japanese soldiers. They mistreat him in such a manner that he dies on the way to Tonowas.

Even in plain view of them, Japanese soldiers commit the most gruesome atrocities against the islanders. During one of these air raids many women, most of whom had to serve in forced prostitution for the imperial army, flee into a roofed-over trench close to the harbor. The commander in charge fears that the invasion of the American marines is just about to take place and he also fears that the island women he abused could speak out as witnesses against him. He therefore gives orders to kill the women. He calls three corporals to the trench. These fire their machine guns through the entrance into the deep darkness inside until the screams of the women are heard no more. With the help of a flashlight they then count about seventy bodies lying there in their blood.[23]

Several times Wilhelm is pleading that he and his family may go to Wútéét. Regularly, permission is refused. They gain the impression the Japanese want to keep them in the battle area purposely so they might get killed.

Waltraud is getting very sick. She is emaciated and cannot help constantly vomiting whatever they give her to eat. In this desperate situation they again ask to be allowed to fly out to Japan. This request, too, is not granted, in spite of a doctor's certificate regarding Waltraud's state of health.

"Lord, have mercy on us!"

Meanwhile together with Richard Neumaier, Wilhelm has constructed a better shelter for them on the hillside a little above the house. There they are safe whenever the sirens begin to wail. This is difficult especially in the dark. In the meantime, the Americans have started to fly their attacks even at night between two and three o'clock.

Not only the missionaries but the islanders also are clinging to the rumour that the Americans will invade and occupy the atoll on April 15. Amazing, what people will hope for in such situations!

---

[23] http://www.kouro.info/war/WWII-1944.pdf (4.5.2005)

Good Friday of 1944 is anything but good for them. Wilhelm is sick; he has a fever. Two days later it's the same with Elisabeth. But she still summons her iron will to take care of the family. On Easter Sunday she breaks down unconscious on the porch, overcome by weakness. When she comes to again, a heavy air raid is starting. Her husband has to carry her on his back up the hill to the shelter in a hurry.

The way up there is simply too far, for by now the air-raid alarm is given several times every night. So the men build a primitive house next to the shelter where they can crawl in at night and try to get a little sleep.

A few days later, a bomb strikes at close range. Scared to death they snatch their children from their sleep and flee into the shelter. The experience is so horrible for them that they beg the authorities again for permission to leave Kuchuwa. In vain.

Instead, the soldiers pile up boxes with ammunition in front of their house. The Germans are a burden to them and in their way, but to put them up somewhere else is more than they want to do.

It is impressive to see the optimism and trust in God voiced in Elisabeth's diary in spite of these abysmal disappointments: "If it is God's will that we remain here to the end, then he can also carry us through these hard times."

Her husband describes his wife's virtually unbending will to live in his usual self-ironic way, and yet with touching words. In a report contained in the magazine "*Anruf*" *("The Call")* from 1988 on the life of Wilhelm and Elisabeth Kärcher, he says about himself and his colleague Richard Neumaier:

"Both of us men sat on a trunk of a coconut palm and were totally discouraged. One of us had the world coming to an end from this direction, the other from that. My wife was standing in the hut, about two yards (metres) away, one child on one side of her skirts, the other on the other side. And she just said, 'I just can't believe the world will come to an end simply because you two men determine so. There is someone totally different who takes care of that. The world will not come to an end, and we will get home again!' And that's how it happened. Sometimes, women also have good thoughts and – faith."

In mid-April the attacks happen noticeably less often. But to find anything to eat is getting more difficult. By now, all are severely undernourished. Occasionally, onions and tomatoes that have been thrown away by the soldiers are floating in the shallow waters by the beach. These they fish out. From time to time, Winiyam, a pastor from the island of Paata, brings them a few taro roots. The rain is just enough to provide for sufficient drinking water. And among the soldiers there is even one who at times gives them some leftover fish.

The shelter is teeming with rats and snails. In the meantime Wilhelm has covered the girls' sleeping boxes with mosquito wire. The wire he had found by chance. This way they can sleep more peacefully again, after increasingly showing signs of being traumatized during the past weeks.

By the end of April, the attacks start again in full force. One night, incendiary bombs are dropped. Everything around them is ablaze. But their house is miraculously spared.

On May 1, 1944, they have a close brush with death. A bomb hits the breadfruit tree camouflaging their shelter. One of its branches breaks off and squashes the primitive shack. The bomb explosion hurls a big stone with full force against the staircase of their little dormitory and shatters it. After that, the two men build another shelter higher up on the hill, under an overhanging rock.

Again and again they see little glimpses of hope. At the end of May they are invited by a Japanese officer to watch some slides. Among them are several from Germany.

Until well into July they wait and hope for an end to the torment to which the constant air raids have been subjecting them. They never have any rest. Elisabeth's journal is full of despair. All of Enin has been destroyed and their *"Häusle"* (little house in Swabian) next to the shelter stands in tatters. It is remarkable that, so far, no one has come to physical harm.

Once again, Wilhelm asks in vain for permission to leave Kuchuwa. Patiently he starts to build a new *"Häusle."*

The memorable boat trip to Wútéét

Finally, on July 25, they get relief. They are being evacuated to Wútéét. As usual, everything has to happen in a hurry. This time, too, they can only take the bare necessities along; they don't know whether they will ever see the things again that they have to leave behind.

The landing craft that is supposed to take them to Wútéét, doesn't offer much room and is open to the sky. Elise Zuber, Anna Dederer, Elisabeth and the children sit under an umbrella. Wilhelm sits next to her, without cover, without any protection against being seen. His white shirt is clearly visible. When the boat comes alongside the island of Párem, it is 10 o'clock in the morning. That is the time for the American bombers to begin their attacks.

Today also they are punctual. In front of them, flying low, they see thirteen four-engine bombers coming directly towards the boat on which, besides the missionaries, there are also a few soldiers and two artillery guns that are being transported to Wútéét and Toon. Wilhelm is gripped by panic. He can already see them all killed. But the incredible happens.

Almost at the same moment as the skipper of the boat tries to move it to the right, the planes bank sharply to the left and unload their bombs all along the island of Párem.

What nobody knows at the time, Wilhelm learns several months later, when he meets the American officer who had been in charge of the attack on Párem. The moment he had the boat in his sight he noticed the man in the white shirt: "That cannot be a soldier; it must be a civilian." So he immediately gave the order to leave the boat unmolested. Wilhelm's commentary (1950:25): "Did not our merciful God shelter us under his wings in so many dangers!"

A Little Bit of Happiness on Wútéét

A sigh of relief! They have escaped the seething cauldron. But at the pier on Wútéét there is no one to help them disembark and unload. The islanders are officially forbidden to have any contact with missionaries. The Germans are still being treated like spies. People are not even allowed to greet them. That is especially hard for Elise Zuber who, with one absence of eight years, had been working on Chuuk since 1909 and knew the adults on Wútéét right from when they were children.

A few weeks later they are living in their own quarters in the village of Mwáánitiw. It is not really a house they have been given in a swampy area, but a wooden shack that Wilhelm is able to make into a viable human dwelling with a floor space of thirteen by thirteen feet (four by four meters). He even does the carpentry for a little kitchen and a porch. The tin roof is anything but watertight.

The other missionaries, too, are getting some kind of wooden shack in which to live.

Together they clear the land around their huts of tree roots – a sweaty and strenuous labor. Nobody owns proper shoes anymore. Barefoot, they plant and weed yams, tapioca, and vegetables. But without the right kind of fertilizer the ground does not yield much. Their crops are rather measly and, to cap it all, others often steal the fruit of their labours.

Wilhelm tries everything possible to bring variety into their meagre menu. Sometimes they even eat the roots of papayas (usually only the fruit is eaten). He climbs into breadfruit trees to pick the fruit, and finally also up coconut palms in order to nick the leaf buds from which they can garner *áchi*, that sweet syrup which we know already from the Mortlock Islands. Three times a day he harvests a quantity for the children in this way; but his feet suffer greatly from all the climbing.

With the conquest of the island groups of Palau and the Marianas by the Americans, the chaos of war visibly calms down. The Japanese on Chuuk are isolated and militarily cut off. But the food situation becomes critical, since not a single supply boat reaches the lagoon anymore.

Elisabeth has no more sugar or salt. At this time of the year there is no ripe breadfruit. A bit of rice is still available, but if there is nothing else but rice every day, the diet is too one-sided. On occasion she can buy vegetables. Secretly, the islanders keep bringing her fish, in spite of the ban on contacting them, even though they are actually guarded by soldiers night and day.

Among those who bring food to them, sometimes endangering their lives, is a young man by the name of Kumo Epineyiser. Later, he was to be one of the most important pastors of the church on Chuuk and, in 1970, would also travel to Germany together with Wilhelm for some time – something no one could even guess in those days.

In Memoriam

Elise Zuber is critically ill. The strain of the internment has worsened her stomach ailments. For a few months she is still holding up on Wútéét. On the morning of October 15, 1944, she dies a painful death from cancer in her wooden shack, without medical help, and without any painkillers. There is not even any material to make a coffin for her. When Wilhelm starts to tear off a few tattered boards from the hut, the chief and the pastor of Wútéét appear bringing some boards they had hidden away in the interior of the island. Because of the funeral the soldiers make an exception. For a few hours all islanders are allowed to meet with the missionaries. They carry the coffin on one of the hills. The path leads through tank trenches and even through a stretch of knee-deep water on the reef in front of Wútéét. Elise Zuber is buried in the cemetery right among the members of the chief's family. Richard Neumaier gives the funeral message: "Blessed are the dead who die in the Lord from now on. 'Yes,' says the Spirit, 'they will rest from their labour, for their deeds will follow them'" (Revelation 14:13).

The grave of Elise Zuber on Wútéét is still being looked after by the islanders.

Life Goes on

On November 22, 1944, Elisabeth is thirty-two years old. On this birthday she is not in the mood for celebrating. She feels closer to tears than to laughter. Her mood also seems to extend to her diary. The time intervals between her entries get longer and longer. It is a miracle anyway that she still has her fountain pen and ink.

Christmas 1944 she experiences as a beautiful holiday. She was somehow able to get hold of flour and has baked cookies. From a Roman Catholic padre – they are also interned on Wútéét – she begs a few candles he still has. The children are beside themselves with joy over their Christmas present. She has painted a small picture book for them.

In mid-January, bombs are starting to fall again. Richard Neumaier's house is badly damaged. The Kärcher family home is barely spared. And once again they spend whole days and nights in a bombproof shelter under a rock.

At such times their house is unguarded. The kitchen cannot be locked. The thieves know that, too. One night, a young man steals the remaining Christmas cookies. The flour, too, that Elisabeth has been guarding, has gone. The fellow is indeed found out, but what he has eaten cannot be brought back, of course. By now, the missionaries who always seemed to be so rich in the eyes of the islanders, are much poorer than they are themselves.

In the Shelter

In April, Elisabeth is expecting their third child. Hannelore can hardly wait until her "brother" arrives. "He" is born on April 28, 1945; but for obvious reasons "he" will be called Anneliese.

The circumstances under which she comes into the world are dramatic. On this day an air attack takes place early in the morning. Elisabeth is transferred to the shelter with birth pangs. She cannot give birth there. Around noon, they carry her back into the house, and Anneliese is born while the Americans are bombarding and the projectiles of the Japanese anti-aircraft guns zoom over their roof. The following days the baby, together with her mother, has to be carried to the shelter on a stretcher. Three times the two of them stay overnight in a hole in the ground.

When the attacks decrease again, the diary reports that, in spite of it all, Anneliese is doing well.

The Horrors Come to an End

The missionaries are informed by a Japanese military doctor on Wútééet that Hitler is dead, that the Third Reich no longer exists and there is a ceasefire in Europe.

On Chuuk, however, the war is continuing with a vengeance. Until well into June, the alarm sounds two or three times a day. One islander, who had always brought them some fish, is badly wounded by explosives while fishing. The charge goes off in his hand and tears it off. He also loses his eyesight forever.

Constantly, one or the other in the family gets sick, except little Anneliese. She couldn't do better, even though there isn't even a pacifier for her.

On August 20, 1945, the pastor from Wútééet brings them news that the war between Japan and the United States is over. This is a ray of hope for everybody.

And yet, the Japanese military remains extremely suspicious towards the Germans. Even though the war is over officially, the missionaries' houses are thoroughly searched once again at the end of August. At that time there is a dramatic incident. One of the officers not only finds the letters Elisabeth has carefully kept, but also – what a disaster – her journal.

The officer has hardly picked it up when Elisabeth tries to snatch it back. She is fiercely determined not to let go of any letters and personal records from the past years, under any circumstances whatsoever. Gnashing her teeth, she screams at the man in uniform, telling him that this is something that concerns only herself. The tug-of-war goes back and forth, until Elisabeth emerges as the winner. Though angry, the officer finally gives in.

The fact that grown-ups keep so many things secret and hide them also has its effect on the behavior of the children. By now, Hannelore fears for the fate of her dolls, so she tries to get them to safety right away whenever she sees a man in uniform approaching.

Immediately after these events the rumour is going round that the American navy will take over Chuuk from the Japanese on September 1st. The missionaries gain in confidence that soon they will be allowed to return to Germany. They pack, give away the few belongings they think they will no longer need, and they wait. But the month of September goes by and nothing happens.

On October 2, they are told that they are now free to go anywhere they want to. The Catholic padres had already been taken to Tonowas the night before. Why they haven't also been taken, no one knows.

They are waiting all through October. The atmosphere is hopeless. They sleep, get up, eat yams and vegetables – if they have them. The rest of the time they sit around and wait. By Tonowas several American warships are anchored, but nothing happens on Wútéét. Since there are no longer any matches, they get fire for their cooking from the Japanese soldiers, taking care that it will remain burning all day long.

A High-ranking Visit

Again it starts with a rumour. On November 15, 1945, they – the Americans – are supposed to come to Wútéét. Everything on two legs is assembled at the beach in order to welcome them properly. But they are not coming.

Then, on November 24, they are indeed coming. It is the admiral himself, who comes ashore with several other officers. It is to be a memorable encounter. Later Wilhelm described it in an interview in 1970 with a recording team from Second German Television as they visited the Philadelphia School on Toon: He greets the admiral in English and identifies himself as a German. The astonished response of the high-ranking officer comes in perfect German: *"Und was machen Sie hier?"* (And what are you doing here?) It turns out that German is his mother tongue.

Also in his retinue is the former Japanese governor, now a prisoner of war. The first visit of the high-ranking delegation is to the missionaries. They all sit down on the porch. And they do not come empty-handed. They bring a magnificent present for the hosts that Elisabeth, for one, is very interested in: rice, milk, meat, sausages, fruit, and also cake, wine, soap, and stockings. To crown it all, there is even a pair of gloves among the gifts. She is especially happy about the milk, so urgently needed for the children. What a blessing!

Wilhelm is introduced to the commander of the admiral's ship, a Mr. Wulf. His parents, too, were Germans. Right away he takes care that telegrams and letters are sent to Germany. A few days after their first meeting he sends the missionaries a copy of a letter he has forwarded to the missionary leaders at Bad Liebenzell informing them about the present state of things on Chuuk.

In December – the United States have by now taken official possession of the islands – an American chaplain comes to visit them, accompanied by three medical doctors. Again there are culinary treasures in abun-

dance: milk – forty-eight tins of it, flour, sugar, bread, salt, tea, and coffee. Elisabeth describes the event as an enormous joy; and no wonder
when one considers for how many years she had to do without such
things.

But there is still no news from home, no letter, no telegram. In Germany, post-war misery holds sway. Home lies in the far unreachable distance. Months of waiting go by.

Sometime at the beginning of April 1946, a letter from Wilhelm must
have reached Mühlhausen. It causes joyful excitement. Lina, Wilhelm's
mother, calls it "a bright ray of light," reports its contents to Waltenhofen,
and asks Marie Wagner to answer it immediately from their side as well.
The only problem is that the German post office is unable in the present
circumstances to deliver any letters, let alone to a foreign country.

The Kärcher family at the end of their internment with their children
From left: Waltraud, Hannelore, and Anneliese
On the right: Rich-ard Neumaier and Anna Dederer

Wilhelm, too, is able to send a telegram to Bad Liebenzell: "We are still alive. What should we do?" The reply after a long time of waiting: "Stay – whatever the circumstances!" This may sound harsh, but it is easily understood. Right after the war, the family, which has meanwhile grown to five people, would not have had any secure livelihood in Germany either.

Freedom to Travel

In February 1946, they are informed that now they can move freely again in the Chuuk area. For Wilhelm this means that from now on he can again take care of his work in the churches, albeit in a limited way. Simultaneously with the news, the equipment necessary for such undertaking arrives – free of charge, from the supplies of the American Navy: condensed milk, hardtack, shirts, trousers, bed linen, field beds including mosquito nets, and plates. By the end of February Wilhelm is on his way to the Mortlock Islands, accompanied by American GIs.

Richard Neumaier, too, makes use of his new freedom to travel. He visits the churches on the Hall Islands.

During this time, Elisabeth receives a visit from General Blake and a reporter of the New York Times. There is an interview and a photo appointment with the children.

She herself is much in demand in other respects as well. Since she can speak English, she is often asked to serve as interpreter, whenever the islanders or the Roman Catholic padres have to communicate with the Americans.

Wilhelm also has become an important mediator. From time to time, American scientists come to Chuuk in order to do research. For this, they need a translator. And who could be of better use to them than a missionary like Wilhelm Kärcher with his intricate knowledge of the language and culture. During these weeks he accompanies the two economic ethnologists Edward T. Hall and Karl J. Pelzer. He willingly helps them in their research and questions on agricultural matters affecting Chuuk.

The literary contributions of these two gentlemen, appearing a little while later in academic publications, strangely do not mention so much as a word about their translator.

10

A New Beginning of Church Work on Toon
(1946–1952)

From Wútéét to Toon

Finally, in April 1946, Wilhelm can look for a possible piece of land on Toon, where he and his family can live and start again after all the horrors and destruction of the past years.

Things look wretched on the island. The Japanese occupational forces had broken down all the churches and Mission buildings and used them for their own purposes. The former station of Pataaniyen in the village of Fóósón is totally devastated. Where the Mission House used to be is now a Japanese military cemetery.

A man who is to play an important role in the reconstruction work of the coming years, which Wilhelm and his wife are about to begin again, makes their return possible. Wupwiini, at that time head chief on the islands in the western part of Chuuk, does not want to be separated from the German missionaries as the conquered enemies of the United States of America, but right away declares that as far as he is concerned they would be welcome to be involved again.

To facilitate this, he makes a larger piece of property available to them at the outskirts of the village of Chukiyénú. The location on the hillside of Mount Winipwéét is very favorable and has access to the sea. This is important for the provisioning and maintenance of the mission station that is to be established here.

The Enterprising Spirit Awakens Again

Elisabeth describes the first months on Toon as a "steep climb." The girls and she herself are often sick. She feels listless and on some days even miserable. One day she carelessly reaches for something and gets stung by a scorpion. An American medical officer consigns her to the navy hospital on the island of Wééné for ten days and prescribes a health cure for her, after which she feels considerable better.

This gives her a boost of energy. She starts to sew dresses from American flag material. The effect is quite colorful, as she expresses it. On one occasion she makes herself a dress from an old tablecloth. The sheer misery of the past years has often served to make her quite creative.

Her husband and Richard Neumaier are tireless in undertaking various trips over these weeks, primarily to the Outer Islands.

Mourning for Ernst

During these months of new beginnings on Toon, letters start arriving from Germany. Elisabeth is overjoyed by a message she receives from her "Klub" in Berlin shortly after her thirty-fifth birthday.

Her feelings change completely when she opens another letter. It informs her that her family in Waltenhofen is doing well, but it also contains a fateful clipping from the "Allgäuer," a daily newspaper published in Kempten. It is an obituary notice, which reads:

In memory of my beloved husband, our dear son and brother, Staff Sergeant Ernst Wagner, b. May 2, 1914, d. April 8, 1945, in Pillau. Faithful, even to the point of death.

Elisabeth is deeply shocked. Of all her brothers Ernst was the closest to her. She feels like David at the death of his friend Jonathan: "I grieve for you, Ernst my brother" (2 Samuel 1:26). With these words she writes her grief into her journal.

After that, she doesn't write anything at all for a number of months. Her next entry first mentions Hannelore's sixth birthday. But more important is something totally different.

Rejoicing Over Ernst

He is Wilhelm and Elisabeth's fourth child. On July 17, 1947, she gives birth to him. Finally, the long-awaited brother, at least as far as Hannelore is concerned, has arrived. His mother calls him an "accomplished screamer." But at night he sleeps peacefully. Soon he even sleeps through.

New Difficulties

After Chuuk was taken over by the Americans, the German missionaries are obliged to hand over the leadership of the work to an American mission. This is the former Boston Mission, at the time calling itself the "American Board of Commissioners of Foreign Missions," and later the "United Church Board for World Ministries."

Under the American Administration the traditional division of church work on the islands between the Liebenzell Mission and the Nan'yo Dendo Dan is retained, but communication problems crop up. These are less of a linguistic nature, because the German missionaries do speak English; rather, it is a difference in the perception of goals, i.e. they are not united in the objectives to be reached and in what means should be employed in reaching these goals. Tensions arise, moreover, from the simple fact that the American colleagues are relatively young and inexperienced. Above all, being newcomers, they speak the language of the islanders much less fluently than the German missionaries who, moreover, can look back on years of experience in living together with the islanders.

Wilhelm, who is busy expanding his new mission station, trying to build it on a larger scale as he envisions the future of the indigenous church, gets in trouble with the American missionary in charge. This man does not want "to fork over any materials" urgently needed for the completion of the missionaries' residence on Toon. Still, Wilhelm keeps a certain confidence going: "We are trusting God. He will help us also in this. He is able!"

But there is yet another reason why the American missionary – presumably Dr. Clarence Gillet – is spreading uneasiness among the German missionaries. He figures that they will all shortly have to leave Chuuk. The fact that he openly tells them his opinion, or at least lets them feel it, makes their situation hard to bear, since everything is in such a shambles and a new start has to be made. In addition, Anna Dederer drops out for a longish period; she is sick and in hospital awaiting an operation.

Afterwards, she leaves the Liebenzell Mission and enters the American mission organization.

Once she leaves Wilhelm and Elisabeth Kärcher are left alone with the responsibility for the work on Chuuk, since Richard Neumaier also has left Chuuk for good sometime in 1947.

The image of a missionary has changed completely. Wilhelm describes this very vividly in one of his first newsletters to reach Germany: "No longer are there any white suits. The missionary is just as dirty as the islander. Likewise, there are no longer any servants carrying things behind you. But this is a healthy thing because now you are respected for it. You do not lose face, as the old missionaries had feared."

Even in earlier times, Wilhelm and Elisabeth had been unhappy with the fact that during church services missionaries and their families would sit on the *róóng*, an elevated platform where the altar stands. They themselves had never made a habit of it and would not do so in future either. When Elisabeth has no particular ministry role, she sits with her very small children way back on the last bench with the women who also have little children. The three little girls sit with the island girls in the sand, learn lessons with them in the children's club, and recite what they have been learning in the same way.

Also definitely positive is the stance of the American military administration on Chuuk when helping with the reconstruction of the church work on the islands. They are open to helping the missionaries whenever a need arises. Working conditions are thus, paradoxically, exactly the opposite from what they used to be under the Japanese military administration. Whereas the Japanese, who had been politically and militarily allied with Germany, had demolished churches and interned the missionaries, the Americans, who are officially enemies of Germany politically and militarily, now have totally reversed the circumstances. They are helping to rebuild the churches and they are allowing the missionaries to move about freely; more freely indeed than the Germans are permitted in Germany at that moment. The country sank into chaos during the last months of war and is now divided into occupational zones, administered by military governments. As long as he lived, Wilhelm remained grateful to the Americans for this exemplary attitude of helpfulness.

But the physical support of the German missionaries is also being assured from another side. It is taken care of by the International Missionary Council that has been founded in the meantime.

The Philadelphia (Finaatenifiya) Mission Station

It is located at the end of a small bay by the name of Neepinómw in the immediate vicinity of the village of Chukiyénú, in English: "Ghost Mountain." With its *woroor*, a pier reaching far out into the bay with places for mooring boats, it constitutes something like a traffic link.

At the end of April 1947, construction of the church on the new Mission property is complete. It has a seating capacity for 500 people and is the first sign of the optimism and vision that are to determine the church work in the future.

Noteworthy is the scaffolding supporting the outside walls of the church. In a letter, Wilhelm calls it "the bones of the church." The walls are made of concrete and contain high-quality steel. The Japanese had laid railroad tracks on Toon that had come from Germany. They still bear the clear inscription: "Made in Germany, Krupp, Essen, 1926."

The American mission contributes money for the corrugated aluminum roof. The churches delegate workers to the construction site, and at its dedication the church is debt-free.

August 22 is a festive day: The opening of the new Philadelphia Mission Station is being celebrated. The place is in a favorable location, surrounded by three Protestant villages. The missionary residence is somewhat elevated, with a beautiful view over the bay and the hillcrest of the peninsula of Féwúpé.

Head chief Wupwiini has a special role in building the missionary residence as well. From the time of the Japanese occupation the military government had left him a larger hospital hall for further use. Wupwiini had made the wood from this hall available for the building of the house.

On the day of dedication about one thousand people have come together. The young American missionary Charles Heuser who had meanwhile taken up his work on Wééné, is coming the night before, with all his students, for the festivities on Toon.

All night long – the moon is shining brightly – people arrive at Philadelphia in their outrigger canoes. In the morning there is an armada of boats round about the pier. In the face of the crowds and so many boats, Wilhelm is reminded of the mission festivals in Bad Liebenzell.

The church cannot hold all the people. Many have to sit outside in the sunshine. Long before the service starts, choirs can be heard rehearsing their songs.

The girls and women have crocheted an altar cloth with an antependium (an altar frontal) on which are written the words "Holy, Holy, Holy."

The festive service starts at 9:30 a.m. and does not end until 12:30 p.m. All the pastors and all the chiefs want to give speeches. But the three to four minutes allotted to each usually grow to ten. South Sea Islanders are just not time-oriented people like we are as Europeans and Americans but event-oriented and person-oriented.

At the end of the service, Namiyo Eyas, pastor of the church in Chukiyénú, is downright overwhelmed in his enthusiasm. He asks Wilhelm the question, "Please tell me, does the pope have a better church than this one here? Nothing can be better than my church!" Beforehand, when the doors of the church were being painted green, he had been awestruck and said, "These doors are almost like the doors leading to heaven itself." Charles Heuser takes Namiyos statement as topic for his sermon.

Afterwards, an abundance of food is being served, such as only the Chuuk islanders can prepare. They eat as long as the service lasted – for a full three hours.

A Strange Episode

In the meantime, the Roman Catholic Mission on Chuuk is also beginning to rebuild their church work. Surprisingly one of the padres also tries to get property in the village of Chukiyénú in order to build. He attempts to win head chief Wupwiini for his purposes by suggesting to him that they could furnish the whole village with electric power, for free. But the chief refuses the tempting offer.

The padre should really have been aware that the German missionaries would have little or no sympathy for his attempt to gain a foothold in close proximity to them. But he keeps on trying and, one day, calls on Wilhelm personally. The latter simply reads to him from Romans 15:20, where it says, "It has always been my ambition to preach the gospel where Christ was not known, so that I would not be building on someone else's foundation…"

Thereupon the padre settles on a piece of land a few miles further away.

Fellow Workers, Helpers, Friends, and Others

Without these people, Wilhelm finds it impossible to tackle the mountain of work piling up in front of him every day. Friends are found mostly from among the officers of the American navy. He has to make one trip to the Mortlock Islands on an overloaded boat. The commander in charge is a navy officer. He offers Wilhelm the office in his own quarters as a sleeping cabin. Wilhelm is reminded of the Roman captain Julius from the book of Acts, who allowed the prisoner Paul in Sidon, on his voyage to Rome, "to go to his friends so they might provide for his needs" (27:3).

On various islands he is to discover that the people have gone back to their old religious rituals again, because of the troubles they faced during the war. Mothers, whose children had fallen ill, have fallen back on their magic medicine again in the absence of a doctor or nurse. Such behavior is not unusual in first or second generation Christians. But it also shows that a church planted by a mission should not be left on its own too early.

Wilhelm knows all this. By now he has learnt to refrain from any harsh criticism. In a report a few years later he describes the case of a father from the village of Wóónipw, whose child had died in spite of intensive efforts on the part of the military doctor and many prayers. Wilhelm had buried the child. The next afternoon the father comes for confession. Asked whether he has not had recourse again to magic medicine he admits that he has. This time, Wilhelm does not react as he did on Téé. He knows: "When things get tough, faith often falters." People are certainly not afraid of a counselor who has this attitude, when they want to be open with him.

Kumo Epineyiser, in the meanwhile pastor of Wóónipw, tells Wilhelm his troubles. The rafters of the church all have to be sawn by hand, a work that needs strong men and only proceeds with difficulty and very slowly. Kumo thinks the people tend to be rather lazy when they have to work alone with him. How different, if the missionary were to work along with them. So then, Wilhelm spends a lot of time in the construction of the church in Kumo's parish. Three days a week he is on the go as carpenter. Many things needing his attention thus remain undone.

At night, when he lies on a field cot under a mosquito net in one of the villages, it often takes him a long time to find rest and to distance himself from all he has experienced during the day. At time it is a heavy burden that weighs on his mind and allows him only some restless sleep.

One of the fellow workers Wilhelm can absolutely rely on is his wife. Primarily she holds children's clubs and women's meetings.

Dr. Gillet, the American field director, and his wife Marion, leave the islands after a term of only one year, never to return again. His position as field director is taken over by Charles Heuser, who initially has proved to be very cooperative with Wilhelm. He is only twenty-six years old and very inexperienced. That may be the reason why he starts to let the German missionaries feel that he has the last word here. Wilhelm, in any case, occasionally feels "talked down to" by him.

An Enormous Work Load

In mid-October 1948, the church in Wóónipw is dedicated. It is arranged in the same manner as the one in Philadelphia, just a bit smaller; and it has something that distinguishes many churches on Chuuk and its islands even today: On the ridge of the roof it has an elegant looking little spire, which one could call a "Kärcher spire," so characteristic of his architectural style. In Wóónipw it contains even a little bell, financed by the so-called "Kinderbund" (children's league) in Kolberg, Germany.

Between now and Christmas it is hoped that the church in Paata will also be completed. Further church buildings are under way.

On two weekdays on the Philadelphia Mission Station, young men have classes from 8:00 a.m. until noon and from 2:00 to 5:00 p.m. On Saturdays, the pastors come from various villages nearby in order to prepare for the Sunday service. On Sundays, Wilhelm himself goes from island to island to hold services and administer baptisms and communion.

Elisabeth is likewise occupied. On two days a week she teaches the young women, and the rest of the week her own children. Sometimes she is called to serve as a midwife. Both are so busy with the work on the mission station that they can only find a little time for each other in the evenings, once the children are asleep.

The Christians are extremely motivated to make a new start. Church attendance is impressive. Ninety to ninety-five percent of the islanders come to the services. Very many go to the communion services, among them especially many men.

It is still not clear when the family will finally be able to go home on their first furlough. By now they have endured twelve long years on their field of service. But still the time to go home has not come. Economic conditions in Germany do not permit a return of the family, and appointing a younger missionary couple to relieve them is out of the question at the moment. The U.S. military government refuses entry visas to the Trust Territories to all civilians. The return of Johannes Rattel and his wife, planned for 1950/1951, likewise comes to naught. So Wilhelm and Elisabeth carry on alone.

After completion of the church buildings they add another school day. Wilhelm especially finds this more "satisfactory," but not so as to take it a bit easier for himself physically while he is teaching. He is rather of the opinion that a mere two days of schooling have little lasting effect on the students; by Friday they will have forgotten most of what they learned on Monday.

At Christmas, 1948, the children get a lot of presents – for the first time in their lives. Christmas packages have even arrived from Germany. Little Ernst, though, finds Christmas rather threatening: when he sees the burning candles he breaks out in tears.

Three Kinds of Island Christians

Of interest is a letter written by Wilhelm at this time. In it he tries to formulate a typology of the Christians among the islanders. He distinguishes three kinds:

"The first group is formed by those who are serious in following Christ. Every morning they will go to church for a chapel service, and every evening, before going to bed, they pray a learned prayer or one from their hearts. They trust Jesus and find refuge in him in times of sickness and need. It is not exceptional for them to sometimes be overcome by anger, especially as they have been able to have their own way since childhood; and so they find it very difficult to submit to the will of God. But before every Lord's Supper they come for a one-to-one counseling talk when we can pray with them.

"The largest of the three groups are those who only come to church on Sundays. They live in a mix of Christianity and paganism and make a great effort to combine the two. They especially hold on to heathen customs and their magic potions, thinking they can't live without them. If they plant a new garden, they first have to make *sáfey* or 'medicine' – by which they mean a magic ritual – and likewise, when they build a house, or move into a house, or fell a tree to build a canoe, when they take a canoe out on the ocean for the first time, and especially when going on a trip. One always has to protect oneself from evil spirits through 'medicine.' Already as pregnant women, mothers feel they have to take various medicines (understood animistically) for the good of the unborn baby. One man in the village of Fóósón told his son-in-law who didn't want to follow this practice anymore, 'Kanep, with the help of these medicines you and all of us were born and have grown up. Why do you now want to make an exception with your child?' This group still has to experience what once happened in Ephesus (see Acts 19:18–20).

"The third and smallest group consists of those where nothing can be done, try what you will. Their minds must simply be darkened. They cannot internalize anything higher than eating, drinking, and doing nothing. When you visit them in their huts and ask why they won't come to the services, they invariably reply, 'I have nothing to wear.' If you then give them clothes, they will come for a while because of a sense of decency, but they soon will stay away again. If you finally get to see them again and inquire, they say they had been sick or away on a trip …

"… One woman quite close to our house who belonged to this group died a short while ago and was buried according to heathen tradition, too. Because she had been the oldest woman and thus the head of her large family, they were all afraid that her dead spirit would persecute her relatives if they did not follow the ways she had followed. But now she has been in the ground for a number of weeks, her oldest daughter Fetiyong – herself already a grandmother – has seriously decided to become a Christian. This is not so easy for her as she learned black magic from her mother and knows how to mix magic medicine potions. Her husband Emok is just like Esau, roaming about the bush on Sundays to catch wild chickens that can still be found here and there, wherever the Japanese soldiers had their barracks."

Occasionally, he speaks of "turtle Christians." One day, he preaches on different verses from John's Gospel that talk about the light in which we have been placed as Christians in order to lead our lives well. That is a comparison that needs explaining not only to South Sea islanders. In order to show his students what a Christian is like, constantly leading his life in the light, in contrast to those who occasionally vanish into darkness, Wilhelm uses the behaviour of the turtle as an illustration.

His listeners know a lot about sea turtles. From time to time these come out of the darkness of deeper waters to the bright light at the surface in order to catch a breath of air. Some remain up a while longer than others. But they always dive down again because they feel more comfortable in the darkness of the depth than in the light of the sun.

Of course, the comparison is not altogether adequate, because the way sea turtles behave is the way they were naturally created. God wanted them that way. But the students understand anyway what John the Evangelist means: He would have refused a combination of animal conduct with the conduct of a Christian. Sea-turtle Christianity is a useless mixture.

Itinerant Ministries on the Islands

In the meantime it is April 1949. By now Wilhelm has been aboard a government ship for two weeks. With a group of islanders he camps out under a tarpaulin hung on deck. During the day the sun burns down from the sky, overnight it is windy, and they also get wet constantly. "When, in addition, someone seasick cannot help vomiting, and the whole contents of their stomach and gallbladder is splattered over boxes, suitcases, bundles of clothing and mats, it is best not to look at it but stay perfectly calm, close your eyes, and make an effort to think of something appetizing."

Something appetizing does indeed happen to him once in a while. He is being invited to eat in the officers' mess. That's a "princely" affair, as he calls it. It always reminds him of a missionary who used to work on Chuuk and quote from Philippians 4:12–13 in such cases, "I know what it is to be in need, and I know what it is to have plenty. I have learned the secret of being content in any and every situation, whether well fed or hungry, whether living in plenty or in want. I can do everything through him who gives me strength."

On the islands he experiences first hand what damage the war has caused while he had been condemned to sit idly on Tonowas and Wútéét. The best impression is given by the churches on the Hall Islands whom he hadn't seen for twelve years. He realizes more and more that a lasting work cannot be accomplished in the churches if he has to take care of such a large field of service as Chuuk without a bigger staff of workers to help him.

In November 1949, he is once again on the way to the Mortlock Islands. He is traveling on board the sailing boat "Nomad," ten feet wide by 50 feet long, owned by the "Truk Trading Company."

On Némé there is a dispute about the correct sailing course. Because of the wind causing the "Nomad" to drift badly a course of 150° is to be maintained. At the end of the six hours that were to take them to Nómwuluuk, there is no island to be seen anywhere. Finally someone discovers that they had followed a course of 250° instead of 150°. Because of it they have sailed almost forty-five miles (c. 70 km) on a mystery tour. After another six hours they do finally reach the island.

Nómwuluuk gives a depressing impression. After the death of the former pastor, the church fell more and more into a state of neglect. Animistic elements exerted their influence again. Hardly any man comes to the services – they get drunk every night on palm wine. Wilhelm has the feeling that he cannot do much about it and, much concerned, departs again.

On Ettaal things are hardly looking any better. Of over one hundred church members from the pre-war time, only twenty-six are left. Wilhelm experiences "some strenuous, joyless days." The other islands do not give him such a bad impression. Only the church roofs need repairing. That's where he is in demand as a carpenter, and he does not spare himself but works until he is quite exhausted.

He describes his exclusively missionary workday by using Woneyopw as an example. In the mornings from eight till ten he works on a text from the New Testament; afterwards the islanders can ply him with questions about the Bible for an hour. Afternoons from two till four o'clock he tells a story from the Old Testament, and from four thirty p.m. until sundown he asks them questions himself. After supper he tries to get them enthused about the new hymnbook – he has brought along a whole stack of them. With them he practices the tunes that they don't know. Sometimes he tells them a story one could use as an illustration in a sermon.

Wilhelm Kärcher performs his tasks as a missionary with amazing conscientiousness. He does not neglect his family, and his wife agrees with him that they should "seek first the kingdom of God" (Matthew 6:33; Luke 12:31); but this attitude cannot be maintained without pressures, especially pressure upon the children. Primarily Hannelore, Waltraud, and Anneliese will have to experience this in the years to come. For now, it is little Ernst. After a two-months' absence he doesn't recognize his father anymore, when he comes ashore on Toon.

A Visit by the Mission Leaders

In November, Mission director Paul Gerhard Möller comes to Chuuk on a tour of inspection. This visit is regarded as an "unprecedented joy" by both missionaries and churches alike, as Wilhelm writes in his report of December 1949.

The islanders, of course, only know very vaguely what a mission director is. Even pronouncing the word is a tongue twister for them. High-ranking representatives from foreign organizations are to them people like their highest title bearers, the head chiefs. So they call Paul Gerhard Möller *samwoonnapen misin*, which means something like "head chief of the Mission." For such a title bearer the reception just has to be magnificent and must be celebrated. At first, though, there is a problem with this.

No one on Chuuk has ever before seen the mission director, not even the missionaries. Will they recognize the right one when he comes down the gangplank from the boat onto Wééné Island? Elisabeth urgently suggests to her husband that he look again at a picture of Paul Gerhard Möller in the "Ebenezer Herald," an American news magazine, to make sure he will recognize his boss. Wilhelm thinks he would probably not be dressed like an officer.

The fact that he does not know him seems very strange to the commander of the military government, with whom he has to register the German visitor. To the officer it is not at all clear that German missionaries had been detained on Chuuk for the past thirteen years without interruption and that they could, therefore, never even have seen their present Mission leaders.

Wilhelm recognizes Paul Gerhard Möller immediately. Both of them promptly get on their way to Toon, where they want to arrive before sunset. Because it is never quite certain whether a visitor will arrive on a certain island at the scheduled time, and as it is impossible to announce his arrival on Toon by telephone, they arrange to have the ship's siren sound five times once they are in hearing distance if Paul Gerhard Möller is in fact on board.

After that, the villagers living close to the pier still have sufficient time to flock to the shore. The crowd is immense.

In all the communities on Toon and the other islands that the Mission director can visit, the pathways are being weeded, churches adorned with ceremonial arches and magnificent decorations.

For Wilhelm and Elisabeth this visit means far more. After many years they can finally talk to a person again who thinks and feels like they do and with whom they can speak, as it were, heart to heart: "Best of all were the evenings, when we could share all our questions, doubts, and worries concerning our work."

Number Five

On January 9, 1950, Helmut is born. He is neither born in a hole in the ground like his sister Anneliese, nor at home like his brother Ernst, but in a downright distinguished setting – at the Navy hospital on Wééné. His mother takes a long time to recuperate from the strain of the pregnancy and the birth of her fifth child. She feels a nervous wreck and is constantly tired because of so many sleepless nights.

It may have been due to the overload of work that neither Wilhelm nor Elisabeth make any journal entries about what is happening in their lives for over a year. It could also have been due to the fact that little Helmut is passing through difficult phases of sickness during his first year of life. Elisabeth still reports sleepless nights. However – and this is characteristic of her optimism and her positive attitude to life – she only writes about troublesome experiences when she can add, as in Helmut's case, that things are getting better. That is how she always dealt with such situations, even when the girls were sick.

Around this time they once again air the hope of returning to Germany: "Our substitute has now been granted the entry visa, after it had initially been refused. We are wondering: Will we still manage to get home this year?"

The political situation in the Far East, however, has once again slid into a difficult phase. The United States have not reached their desired objectives in the Korean War, and the so-called Cold War leads many people to fear a new worldwide conflict.

The Pastor's Child

One topic that still frequently bothers the islanders is the problem of soothsaying, and recourse to magic potions, and witchcraft when building houses or boats. Wilhelm constantly brings up the subject at pastors conferences. The younger ones are on his side; the older ones wrap themselves in silence because they are directly affected by this.

Among the younger ones is Namiyo, the pastor of the church in Chukiyénú, to whom the new church seemed much more beautiful and magnificent at its dedication than St. Peter's, Rome. His family is hard hit when one of his children dies. A short while later another one of his children gets terminally ill. Namiyo is desperate. In such troubles there is a great temptation among the islanders, even for an ordained minister, to make use of any and all means in order to save the life of his child – and not only scientific medicines but also the traditional, magic ones.

Namiyo does not want to give in to this temptation. The missionary tries to encourage him in this. Wilhelm visits the child several times and prays with him. One evening, Namiyo knocks at the door of the missionary residence and says, "He will die tonight. I will come and tell you when he has died." After that, Wilhelm, Elisabeth, and Namiyo again pray very earnestly for the child. Very early the next morning, the father comes up the stairs and says, "I just wanted to let you know that my child is no longer sick." He got well again without *roong* (magic medicine).

Missionary Work Is Modernized

In June of 1950, Wilhelm once more travels to the Mortlock Islands. In his luggage he has some of the latest modern technology. From an American colleague he was able to borrow a kerosene-gas projector and quite a number of pictures. Moreover, he had been able to hide a series of photos from the beginning of his missionary activity on the Mortlocks from the suspicious eyes of Japanese officials and soldiers. And he can show pictures of Paul Gerhard Möller's visit. After it gets dark he makes quite an impression on the islanders using this equipment. No one is going out to fish at that time or working in their gardens. On each island, young and old sit in front of the bed sheet which serves as a projection screen. Even Roman Catholics cannot stop themselves from surreptitiously glancing at the pictures. Some of them get a bad conscience from this and later go to confess to the padre that while with the Protestants they had been "watching".

Wilhelm is also impressed by his new medium of communication. If only he had such a gadget, too! Missionary work would be much easier that way. Islanders who cannot read or write could be taught by this means with much fewer problems and much more graphically.

On several islands he has heated discussions with the men about the taboos they observe when fishing for fish and crabs with weirs – a kind of fish trap – because they still believe that with these taboos they can positively influence their success rate: "I noticed that so many young men sat in church with shaggy beards. Some did not even cut or comb the hair on their heads, so that they looked like apes from the forest." He discovers the meaning of all this one Sunday from one of those "unkempt ruffians" who comes to him to talk things through. The men indeed believe that their weirs will fill up more abundantly when they neglect their outer appearance.

Meanwhile, there is no longer a church building on Ettaal Island. In the face of great difficulties Wilhelm starts a new construction. Hardly anybody wants to help him; often he only has breadfruit and salt to eat. He has to drag in the blocks of coral, as rough as sandpaper, with his own hands; his hands are so full of sores from doing this that he can only work by applying band-aids on all his fingers. Unfortunately, there is no hardware store around to get working gloves.

The Western Islands

At the beginning of 1951 he starts a difficult project. The islands around Pwolowót are situated about 200 miles (c. 300 km) west of Chuuk. Their inhabitants speak a dialect that is not essentially different from the language spoken on Chuuk. These islands did occasionally get visited by some missionaries, but their inhabitants have had little contact with Christianity; quite different from the Hall Islands where Wilhelm Kärcher and Richard Neumaier had already made intense efforts in the 1930s to take the gospel to the islanders.

Now we see him on his way to Pwolowót. It is to be a journey with many setbacks and stormy seas from beginning to end. Shortly after leaving Toon, Wupwiini's boat runs aground. Only when the tide rises can they get it going again. The next day when they hurry to get through the passage to the open sea before nightfall, the boat suddenly starts to tremble with a booming noise. At the same moment they are stuck on a coral bank that had been lurking under water. The four diesel motors are revved in full reverse power. Little by little the boat jerks back into deeper waters. Much time goes by because every fifteen minutes the ship's hull has to be investigated to see whether any water is leaking in. Only when they are sure there is no leak do they dare venture out in the darkness through the passage into the open sea.

They reach the island of Sowuk by eight o'clock in the morning in pouring rain. The old chief Ikeniyong had asked that a church be planted on his island. The Bible is almost totally unknown on Sowuk until that time.

There had been an attempt years before to send one of the church elders from Chuuk to the island. That man was judged to be willing, capable, and motivated. He even had attended school under Ernst Dönges for a while, a Liebenzell missionary who had worked on Chuuk between

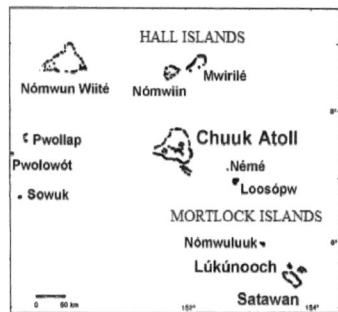

1909 and 1916. But somehow the project had run aground. Wilhelm was of the opinion that this happened because they had not paid attention to how the apostle Paul as a missionary had "spurred on" his fellow workers – not with words such as "Take it easy" or "Go slowly at first," but with urging encouragements like "Do your best!" or "Make every effort!"

Now he has come in person. He visits the people in their huts, and at night has a meeting in the *wuut*, the "community hall" of the island. The number of listeners remains modest at first. Three men, one woman, and eight adolescent boys that are almost naked because they have no clothes to wear, have come. He expounds to them Matthew 28:18–20 where Jesus speaks of the power given to him and of the Great Commission to spread his teachings in the whole world. Wilhelm's pulpit is one of the outrigger canoes stored in the *wuut* whenever they are not out on the ocean. Ikeniyong, the old chief, finds the meeting rather boring, even though it only lasts for half an hour. He is constantly glancing at a carton of cigarettes he received from an American.

Several days later, Wilhelm finds a small congregation on Pwolowót that had obviously well been cared for by Nelson, a pastor from the East Micronesian island of Kosrae. The islanders make a vibrant impression on Wilhelm; they have even constructed a church building for themselves.

In the course of this missionary journey, Wilhelm seems to have formulated a concrete plan, thinking it was about time to introduce the Christian faith to the inhabitants of the numerous little islands between Chuuk and Yap also. These islands are called the "Central Carolines", scattered in a belt of varying, though comparatively narrow breadth, like a road of about 920 miles (c. 1500 km) length a few degrees north of the equator. These islands, without exception, are flat sand islands, and because of their geographical location Wilhelm liked to speak of the "road of islands." (See map on page 63).

About ten of these islands are inhabited. The others are populated by turtles, providing meat for the islanders of the Central Carolines. Among the inhabited islands, Satawal is the one Wilhelm focuses on especially. Its inhabitants speak a language very much akin to that of Chuuk; so there would be no great communication problems if he tried to start a work there. At the moment, however, such an undertaking is rather illusory; no useable traffic link exists with the island, and without fellow workers he could not think of starting this task.

Trials

After long weeks of absence, he arrives back on Toon with his luggage totally soaked through. He does not even recognize his children right away, since by now they are wearing clothes from America.

The first news he receives is the death of his mother. Karolina Kärcher had died on February 13, 1951, from jaundice. She had hoped until the end to see her son and his family once more. She had firmly reckoned with their return to Germany that very spring. It is not to be.

After that, Wilhelm and Elisabeth once again had to be patient souls and wait for a younger missionary couple to get entry visas for Micronesia in order to relieve them.

Several weeks later, on the evening of May 14, 1951, Elisabeth returns from the island of Wééné with Hannelore and finds a distinguished visitor at their home. It is Admiral Miller. He has come to inform them that in future no more German missionaries will be allowed to enter the country. The news is devastating.

The Last Months Before Their Voyage to Germany

On May 9, 1951, Wilhelm is travelling by plane for the first time. He is on the way to this year's missionary conference for all of Micronesia, taking place in Pohnpei. Since Admiral Miller, the highest-ranking military chaplain in the Trust Territory, is taking part for a few days in the conference, they fly in an amphibious airplane belonging to the American Navy; it can take off and set down on land as well as on water. Wilhelm is totally enthralled by this technology, but still rather cautious, for he is sitting right next to the entrance and exit door. Because the weather is so very nice, the pilot leaves the door open, so Wilhelm has a magnificent view of the islands and the ocean during the whole flight. When Némé and Loosópw come into view he is reminded again of the many restless trips on the sea that he survived during the past years. "How nice to be able to fly!"

(courtesy of Alan Pipkin)

Three hours later, Pohnpei appears. Since there is still no landing strip, the airplane sets down on the water – a spectacular experience for him. He is downright sorry to be back again on cumbersome ground.

Around sixty Christians have gathered to welcome the conference participants from Chuuk. Everyone wants to prove his or her language skills: Chuukese, English, Japanese. One of the pastors who decades ago had helped Liebenzell missionary Adam Syring (1883–1963) in Japan to translate the New Testament into the language of the islanders of Pohnpei, even manages to show off to Wilhelm his knowledge of German.

On Pohnpei Wilhelm finds unusual luxuries: the American missionary family has a fridge, and their apartment is much more spacious than his own on Toon.

Here they have a sizeable colony of islanders from Chuuk and the Mortlocks. One night he shows slides in their church. He also finds traces of the earlier German mission station and the statue of Henry Nanpei, the head chief who had once visited Bad Liebenzell during German colonial times and had sent his sons Enter and Robert to Germany for education.

Two weeks later, on his trip home, he is quite enthused again about the spray foaming up at the engine of the plane, which doesn't lift into the air until they are almost at the great coral reef: "O Lord, my God, when I in awesome wonder consider all the works thy hands have made!"

At this missionary conference the decision is made that the Kärcher family should return to the mission field after their forthcoming home furlough. They even discuss a possible transfer to the American mission, reasoning that this would be best for all involved. But this is not to be.

In the village of Féwúpé on Toon a church is being built. Originally, the congregation wanted to build the concrete church walls to only about 2 feet high (about 60 cm). At some time they must have felt like the Israelites in Nehemiah 4:6, where it says: "So we built the wall till all of it reached half its height, for the people worked with all their heart." The people of Féwúpe go even further: The walls are to be made of concrete all the way up to the roof. Even women and children are helping. They carry the required sand in palm leaf baskets on their heads from the beach up the mountain.

On Ruwó also, one of the Hall Islands, people are busy building. Aakos (which would be "August" in German), the pastor, has motivated his congregation to build a church on their own initiative.

Finally the time has come for Wilhelm and Elisabeth Kärcher with their children to venture out on their long journey to Germany, in order to see their relatives again – or, in the case of their children, to see them for the first time. For Wilhelm, it has now been fifteen years since leaving Mühlhausen.

However, the journey is postponed once again; the family prefers not to be in Germany for Christmas so that the children would not have to endure the winter. They are to start their trip home in the spring of 1952.

11

Home Furlough and New Departure
(1952–1954)

On Board the Great Ocean Liner

The voyage, they are all looking forward to, has a rather sad beginning. Close to the Kärcher family home people are sitting around watching them without a word as they go about their packing. Especially the older ones want to say their good-byes to the children; many of them are thinking wistfully that they will perhaps never see the family again. The whole scene gives Wilhelm the impression of "being at a funeral service."

Hannelore, who by now is almost eleven years old, has very mixed feelings. She finds it hard to accept the separation from her many girlfriends. Having to say farewell really upsets her.

There is a final service at the church in Chukiyénú. In moving tributes the pastors from the villages on Toon are thanking Wilhelm and his wife for their ministry among them throughout all the past years.

At the pier on Toon many people have flocked together as Wupwiini's boat is casting off. Nobody knows exactly whether the Kärchers are leaving forever or whether they will return, not even the Kärchers themselves. As they cross the lagoon, their home, the school, the church, and finally the cross on the little church spire are one by one vanishing behind the mangroves. Numerous boats are following them to Wééné, so the people can say good-bye to them there once more.

On Wééné things are as they often are on the islands. The ship, the "Chicot," which is to take them on their first leg to Guam, is coming from Pohnpei and is late. The departure time is postponed twice. Until then the Kärchers live in the house of an American family, which is constantly beleaguered by people in the following days. All the pastors who had come to Wééné in order to say farewell to the missionary family, are returning to their congregations on Saturday night, so they can have their Sunday services. But on Monday morning they are all assembled again in full force.

Wupwiini, especially, does not want to leave their side. Again and again he appears in order to take little Helmut on his lap. "I am just coming to see you all once again. From now on the white children will no longer be at the pier when I go back to Chukiyénú." They had often waited there for Wupwiini and caught the rope he threw to them to tie up the boat.

All night long, from March 19 to 20, the "Chicot" is being loaded with cargo. Around six o'clock in the morning – the sun has just risen – Wilhelm, Elisabeth and the children are standing at the stern of the ship. All of a sudden two little rowing boats appear. The pastors from Toon with their wives want to call out to them their very last *Éwúnee feyinnó* and *kinissow chaapwúúr*: "Farewell" and "many, many thanks!"

The anchor cables rattle, the ship's siren begins to sound, the engines start, and a trembling goes through the ship. The Kärchers are waving to the islanders in the many boats that still accompany them. If only they could know for sure now that they will be returning! The parting would then certainly be easier for them.

Wilhelm is very much concerned. He neither knows for sure whether he himself will be able to continue the work he has built up, nor are there any prospects at the moment that a younger successor will come to Chuuk in his place. He is afraid that much of what has come into being under his care will break apart again because he is unable to secure it to last. He sees himself in almost the same situation as when the Japanese had interned him and his family, thereby hindering him from doing his work in the churches. But Wilhelm is trusting God, firmly believing that he will find a solution in all of this.

His fears are justified. The world, in the meantime, has been divided into two great blocks. The so-called Cold War has started. What he cannot know: He will come again, and soon enough. But for now he is looking back from the ship passing through the opening in the great coral reef close to the island of Piis shortly before half past seven, and reaching the open sea.

Slowly Mount Winipwéét on Toon is disappearing from view in the haze on the horizon. In the evening light he stands on deck once more, looking out on two smaller islands – the last ones belonging to the Chuuk District – and thinks back: "The ship with its long and narrow body was plowing through the ocean, leaving behind it a white, foaming pathway that led back to Chuuk." In spite of looking forward to seeing their old home country again, he and his wife are nostalgically conscious of the fact that Chuuk and the sea, which they had so often traveled in mortal danger, are now behind them and a new chapter has started in their lives. Wilhelm describes their emotions with these words: "There is still a very open wound in our hearts."

Among the fellow travelers is an American, Dr. Harold Hanlin, also a missionary. This man, although at the moment of no great consequence, was to pose – to express it positively – a considerable challenge in the coming years, especially for Wilhelm.

When dusk is beginning to fall, Waltraud can't imagine why they won't get ashore someplace soon to go to bed. That is how she was used to it being on boat trips around the islands. She also wants to know why such a big ship doesn't fall over, seeing that it sticks out so high above the water. One of the two boys is puzzled about the "big barrel" towering so high above the deck. For him, ocean-going vessels never used to have a chimneystack until now.

Shoes and Other Unpleasant Things

On March 22, they reach Guam safe and sound. A first surprise awaits them there. At the pier are not only the two military chaplains of the American Navy, Captain J. H. Heintzelman and Lieutenant James R. Beamer, to pick them up, but also two German doctors. Thanks to the presence of the two officers, all their luggage and transport problems are solved. They also do not have to worry about their documents for their onward travel, which would have taken them more than a week in paper-work had they to sort it by themselves.

One of the big problems plaguing all the family is caused by the blis-ters they are getting because for years they have not been used to wearing leather shoes.

March 23, 1952, is a Sunday. They take part in the service held in the navy hospital chapel. Here they count as VIPs! Wilhelm reports about his work on Chuuk. And, of course, everybody expects from Hannelore, Waltraud, Anneliese, and Ernst – Helmut is still too small for this – to hear what all the world wants to hear from missionary kids: a song sung in Chuukese. Nothing could be easier than that, and everybody is delight-ed! Afterwards, their father grants several journalists an interview for a report in the military newspaper published on Guam.

The report, published three days later in the "Marianas Mariner," is full of mistakes and bias. It not only contains a picture of the family in front of the military hospital, accompanied by the two officers, but also murders the spelling of the names of Waltraud and Anneliese beyond recognition. They are given as "Weltereaut" and "Anneiese" respectively.

Besides, the author of the report states at the end that the children can speak Chuukese and some German, but no English.

The following Monday things are turbulent. They are bussed to the harbour where they board the ship that will take them from Guam to San Francisco across the whole Pacific Ocean.

The "General Edwin D. Patrick" is a troop ship capable of carrying two thousand GIs including all of their gear. It is 608.8 feet (186 m) long, has over 400 cabins und bears the name of a general who had been killed in action during the Second World War near Manila in the Philippines.

The "General Edwin D. Patrick"

Wilhelm is being shown the ship's technology. The giant engine room is especially interesting with its transmissions and a technical device that allows the crew to produce drinking water from seawater.

Their luggage is already waiting for them on board ship in their spacious cabin. The children are mightily impressed. Not only are they excited by the many cars everywhere on Guam's streets, but their attention is also drawn by the two bands they can hear; you could not find such things on Chuuk.

In the end the two little boys feel threatened. "While the general who was traveling with us inspects the troops, Ernst flinches with a start each time the cannons blasting their salute to the ship. Helmut starts crying and only calms down when his father takes him to the other side of the ship where he can see the ocean and the little boats he is used to from Chuuk. With them, his confidence in the world returns."

At eleven o'clock on the dot the tugboats start moving and manoeuvre the big ship out of port.

Off to San Francisco

For over a week they proceed eastward. The crew's attitude to them as Germans is totally different from what they experienced with the Japanese. "I must say, they did not just treat us as passengers but as guests." The ship's purser speaks excellent German as he has lived in Germany for a while as a younger man. He likes to talk to them. One evening, he has a table prepared with many gifts for the children, just as if it were Christmas.

On March 31, the ship reaches Honolulu on Hawaii. An old acquaintance, who had been an official on Chuuk, shows them the island of Oahu. Wilhelm's ironic comment is: "He gives himself the pleasure of driving the village folk from Micronesia by car through Honolulu."

The children marvel at a department store. So many things! "Why don't you just buy them all?" they want to know from their father. And especially the escalator! What an exciting adventure! After reaching the upper floor, Waltraud jumps off the last step she stood on and looks back to see whether the thing will perhaps pursue her further or not.

In Honolulu zoo they are seeing elephants, crocodiles, zebras, monkeys and giraffes for the first time. They constantly draw the attention of other visitors because they express their amazement in Chuukese. People think they are Swedes or Poles. Some take them for East Indians because of the jabbering of the children.

Once Honolulu lies behind them, the weather cools down as they travel northeast. The tropics are soon left behind.

On board, the children are not alone by themselves. There are about seventy other young passengers. A party is being organized for them on the way to San Francisco, and again they have to sing songs in the Chuukese language. The performance of the Kärcher children is even transmitted via loudspeaker into all the cabins. One of their "hits" is an evening song. When asked, they will sing it for people any time of the day.

On April 5, 1952, in the morning they reach the American mainland. It is very foggy. The captain asks them to come to the bridge and explains to them the difficult manoeuvres entering San Francisco Bay. Suddenly above them they can see the arch of the Golden Gate Bridge. This structure that had the longest span in the world at that time is an overwhelming sight.

Here too, in San Francisco, they are expected and taken care of by friendly people. They drive over the bridge that has a center span of 4,200 feet (c. 1,280 m), an overall length of 9,266 ft (2,824 m), two decks, and six lanes, connecting San Francisco and Oakland with the American mainland via the Golden Gate inlet into the bay.

Straight Through the United States

On April 8, they are sitting in a train that is to take them straight across the United States to Newark in seventy hours. Traveling through the Sierra Nevada the children see snow for the first time in their lives. The whole family catches a cold during this trip. In spite of this it becomes an unforgettable experience. After passing through the American desert on the second day, the train takes them on the third day through the Midwest with its fruitful land and many farms.

From Newark they get to Schooley's Mountain, the American Branch of the Liebenzell Mission, by car. The children are more and more bothered by the fact that their skin no longer is so moist as it used to be on Chuuk, but unpleasantly dry. And always these stupid shoes! Isn't that a bit much?

When Do We finally Get to Germany?

They stay for five weeks in Schooley's Mountain. On May 15, they find themselves in Montreal in Canada. From here their journey takes them to Bremerhaven in Germany. As they travel by ship down the St. Lawrence River and across the Atlantic, a trip that takes eleven days, nothing special is happening; the children are bored and keep asking the question that usually gets on their parents' nerves: "When do we finally get to Germany?"

When the ship reaches the European continent and the North Sea, the children think Germany must be something like a long stretched-out island without an end to it. They suddenly miss the ocean that in the South Seas is always nearby wherever you are.

In Bremerhaven they are picked up by Elisabeth's aunt Elise Grentz from Berlin. They take the train to Karlsruhe, and from there go by car to Bad Liebenzell.

The drive through Pforzheim is depressing; everywhere there are only ruins and destruction, the legacy of the severe air raid in 1944. The Nagold valley and the "Mission Hill" appear in sharp contrast to this. For the children who have never seen Germany before, all this is an experience that gives them mixed feelings.

What Happened in Germany

At the cemetery in Mühlhausen Wilhelm and the children are painfully made aware of the fact that his parents – their unknown grandparents – are no longer alive.

Ernst, Wilhelm's youngest brother, had been killed in action in 1942 in Russia. Shortly before Christmas of 1944, Wilhelm's mother had found her husband dead in the stables. A heart attack had unexpectedly brought an end to his life. Wilhelm's brother Karl had been taken prisoner of war; but he had survived and, in sometimes adventurous circumstances, had struggled back home. His brother Franz had fled from Silesia with his family, reaching Mühlhausen after walking for many weeks, almost without a penny to their name.

Wilhelm's mother had been ill with cancer and fought for several years with great energy against the limitations placed upon her by her sickness. She had longed to see the return of her son to Germany. Finally, she succumbed to jaundice that robbed her of her last strength. She died at the age of seventy-two years.

Discoveries and Experiences

Ernst, who by now is five years old, thinks Germany is absolutely too cold and that the *fénúwen misin*, the "mission property," as he called the "Mission Hill," is clearly less attractive "than ours." By "ours" he means Philadelphia on Chuuk.

The girls, on the other hand, discover many exciting things, like horseshoes, for example. The horses (at that time the Mission still maintained a farm), they say, are wearing real *geta*, Japanese wooden sandals, and they want to know who will put them on the horses every morning.

They are also amazed that his father has so many "brothers," because they are not used to hear him and his colleagues being addressed like that as if they are relatives, not only in Bad Liebenzell but also everywhere else in the churches and fellowships.

A propos relatives! The children are having great difficulty remembeing who is their uncle, aunt, or cousin for whatever reason. Ernst insists on finding out among all his relatives who really is his mother-in-law.

Mühlhausen is of special interest to the children. Here they can learn to ride a bike, chug into the woods on uncle's tractor, and climb up and down the many steps in the hilly vineyards on the river Enz.

In Waltenhofen, however, they do have grandparents, who own cows with bells around their necks as they graze on the meadows. Close by is a little wood where one can play to one's heart's content, almost like on Toon. But the freedom they had there has its boundaries here. The children do not know that meadow grass in Germany is precious. On Chuuk nobody has to make hay for cattle to have feed during the winter months. Unconcerned, they run across the meadows in the neighborhood and are totally surprised and frightened when they are being scolded by the farmers for doing it.

1952 goes by with its deputation work and slide lectures all over Germany. As of August 1st, the family of seven lives in Eutingen near Pforzheim. An acquaintance and friend has managed to find them a house that they can buy at a favorable price and also furnish comfortably with the help of their relatives. Wilhelm and Elisabeth give it the name *imwen kinamwmwe*. That means "house of peace, of quietness." The writing is still there today in Pforzheim-Eutingen, Brömachweg no. 27, on the house wall next to the front door.

For Hannelore, Waltraud, and Anneliese the school year has started and with it a stressful time. They struggle with the same adversities as most missionary kids. Hardly anybody can fathom what it means for a child at this age to get along with other children in a classroom from one day to the next, lacking the prior experience of a kindergarten. Nobody knows you; you have never played with them before; and whatever you tell them of your experiences in the South Seas is so unbelievable that you are quickly branded as a dreamer, a show-off, and liar. They encounter the many little unknown details in a school in Germany that a child cannot know if it has not grown up here. To be sure, the parents have prepared them well. But still the three girls experience difficult first weeks at school, as their vocabulary in German is not at the same level as that of their fellow students.

How could it be otherwise? On Chuuk there are no annual seasons like springtime, summer, fall, and winter. Children who have never experienced the seasonal cycle do not know the words to speak about such

things, to share information, and to give them the capacity to think about it. By contrast, Hannelore, Waltraud, and Anneliese know the world of the South Seas and the language skills to describe and talk about the things there. The fact that they are now in Germany – and thus in an environment having a different language orientation – they experience as a shortcoming, and so they feel very insecure. Anneliese, being the youngest, has it the easiest. However, the initial difficulties at school decrease in the course of the first few months and are fairly soon consigned to the past.

A Second Farewell from Europe

Almost a year later, we find an article in the Mission's publication (*"Mitteilungen der Liebenzeller Mission,"* July/August 1953:11–12) written by Wilhelm. It is his farewell address at the mission festival on Pentecost Sunday in Bad Liebenzell before his second departure. As a title it has the two verses from Exodus 40:36–37: "Whenever the cloud lifted from above the tabernacle, the Israelites would set out; but if the cloud did not lift, they did not set out." What follows is worth quoting verbatim:

"Moses knew very well that anytime the cloud lifted a totally new period of travel would begin. So he did not think: I am so experienced in the ways of the Lord and also so well acquainted with the desert that I can risk setting out even without a special sign.

"Fifteen months ago, when we prepared ourselves for our trip home, we had the inner assurance that for us the cloud had lifted as a sign that we should set out. The One who commanded the cloud to lift, had also made the road plain for us in a miraculous way to come home, all the way to Eutingen near Pforzheim. Only then did the cloud settle again.

"And now the cloud has lifted again as a sign to get going. We cannot help but set out in obedience and pray like Moses: Lord, go with us, for a new chapter in our travels and our lives has started!"

He then recounts again the experience he had as a child in the First World War when, at the station in Mühlacker, he saw the soldiers going to war, full of enthusiasm, because the king had called them.

And then he added another experience from his youth:

"In my hometown many years ago, the sheep shelter up from the village was on fire. Since, fifty years ago, the fire department's equipment was not as modern as it is today, and there was hardly any water on the hillside, the whole community formed a long chain of buckets of water from the village fountain up to the burning shed. One person would pass the full bucket of water to the next. At the end of this bucket chain the firemen worked. In this way, all acting as one, the fire was contained. This was not only thanks to the firemen but also to the bucket chain. This is just an illustration for the cause of missions. If you cannot be a missionary, you can certainly play your part in the bucket chain. Today, at this Mission celebration, who would not want to join in the bucket chain?"

It is planned that Wilhelm should travel alone to the States in September 1953, in order to fulfill several demands since made by the American authorities on non-Americans who want to work in the "Trust Territory of the Pacific Islands." This is now the name given to the islands of Micronesia, administered and taken care of by the United States as a mandate from the United Nations. For Wilhelm this means going through some kind of orientation classes, before he can get a visa for himself and his family to return to the islands. Only after taking care of these formalities will his wife and the two youngest children, Ernst und Helmut, follow him to the States. Together they will then return to Micronesia, without the three girls.

A Serious Decision

A family separation? Indeed! And there is a simple but valid reason for it: There is no opportunity on Chuuk for Hannelore, Waltraud and Anneliese to attend a school with a curriculum according to German standards. So the three girls have to stay behind in Eutingen for their school education. In their parents' absence they will be cared for by Barbara Löscher, a Liebenzell sister.

Until way into the first half of the 20th century, children's schooling and vocational training posed one of the greatest problems for missions and missionary families. There were no expatriate German schools in the countries where missionaries were active, nor were there distance-learning courses available to prepare missionary children for vocational school education in Germany.

Originally, there was only one single solution for this problem, in the form of a home for missionary children. That is where they were sent when they were legally required to attend school and their parents wanted to return to the mission field. This meant that the needs of missionary children had to be subordinated to the missionary mandate of their parents.

Very often for the children this entailed a special kind of emotional pressure. Within a short time, in a single phase of their development, they would lose the people they related to most, just when they needed them the most. They had to get along with substitute attachment figures; and building a relationship with them was rarely easy, not to say generally difficult, and often full of tension. It was not unusual to meet missionary children for whom the experience of being separated from their parents was in some ways a traumatic event, for which they blamed their parents their whole life long. Among these children were not a few who turned away from everything to do with being a Christian, from faith and from the church.

Nowadays this is much less of a problem. Missionary children (or "missionary kids" – "MKs" – as they are called) do not have to be separated from their parents very early anymore. There are expatriate schools, long-distance educational programs, and professional care in boarding schools for them.

Under the present circumstances there is no other possible solution to the problem of their education than for Hannelore, Waltraud, and Anneliese to remain in Eutingen.

Outwardly, the decision to separate the family seems to have been comparatively easy for the parents to make. In a farewell letter written by Wilhelm on August 6, 1953, it runs as follows: "We have to leave our three girls behind in Germany on account of their schooling. This we dare to do as we look to Him who said, 'Anyone who loves his father or mother … his son or daughter more than me is not worthy of me' (Matthew 10:37f)."

In reality, Wilhelm and his wife struggle for a long time about how to match the life and needs of their three daughters with the task on Chuuk that they view as not yet complete.

However, it has not come to that just yet. First, Wilhelm the father will leave the family. It will be some time before Elisabeth with Ernst and Helmut are due to follow him.

Bagagli!

Just as in 1937 at his first departure, he stays overnight in Bern at Rosa Mäder's house and then takes the train to Genoa. Once in Genoa, stress is in store: the luggage he had checked in two weeks before in Liebenzell is nowhere to be found. What is to be done now?

After searching frantically for it for a whole day but without success, he sends a telegram to Bad Liebenzell: "Cannot find luggage." There is nothing else but to be patient. Late at night there is a knock at his door; a

policeman is standing outside, holding the reply telegram from Bad
Liebenzell in his hand: "Luggage passed through Chiasso August 16."

Wilhelm can hardly sleep that night. Next morning he starts searching
again for his belongings. Around eleven o'clock, after starting sightseeing
in the city to take his mind off his troubles, he finds himself in a narrow
alley in front of a house that is the office of a small shipping company.

"*Trasporti*!? I could perhaps try here!"

Wilhelm goes into the building. On the fourth floor, in an old and
somewhat grubby room, he finds an Italian sitting at his desk and chewing a cigar. At first he can't believe he will find his luggage here. But
then he can't believe what he is looking at: the man does indeed have the
express waybill belonging to his luggage on the desk in front of him!

At this moment, a German-American lady enters the dingy office,
likewise in search of her things. Both together now try to communicate
with the Italian. That is partly successful, but it still takes over half an
hour before the customs clearance for their luggage has been completed.
But that does not mean that they can now see their boxes and suitcases.

Hours later – by now it is four o'clock in the afternoon and all the passengers have gone through passport control and customs – Wilhelm's
stuff is still at some unknown location. Desperation threatens to grip him
again, when he suddenly sees something he can only describe as "an old
jalopy of a truck." To his great relief he sees his boxes on its tailgate.
This is pure joy to him, just like Christmas. But his joy is misplaced; the
ship's purser refuses to accept the luggage. It is not registered, he says.

By now Wilhelm is furious. He marches from the deck down to the
truck, pulls off his luggage, loads it onto the back of one of the Italians
drifting around, and explains to him with hands and feet that he should
carry the things on board ship.

Now it's the purser's turn to get furious. When he sees the things
standing on deck he tries to use red tape: "That will cost you fifteen dollars cargo fees!" But Wilhelm will not be defeated. He talks non-stop,
explaining to the pedantic official that on every ship each passenger gets
one cubic meter (c. 3.5 cubic feet) of free space for luggage, and that his
"stuff" would be just a bit more than that. But the purser refuses to back
down on his demands. He calls one of the ship's officers who appears
with a tape measure and starts measuring.

Now things really get interesting. Wilhelm soon realizes that the tape
measure is only graduated in feet and inches, but that the officer does not
really know how to figure the difference between cubic metres and cubic
feet. Resolutely, Wilhelm takes the tape measure from his hand and gives

him a practical visual lesson of the size of a cubic meter. To no avail. The officer also insists that Wilhelm will have to pay.

No way does Wilhelm want to do that, and so he takes up the last argument left to him. He explains to both of them who he is and that he wants to get to the Carolines. At these words the officer looks at him again from head to toe and then says, "You are a man of the church. We can do nothing."

Wilhelm's commentary: "After two full days this was finally the end of the *'bagagli'*" (Italian for "luggage").

From Genoa to New York

On September 2, 1953, the Egyptian ship "Khedive Ismael" sets sail from Genoa to New York. Wilhelm shares a small cabin with "a nice 17-year old Arab fellow," as he calls him. Because the young fellow speaks English, Wilhelm reads with him a passage from the English New Testament each night before they go to sleep.

While they are in the Mediterranean, the sea is calm, in contrast to the Atlantic where, on and off, they encounter storms. During the rough and rainy weather sticking strips are attached to the tables to keep dishes from sliding off when the ship pitches and rolls. Not many people are still going to the dining hall to eat.

The unappetizing scenes Wilhelm witnesses and describes on his voyage to New York show in an impressive way how, for him, reasoning and serious take on life are combined with pleasure at what is funny, quirky and grotesque. Yet he never crosses the limits of good taste, even if he gets disturbingly close to them.

One of his meal companions wishes to prove that the ship's pitching and rolling have little effect on him, and that he can keep his poise. All of a sudden he goes white in the face, walks slowly to the porthole, opens it, and sticks his head far out as if to call somebody. He remains in this position for a few minutes, lifting his nose to the fresh air; but then despite his efforts he starts to cough and empties the contents of his stomach into the sea …

Another passenger is so quickly overcome that he "does his thing" at the table itself. Wilhelm's commentary: "If you don't get seasick yourself, the whole matter is rather interesting. But unfortunately, I almost lost my appetite as well."

At mealtimes he often sits at a small table with a Greek lady. She loves to dress up for these occasions. Her lavish attempts to beautify herself seem rather pointless but take so long that she usually appears at the table somewhat late. "The varnish on her nails and toes, her lipstick and her make-up are always fresh. Her long red fingernails almost look like bird claws, and she wears new earrings for every meal – up to two inches (5 cm) in diameter. Actually, all that's missing is a nice big nose ring. She has hardly finished eating when she blows her cigarette smoke across the table right into my face, mixed with the smell of her perfume. One could easily get seasick from this, too."

Also on board ship is a grandmother from Munich in her late sixties, who has never before in her life undertaken a big journey. She wants to visit her three daughters in the States. After the Sunday service led by Wilhelm, she bursts out in tears: "On the ship all I can hear is a hotch-potch of different languages, of which I can't understand a word. But when you preached and prayed I could understand everything."

Wilhelm gets the impression that she is becoming more uncertain the closer they are to New York. She is obviously afraid of that unknown world she is to encounter and wishes to be back in her own familiar sur-roundings. When the "Khedive Ismael" enters New York harbour, she is once again sitting in her cabin crying her eyes out. Wilhelm tries to en-courage her, but she is determined to stay miserable: "Who will help me in America if my girls aren't going to be there?" It is a pitiful sight. Wil-helm accompanies her to immigration. The dear woman is so excited, she is constantly muddling all her papers, even losing some of them. Finally, after half an hour, all the documents are in order and presentable, and they can both risk going ashore.

Down at the landing stage three modern looking American ladies are waiting. Their heads are bowed in deep conversation. Wilhelm assumes they may be the daughters of the old lady in his company, so he addresses them and asks whether this is their mother. The three of them do not rec-ognize their mother right away, not having seen her for quite a while. Her figure also seems to have changed considerably in the meantime. When the light suddenly dawns on them, one of them cries out, "Mother, have you ever gotten fat!" With this statement the world is okay again for the old lady, and one of her daughters presses a five-dollar bill in Wilhelm's hand as a thank-you for his role as mediator.

Studying in the United States

At a college in Connecticut, the Hartford Theological Seminary, Wil-helm completes the orientation course he is obliged to take to qualify for a re-entry visa to Micronesia.

In the lectures and seminars he attends, he gains an appreciation for learning: "If I had to start a missions seminary, I would not only employ good teachers but also furnish it with an extensive library. Here they have a five-storey building with all kinds of books." At that time, the library had over 180,000 volumes. "Every new and worthwhile book that is published can be read here, even many German books. However, if we had had to study so many books in Bad Liebenzell as we do here, I probably would not have gone into missions. But the Kingdom of God would have been built anyway, of course."

People find him interesting, this German fellow with his strange typewriter, who thinks in such different terms from the young American students. And they listen to him with great attentiveness as he tells of his experiences on the islands of Micronesia. For even though American soldiers had taken and occupied the area ten years before, hardly anyone knows, strangely enough, where Micronesia is situated and what is meant by the Carolines. Some react with surprise and are amazed that there should be islands in the States of North and South Carolina.

Wilhelm Kärcher the student learns to evaluate the minimum he should know about a topic before he can join in conversation about it. But he has his difficulties with the academic jargon, the totally different mentality of the people, and the differences between the German and American education systems. One of his letters to his former colleague Richard Neumaier ends with the words: "If I had known beforehand all that one has to learn prior to going into missions and how one can often not even sleep because of all the learning, I believe I would have remained a carpenter. In this trade things had to be learned as well, but it almost fell into my lap, whereas here in Hartford, just like in Bad Liebenzell, I have to struggle hard to get anywhere. Sometimes I am all depressed and ask myself, why I have to go through this. For you this would be just the right place, and it would not even be much of an effort for you as it is for me. I am also lacking the basics. All the students here have graduated from college or some other school of further education. So you can well imagine that I am not one of the best. But when I had 65% [of the examination material] correct in our first test in anthropology, I was really very happy, because many Americans who had attended more schools than I have, were below me. And then the [English] language – that's not so easy either. So then, this school is quite an ordeal for me. I have to "take one bite at a time, one day at a time.""

What it means for him to "take one bite at a time" he describes in a letter dated August 2, 1976, to missionary Klaus W. Müller, his nephew and successor in the mission work: "Friday at noon the canteen was closed. There was nothing to eat from then on until Monday morning. From Schooley's Mountain I received at that time 20 dollars per month. That was my pocket money. The Mission had paid everything else. So then, like the Japanese students, I went hungry throughout Saturday and Sunday. The African students did likewise."

Whenever he has no more money he looks for opportunities to earn a little by babysitting. The people are usually very astonished to see a grown man at his age – by now he is forty-five years old – still doing such a thing as a student. He is suspected of wanting to abuse children and has to prove that he is married himself and a father of five children, in order to allay any such misgivings.

In his letters he uses that expression "to take one bite at a time" [which in German means "to struggle through" something] all through the winter semester. In one letter he even uses it referring to his program: "So, now I won't write another letter until I have 'bitten my way through' this semester."

During his time at Hartford he receives news of the death of an islander whom he regarded as a close friend. Kiriimen had been a long-time pastor on Némé, one of the Outer Islands of Chuuk. The deceased, who could speak German quite well, had earlier told him many things from his eventful life. He had been to many places as a young man, had worked for some time in the phosphate mines on Nauru Island during the German colonial era, and had been one of the first on his island to become a serious Christian.

Moved by news of his death, Wilhelm decides to write down Kiriimen's life story, as far as he knows it, in a brief biographical sketch. In spite of his workload and the difficult circumstances of his life at that time, he begins to work on the manuscript while still at Hartford and finishes it at Schooley's Mountain.

He sends the finished text entitled *"Krimen, ein treuer Insulanerprediger"* (Krimen, a Faithful Island Preacher) to Bad Liebenzell. It seems to have arrived there, but for some unknown reasons it falls into oblivion. Joachim Braun, a pastor from the Württemberg State Church, who publishes a Christian newspaper, prints the story in episodes. Someone in Bad Liebenzell does discover it eventually, and the initiative is taken to publish the story also through Liebenzell's own publishing house. It finally appears in 1960, seven years after the completion of the manuscript.

A Decision that Leaves a Bitter Taste

At the College in Hartford there is a teacher with whom Wilhelm develops a special rapport. He is professor of anthropology and ethnology, and German is his native language.

Dr. Paul Leser, born in 1889, studied ethnology and received his doctorate and qualification as a university lecturer in this subject. Because he was a Jew, he lost his post as university lecturer soon after the National Socialists (Nazis) came to power. He had to flee Germany. Via Sweden he bluffed his way through to the United States where finally, in 1953, he received a lectureship at the Kennedy School of Missions, a department of Hartford Theological Seminary. That is where he and Wilhelm Kärcher get acquainted.

Wilhelm likes to speak up in his lectures and seminars, especially whenever he can straighten out a point that the professor does not present quite in accordance with Wilhelm's experience.

Thus, one day, they talk about the way grain used to be threshed in Germany until a few years back. The statement is made that it always took four people, who would wield the flail in rhythm. Wilhelm just can't not point out that as a boy he used to thresh in a group of six boys.

For an ethnologist like Paul Leser, a grown man like Wilhelm with all his experiences as a missionary, is of greatest interest. They frequently talk about culture, society, and language of the islanders of Chuuk, and Professor Leser gets the impression that Wilhelm meets all the criteria to do a doctorate in ethnology. In fact, he wants to accept him into the doctoral program.

Wilhelm mentions this suggestion to Richard Neumaier in a letter dated December 7, 1953:

"Last week, our anthropology professor urged me to write down all the old stories and *roongen sáfey*[24] very precisely. If I had enough [scientific material] to amount to a book of about 200 pages, [...] then I could get my doctorate with it; if not in Germany, then certainly in the States. That would be something."

He does indeed add that he is still not truly convinced that he should follow his teacher's suggestion but he does not reject the plan outright, especially as he can see that such an undertaking – if he should be successful in it – would give him an enormous advantage. Primarily, he could thereby confirm his position among the islanders. Not that it mat-

[24] Collective term of the islanders for magic procedures for healing of sicknesses, protection against all kinds of misfortune etc.

ters much to him, since he has already gained quite a status over the past years by virtue of his personality and commitment, so that he would be an authority with them even without an academic degree. Much more important is another argument. As a German missionary on Chuuk he will have to work in the future under the supervision of American colleagues. In their educational training, university degrees have been the rule for a long time already. German missionaries, with their training in a trade or profession followed by a seminary course, are therefore not viewed by them as equal partners. Wilhelm knows this very well; so he decides to present Professor Leser's suggestion of aiming for a doctorate to the responsible Mission inspector, Rev. Heinrich Hertel, and get his opinion on it.

Heinrich Hertel had studied theology in Erlangen, Bavaria. In 1926, Heinrich Coerper had invited him to come to Bad Liebenzell as a teacher and adviser. Besides his teaching he had, many years before, taken on the inspecting of the mission fields of Japan and the South Seas, which means he was Wilhelm's immediate superior.

When Heinrich Hertel learns from Hartford that Wilhelm Kärcher has been suggested for a doctorate, he reacts with indignation – not so much against Wilhelm as against "those Americans" and "such a notion."

It is not at all clear why he rejected the idea outright. The argument that a doctorate would be useful in bolstering Wilhelm, strengthen his position among his future American superiors on Chuuk, and would thus make his work considerably easier, is so reasonable that Heinrich Hertel should really have agreed to it. Did he perhaps fear creating a precedent, i.e. would he, in agreeing to it, have come under pressure to allow the same opportunity to other missionaries also? Or must the reason for his refusal be seen in the opinion, prevalent in those days, that South Sea missionaries did not need an academic education?

The present-day thinking of the Liebenzell Mission is, of course, far removed from such an attitude, and one cannot simply insinuate either that Heinrich Hertel had been too narrow-minded. Whatever the reason, it is certain that because of his negative response to Wilhelm's plans for earning an academic PhD. degree, these plans had effectively been thwarted.

Wilhelm Kärcher accepts the decision without contradiction, but it left him with a bitter taste for the rest of his life.

Plans for Chuuk

What really and seriously concerns him during his studies are worries of quite a different kind. He asks himself how the pastors, chiefs, and Christians are managing on Chuuk, where they have had to cope without his advice and experience for so long already. He is afraid that religious groups of other persuasions could gain influence in the churches and cause disturbances. The pastors, together with the American colleagues responsible for them, are writing to him regularly. But their letters contain no news raising concerns.

Wilhelm's former colleague Richard Neumaier, with whom he corresponds regularly, tries repeatedly to get him to take heart and gives him suggestions, especially in connection with plans for a school. If one day the churches on Chuuk are to be independent, their representatives and workers must be trained for it. This requires investment as regards materials and ideas. In numerous letters Wilhelm and Richard Neumaier discuss the concomitant problems that need to be solved. Should the school be built on Toon or rather on Wééné, the seat of the government and administration? Where could the teaching staff come from? What time schedule appears to be realistic?

A Fight for the New Testament

One of the most difficult matters plaguing Wilhelm that he has to tackle in the course of this winter semester has to do with a manuscript still in his luggage.

Let us remind ourselves. Early on, Richard Neumaier had recognized that the translation used so far by the Christians on Chuuk and its Outer Islands contained too many inadequacies for it to be of any future practical use. This motivated him to translate the New Testament in a revised form into the Chuukese language. He had devoted himself to it over many years of patient work, and after his final return from his field of service he had the manuscript prepared for printing.

One might think that the printing and publishing of Bible texts would not be such a big undertaking, once all the groundwork is done. In reality, though, there is still a lot of work involved afterwards. Bible translations have to be tested with utmost care, and that in several respects. Is the text correct? Does it create theological problems because terms in the original language appear distorted and unintelligible by being rendered in another way of thinking? Does the text seem fluent and smooth to the people who read it? Can those who are conditioned to understand by hearing also absorb its contents while reading it and, in doing so, trying to comprehend it? There is a whole range of other questions that need to be answered before a Bible text can appear in print.

As a rule, examinations of this kind are best left to Bible societies who serve as editors and also take care of the financial side of printing. In the case of Chuuk the American Bible Society is responsible. But their representatives view Richard Neumaier's version of the New Testaments rather critically, for various reasons.

The fact that he is not considered to be a linguist and, as a theologian, has not been able to show any university level of training, has been mentioned earlier. However, the standoffish attitude of the representatives of the American Bible Society has a very human background.

Since 1951, i.e. for two years now, the responsibility for the whole work in the churches on Chuuk lies with an American missionary. This is Dr. Harold Hanlin, whom we already know because he had been on board ship when the Kärcher family was on its way home from Chuuk to Europe.

Harold Hanlin is, without a doubt, an impressive personality. He had his doctorate in theology and Greek and had taken courses for Bible translators under a certain Dr. Eugene A. Nida, a renowned ethno-linguist of his time. One outstanding characteristic of Hanlin's is his ambition, a trait that can spur a person on to great achievements when used in moderation. So far, Hanlin's progress in learning the language of Chuuk was rather modest in Wilhelm Kärcher's opinion: "If he were gifted in languages he would surely be able by now, after two years of residence, to hold a chapel service. But he wrote to me that he would still not dare do so." And yet, Harold Hanlin, in the meantime, is working on his own translation of the New Testament. At least, he is intensively planning it.

It soon becomes evident that Harold Hanlin – strangely enough Wilhelm spells his name as "Hänlein"[25] in his letters of that time – wants to prevent Richard Neumaier's translation from being published and introduced to Chuuk. To do so, Dr. Harold Hanlin can avail himself of almost any means. He is the one responsible for the work on Chuuk. His far-reaching authority and his influence are based on one decisive criterion: He knows that his teacher, Eugene A. Nida, who by now has become president of the American Bible Society, is on his side. If Richard Neumaier's New Testament were allowed to be published, this could only happen with his permission.

---

[25] which, in German, sounds like "little rooster"

The task given to Wilhelm for his stay in America is to accomplish exactly this. He is the one chosen to lead the negotiations. In the past, he himself emphasized repeatedly that he would keep his hands off translation work, since the American fellow workers were said to be the better academics. But he also knows that, at the moment, there is no one better informed about the language and social circumstances on Chuuk than Richard Neumaier, and he knows about the special qualities of his translation of the New Testament. But even more important is the fact that it would take years until Wilhelm had access to a useable Bible text for his future theological work in the Chuukese churches if he had to wait for Harold Hanlin's translation to be published.

Wilhelm is fully aware of the tension in relationships, but he is also willing to face the difficult task of getting the finished version of the New Testament he has in his luggage published. From Hartford he writes a letter to Eugene A. Nida with a request for an audience about this matter. Nida sends him word that he will invite him. But Wilhelm waits in vain for an invitation. At one point, his patience has come to an end and he has the distinct impression that he should take the initiative. Under his own steam he travels to New York, where the American Bible Society has its headquarters.

One of his fellow students makes his car available for this trip. The two of them leave early morning at five o'clock. Four hours later they are on the spot. Nida does indeed receive Wilhelm. Their conversation lasts for almost three hours, in the course of which both parties are tough and negotiate doggedly. Wilhelm speaks with the tongues of angels and has to make a tremendous effort to restrain himself; more than once he feels that he could get very angry. Repeatedly he gets the impression that his negotiation partner knows and plans more than he is willing to admit openly. Wilhelm feels unfairly treated in more than one respect.

As he leaves the office of the director of the American Bible Society, Wilhelm has the impression that, although he did not come across badly, he also had not been able to convince his negotiation partner. Wilhelm had suggested getting the opinion of the islanders in this matter before the Society made any decision. Nida had agreed. Wilhelm was tasked with taking the manuscript to Chuuk and leading further discussions there.

It becomes evident that this solution is merely a postponement. The conflict smoulders on, and the whole matter remains a heavy burden on Wilhelm: "I just can't get down to my studies these days as the matter of the New Testament is preying on my mind day and night." And on November 20, 1953, he writes in a report to Richard Neumaier, "Now I am hoping to banish thoughts of the New Testament so I will be able to concentrate on my studies again."

In a letter of December 12, 1953, the American Bible Society yields partially and declares itself willing to copy parts of the finished translation of the New Testament and distribute it among the island congregations for testing. A few weeks later, negotiations with the copying company are indeed definitely under way.

Completion of Studies

By now, Wilhelm has been in the States for about half a year. The studies, the strange language, and the people who speak it, the different college and its system tire him out. But then he doesn't have time to feel homesick, though at times he does feel a bit lonely in his attic room: "I was used to having a family and not just books, tables and chairs." In time, he found friends who were interested in the islands, in Germany, and in his experiences.

The letters he writes to his daughters in Eutingen during this time, show a father full of warmth, understanding for his children, and a subtle, benevolently restrained humor. In addressing the envelope he contracts the names of Hannelore, Waltraud, and Anneliese into one single name. Thus, the three of them are simply called "Hannewaltliese," the same name, by the way, that he gives to one of the boats he uses on Chuuk.

"Hannewaltliese"

The relationship the professors have with their students he could only call very friendly. He loves studying, often working in the library until midnight. He probably has never read as much as at Hartford. His English has improved considerably.

He graduates from his studies with great success. A serious offer made by one of his professors, to go to Africa – to Natal – he turns down. But the most important thing for him is the letter of recommendation handed to him by the director of the Theological Seminary: "Now I won't regret having submitted to this training at this stage."

With this letter he immediately receives the so-called "navy clearance" from the Americans, allowing him as a non-American to re-enter Micronesia. At the same time he learns that Harold Hanlin does not want to see him on Chuuk again, whereas the pastors, who know him best, indeed do! He has heard from them that they are waiting for him and are looking forward to welcoming him again.

Traveling Days

During his studies at Hartford he has been visiting churches that support the Liebenzell Mission, but after graduation his visits increase; he accomplishes a tremendous workload. From February 1954, for three months, he travels by "Greyhound" buses across fifteen states lines.

He finds America tremendously fascinating. He visits the Niagara Falls, and watches the black workers at a meat packing plant in Chicago. In his enthusiastic sounding descriptions we sometimes find the starkest contrasts side by side. For example: "In one hour, one black man alone can kill a hundred and fifty cattle. Streams of blood flowed like water. America is a beautiful land. I like it very much!"

But all this also makes him wonder: "If one is always driving around in such comfortable coaches and upholstered trains and gets used to the soft carpets in the houses, it will indeed be difficult to accept the simple life on the islands again. I can now understand much better why American missionaries have such a hard time working and living on the islands."

The presentations he gives of his work are interesting, true to life, and occasionally carry people away. After all, his life story so far could hardly be more thought-provoking. And people donate money. The amount of finance he raises in his travels far surpasses all that Heinrich Zimmermann (director of the American branch of the Liebenzell Mission in Schooley's Mountain) had been able to achieve by then, as he himself states with admiration.

After a while he is thoroughly tired of this traveling business "from the East coast to the Far West, then again to the North close to Canada, and again to Texas." In a letter dated March 23, 1954, he bemoans the fact that he has to tell his story everywhere until late at night. Besides, he does not like the fact that the departure from Germany of his wife, whom he expects to see as soon as possible, is being "overturned" time and again. To him, that sounds like organizational chaos:

"At first they said we should fly from here to Guam because the cargo ships do not want to take passengers. Then I was told I should cross the Atlantic by boat and meet my wife in Naples, proceed from there via India to Hong Kong, and continue either by plane or by ship. I will be very glad once everything is behind me and I can live in a house again."

How thrifty Wilhelm Kärcher had to be with his funds during this time may be seen from the following: An old friend of the Mission gives him a car. When he does not need it anymore he sells it for sixty dollars; which he sends to Eutingen in order to pay off the last mortgage installment on their house.

Separation of the Family

On May 1, 1954, the steamship "Maasdam" sets out to sea from Rotterdam in Holland. On board is Elisabeth Kärcher with her two youngest children Ernst and Helmut, as well as the young Liebenzell missionary Ingelore Lengning. Hannelore, Waltraud, and Anneliese remain in Eutingen.

Anneliese describes what she and her sisters then experience in differing intensity – and what they at times still feel today:

"… What we felt at that time is hard to describe. Saying farewell to my mother will always remain unforgettable for me. It was nighttime when my brothers came with a car belonging to the Liebenzell Mission to pick her up. We girls stood by the garden gate and waved them off with tears in our eyes. We felt as if our hearts had been cut in two with a sharp knife. It was dark – outside and inside. The deep wound was bleeding.

"Our childhood became heavy and sad through this experience, and today we mostly keep silent about that time because few people if any would really understand – and because we are afraid to touch the wounds that have scars on them by now, as they are still hurting us. In talking with my sisters I became aware of the fact that, for me as the youngest, things were still the easiest at that time. I had been able to hide behind them for protection" (1996:63–64).

She continues to talk about the "burden of being a missionary kid." They are always expected to be neat, well behaved and respectable, whereas they themselves would just want to be like any other children; but they aren't allowed to be. To her and her sisters all this amounted to being robbed of their freedom (1996: 64–65).

However, she does not let this accusation get the better of her:

"My sisters and I did not have an easy childhood, but with God's help we saw that we learned especially through such hard times to accept further difficulties in our lives sooner. God has blessed, kept, and carried our family through everything in a special way" (1996:66).

For her later work as a teacher in New Guinea, where she taught missionary children at a boarding school, her childhood experiences proved to be an absolute qualifying factor for her role: "I […] was able to sympathize with the children whenever they were homesick" (1996:66–67).

Back to Micronesia by Plane

On May 12 – two days later than originally scheduled – Wilhelm is waiting in New York harbor for the arrival of the ship carrying Elisabeth and their two boys.

"Ernst already recognized me from far off and immediately started talking. He conveyed many greetings from our three girls in Eutingen as well as a nice present from Mühlhausen. With Helmut it took about ten minutes before we could be friends."

Two weeks later, the four of them are on their way to San Francisco. In America the era of air travel is beginning. For Ernst and Helmut it is quite an experience to fly in a four-engine airplane. They wish their sisters could be with them: "Why didn't we take the girls along?" On this flight, taking them first to Chicago and from there to San Francisco, they enjoy seeing below them the beauties of the American landscapes, the Mississippi, the farms, the Rocky Mountains, which they had seen already two years ago from a train.

The flight durations of 1954 appear long to us today. At that time there are still no commercial flights by jet planes but only by four-engine propeller-driven planes. New York to Chicago takes them more than three hours and from there to San Francisco as much as eight.

In San Francisco an American officer whom they already know from Chuuk is picking them up, and he helps them with the bureaucratic

paperwork. Even now his uniform serves to shorten all the red tape noticeably. Their long flight taking them all the way to Guam will start from here across the Pacific.

One has to really think about it. Not only did the airplanes not have jet engines but they also were not large capacity. Wilhelm still speaks with enthusiasm of the "Trans Ocean Line" plane: "The aircraft can carry more than thirty people!" And he adds the reassuring words that even if the plane was no seaplane, still, in an emergency it could float in the water long enough until all passengers were safely in the inflatable dinghies. Well, there you are!

Their flight leaves at one o'clock in the afternoon of May 28. It takes them to Hawaii in beautiful weather. When they land in Honolulu at ten o'clock at night, after nine hours in the air, it is already pitch black. For two hours they can walk around, before the next leg of their flight starts – twelve hours to Wake Island. Since the plane is no longer filled to capacity after Hawaii, the flight attendants make up a bed for Ernst and Helmut from two seats next to each other.

One can well imagine the demands made on these two boys on such a long flight, given their wish to be active. On Guam Helmut, by now four years old, simply refuses to get into yet another airplane, "because they always tie you down in a seat."

Back by Ship to Chuuk

Helmut's protest is quite timely. On Guam a ship is waiting for him to start the last stretch of his second world trip in his life, and on this journey he won't be tied down. Again it is the "Chicot" on which he had traveled from Chuuk to Guam two years before, when he went to Germany for the first time in his life.

His parents use the time until their departure – a whole week – to accomplish all kinds of purchases. His father is buying building material he will need for the construction of churches on the islands, which won't be available in sufficient quantities and at a good price on Chuuk itself; for example sheets of corrugated metal – five hundred of them. He also gives missionary reports in different churches.

The trip from Guam to Wééné takes three days. On June 11, the sun has just risen, the Chuuk island mountains appear on the horizon; and when the "Chicot" drops anchor at the Wééné pier an impressive scene greets the four of them. Almost all the pastors of Chuuk are gathered at the harbour. So as not to miss the arrival of the missionary and his family, they had already been camping on Wééné for a whole week. This is not just a way for the islanders to show their affection. For them, in this case, it is an absolute sensation: It has hardly ever happened before that a missionary couple has returned to them in Chuuk for the second time after a home furlough. That has to be celebrated properly. Even the governor has come to the reception. There are no passport and customs formalities for them as VIP guests.

There is only one single disappointment for the islanders in the joy of their reunion: Ernst, now seven years old, doesn't reply to their questions. He has apparently totally forgotten the Chuukese language while in Germany.

That's how it is with children at the age of language acquisition. They have no trouble picking up another language besides their mother tongue. But as soon as the linguistic situation does not force them anymore to use the second language, it will fade within a short time. Once speaking opportunities occur again, the structures of their second language will reappear during this phase of children's intellectual development. So, again, Ernst is soon answering in the islanders' language when they talk to him.

12

Peak Years of Creativity

(1954–1959)

Unwelcome House Residents on Toon

On June 15, at the Chukiyénú Mission Station pier, the sound of the conch shell can be heard several times. At the church they start a spontaneous service. Everywhere people are singing, even at night when the four dead tired "home comers" finally want to sleep. Many islanders inquire sympathetically about Hannelore, Waltraud and Anneliese, who had to stay behind in Eutingen; and they talk in a tone of admiration about the fact that they, their parents and brothers, have made the sacrifice of a family separation.

They have their first surprise when they enter their dwelling that they left two years before. It is in pitiful condition. It has become badly dilapidated on account of the voraciousness of termites; their traces can be seen everywhere in the wood. It has to be repaired.

Ernst and Helmut can remember many things quite well. But they both think it is a bit much to have to live in a house next to resident ants, geckos, lizards, and cockroaches, and such a lot of them. Again and again they discover other vermin that make them shudder. Helmut is the first to declare that he doesn't want to stay there, and after one week Ernst, too, expresses the opinion that they have had enough and it is about time to go back to Eutingen.

But soon they have friends again. A horde of island boys is constantly there and running around. After several months, even Helmut decides once and for all not to return to Germany anymore. Life on Chuuk could not be better!

Difficult Plans

For all Micronesians the 1950s is a decade which provides an effective administration, modern economic parameters, and the infrastructure that goes with it. The United States, mandated with the trusteeship for Micronesia by the United Nations, direct their efforts above all also to establishing a proper school system to give the population the opportunity of catching up in their education, and also in their store of knowledge, with the rest of the world. Future politicians, physicians, economists, and teachers from among the islanders are in need of educational institutions. The same is true of pastors who have to shepherd the island congregations in the future; and, last but not least, also the girls and women whose children will determine the destiny of Micronesia in the coming years.

Those who want to establish a Christian family life have to know what this means. Wilhelm describes what it means for female islanders in the following words: "Fááyichuk, the western part of Chuuk, has more than three thousand inhabitants, but not one school for girls aged fourteen to eighteen, where they can be educated, trained, and led to Christ. For that reason, most of them are married off by their parents, so they will be taken care of, and the young husband can work for the father of the young wife; she is, after all, still a girl. Child marriage!"

Already in 1949, Wilhelm and Elisabeth had undertaken to establish a girls' school on a trial basis. For various reasons the project had foundered right from the start, and Wilhelm occasionally expresses his anger at so many know-alls who had meddled. Now both of them are downright beleaguered by the churches to try it again. So they resolve to create a girls' school during their second longer service term on Chuuk; this time, however, not on Wútéét, as before the Second World War, but on Toon. But that was not all.

On the new and yet to be built up mission station a project is to take shape that will be of decisive significance for the future of the churches: a college for pastors. The realization of this project, as far as Wilhelm and Elisabeth can see, will mean a lot of work and cost a lot of money; but it is to become reality given the agreement and cooperation among the churches. However, first priority is to be given to the girls' school.

Its financing is a story in itself. Heinrich Hertel, whom we already know as the inspector for the South Seas, one day finds a penny and asks God on the spur of the moment to bless this penny. His appeal to collect pennies for missionary work results in a spectacular success that comes to be known as the "Penny Blessing." Essentially it is for the benefit of the girls' school on Palau. For the future Girls' School on Toon Heinrich Hertel starts a second fund, which after a suggestion by Johannes Rattel, is called "Drops of Blessing for Chuuk."

For Wilhelm and Elisabeth this project does not just entail more building activity but also a need to look around for suitable coworkers. These are not just people who are capable of teaching. If Wilhelm and Elisabeth want to be available to run the school, they need at least one missionary couple to take over the work in the churches from them. While still in Germany, they had applied for this, but they do not know exactly who will be involved and when these people will be available.

Cooperation with the American mission in the area of planning for the school proves to be difficult. This is not so much a matter of willingness to cooperate but due to the very different ideas held by Americans and Germans about such a school and its curriculum. Wilhelm, moreover, has the impression that his American "superiors" are only interested "in rushing him into construction," a work he had done in years past to utter exhaustion and which he doesn't want to consider his prime task any longer. He is especially chagrined about the fact that "the big shots always want to pass the problems on to the little guys."

Plans are also made difficult because building material has to be transported, most of all cement and sand. For this, the mission station is lacking a suitable vehicle.

A Suitable Motorboat

The logistics of a mission station on the South Sea Islands, i.e. its maintenance, stands and falls with the availability of a very powerful boat. So far, Wilhelm has always been dependent on being able to request the boat belonging to head chief Wupwiini for transporting material and people. However, for a construction project as large as the girls' school this is not a permanent solution. He urgently needs his own boat, available at all times. Elisabeth wants the same, though for her, questions of safety have priority. On the ocean you need technically safe vessels. For a time she even voices her conviction not to return to Chuuk unless provided with a proper boat. Well, they are to get one in a rather peculiar way; and this story has an interesting prelude.

In those days, the Liebenzell Mission maintains a so-called Mission Show, something like an ethnological museum. It shows the various areas of activity of its missionaries by means of articles from the material culture used by indigenous people in their everyday life: styles of houses, household utensils, tools, clothing, means of transport, and many other things. In this Mission Show, today called Mission Museum, they also have a South Seas department. There a young man from Murr, Germany, one day saw an outrigger canoe as used on Chuuk, and he got the feeling that it was high time to provide the missionary work there with a seaworthy motorboat. His appeal for money for this boat triggered a real boom in donations, especially in the German youth organization called "Christian Endeavor" in the States. Within a few months, 3,000 dollars came together; an enormous amount considering conditions in Germany in 1954.

After this prelude, we now come to the proper story about the first motorboat put into service with the Liebenzell Mission work on Chuuk.

In July, Wilhelm is once again attending a missionary conference on Pohnpei. In the harbor he happens to see a motorboat that almost fits what he has in mind. So he goes to look for the owner, finding him "far back in the bush." The man does not just understand a little English but also speaks Chuukese. Consequently, Wilhelm does not find it hard to negotiate with him. The owner of the boat is willing to let him have the boat for 1,000 dollars; he himself had bought it from the government years before. He is even willing to put new paint on.

Wilhelm successfully applies to the American administration to have the boat transported to Chuuk with the next cargo ship, for the very favorable price of 350 dollars. His American missionary colleague even advances him the purchase price.

So far, everything has gone smoothly, and Wilhelm reckons with the use of his new boat by the coming August. But things turn out differently, as is so often the case.

Instead of the boat, the freighter delivers a letter to Wilhelm, stating that he will have to come back and negotiate further. So, in September, he again travels to Pohnpei. There he finds "his boat" left, lying on the beach, in the same slightly neglected condition he had seen it in before. The diesel engine doesn't work very well, and that is the reason why the boat cannot be brought on board the ship to Chuuk. What is to be done?

Wilhelm doesn't deliberate long. He decides to repair the boat himself since he really wants to have it. This means three weeks of hard labour. For outside repairs he constantly has to stand in the water. He scrapes his feet on the coral blocks until they bleed, and his hands are full of blisters. After working on the diesel motor his whole body is always so dirty that he has to clean himself first with kerosene before he can take a shower. But finally he can successfully complete the extensive repairs. The first test ride shows that all his efforts have been worthwhile. Wilhelm feels he is close to reaching the desired goal.

But now new obstacles are placed in his way. The now splendid looking motorboat, which nobody was interested in before, is suddenly drawing the attention of the public on Pohnpei. Buyers appear offering the former owner more than the 1,000 dollars paid by Wilhelm. The greatest difficulty is because the boat has caught the attention of the American governor of Pohnpei. He wants to have it back, but this is not possible for him through normal channels, for Wilhelm has correctly concluded the purchase and put in an enormous amount of work to get it going again. So the governor tries a dirty trick.

He knows that Wilhelm cannot transport his boat to Chuuk without loading it on to the big government cargo ship. So he hikes up the freight costs, originally promised at 350 dollars, in sheer harassment, until they are finally up to 1,782 dollars, an amount that is almost double that of the purchase price. Wilhelm, of course, cannot come up with this amount.

In his desperation he tells the governor's secretary how the money for the boat has been raised together, and he points out to him that he wants to use it exclusively for the benefit of the islanders and not for his own pleasure. Such high freight would surely be totally excessive.

Surprisingly, the secretary is of the same opinion and, indeed, obtains permission to get the boat shipped to Chuuk at a cheaper rate for the Mission, namely for 750 dollars. What an answer to prayer for Wilhelm!

It arrives on Chuuk in November, a bit damaged, but still in a seaworthy condition. On Toon it is welcomed with the hymn *Sipwe mwaareyiti Koot reen awach me neetipach* – "Now thank we all our God with heart and hands and voices." The Young People's Society of Christian Endeavor on Chuuk makes Willi Lutz, the initiator of the fund-raising campaign, an honorary member, and even makes Arno Pagel, the association's head pastor at that time in Germany's Christian Endeavor, an honorary chief.

The boat itself is named "Jugendbund EC" ("Young People's Society of CE"). For Wilhelm and his work this is:

"… something without precedent. Only someone who for years has stood on the road thumbing a lift, and then all of a sudden is given his own car, can understand how we feel today as the boat is now anchored down there at the pier and we can use it any time without having to ask anybody beforehand."

It has a length of about 33 feet (10 m). Its motor reaches a performance of ten horsepower, needs little fuel, and is easy to handle. The front-loading capacity amounts to two tons of cargo, and ten people find room in the cabin on the afterdeck. Its deployment, however, is limited in one respect: It can only be used for trips within the Chuuk Lagoon. It is unsuited for the open ocean outside the barrier reef.

He cannot expect a financial maintenance allocation for the boat from the Mission; and there is also nothing that could be put aside for it from the station's funds. It has to be self-supporting. Wilhelm employs a man who will only be paid for the days the boat is actually being used. The payment is one dollar and free food for him and his wife. But this man only does the practical maintenance; the boat's skipper is Wilhelm Kärcher. The pastors who can go on various trips with their wives, also help with the practical work if necessary, for example while casting off or docking.

Every Monday, Wilhelm goes to Wééné, accompanied by several students, in order to pick up mail, go shopping, and go to the authorities. The "Jugendbund EC" is used in this way for over ten years.

The Girls' School Is Established

Construction starts in October 1954. It is almost ten years since the girls' school on Wútéét was destroyed in the war.

At first, there is no money for building materials, let alone for the missionary to pay the wages. The start of the construction is a step of faith, and the "Drops of Blessing" come later. First come the beads of sweat running down the builders' skin!

Nothing happens without the help of the churches. Men and women organised into six shifts work to put up the building; the lower floor is for the schoolrooms, while the upper floor is to contain a dorm for the girls and a small apartment for two missionary ladies.

Stones of basalt and coral have to be hauled up. The sand needed for the concrete parts of the building is brought in by boat from uninhabited islands. Men on the Mortlock Islands saw by hand the beams that are going to support the roof.

500 Miles (800 km) and No Coworkers

Since the girls' school is to be ready by October, Wilhelm is again working to the limits of his strength. He does not neglect the work in the churches during his construction activities. He often prepares his sermons with hands made oily from repairs to the boat's motor. "At the present time, my Bible and my measuring stick are two important things on my desk."

What he and his wife are achieving in all this is enormous. Just imagine: a ministry to thirty congregations lying scattered in a radius of 500 miles (800 km). In the past eighteen years, six new ones have been added, but there was never an additional coworker. If he stopped over in each congregation for just one single week, he would need a whole year (including traveling times) just to get around once. Without fellow workers this is impossible to do. The Mission leaders in Germany and the United States are also aware of this. But there is a hitch.

The U.S. Department of the Interior, also responsible for the Trusteeship of Micronesia, has meanwhile decreed that only persons with American citizenship may work on the islands. Young Germans who feel called to missionary service on the South Sea Islands, will no longer be able to love father and mother less than the Lord, as stated in Matthew 10:37, they will also have to give up their German nationality. There are such people, and some of them are already on the way. It is just that Wilhelm and Elisabeth have only heard rumours about the details. Erwin Pegel, one missionary who has just finished his training, is already in the States in order to get his citizenship, and two lady missionaries are said to join him there.

Among the pastors of some churches there are difficulties of a specific kind. In the meantime, various other religious groups have started to work on the islands. These are making promises to them in case they want to go over to join them. If such promises involve material advantage or money, not only is the temptation for pastors great, but equally great is the pressure from their church for them to take such a step. Wilhelm sometimes has a lot of trouble preventing the "foxes," as he calls them, "from forcing their way into an unlocked henhouse." Occasionally, he meets with open hostility in this regard.

On Nómwuluuk there is a man who has been deliberately avoiding him for some time. When Wilhelm wants to visit him in his hut, he is never present. Wilhelm stubbornly refuses to give up, until he finally succeeds in talking to him. When the man sees him coming, he lights a cigarette and, without saying anything, blows the smoke into Wilhelm's face; a behaviour that islanders themselves would regard as arrogant and totally unacceptable. Anyway, Wilhelm knows immediately what to think of it. He is not welcome.

Still No New Testament

Wilhelm keeps up a lively correspondence with Richard Neumaier, asking him for his advice in important decisions; and he regularly receives donations from Richard to support his work.

In a letter to him dated November 16, 1954, Wilhelm complains that everything would be much easier if he at least had the Gospel of Matthew in a useable form. But the American Bible Society is still holding back on the publication of its New Testament. Parts of it do indeed appear from time to time in mimeographed copies. But beyond that nothing is happening.

In the meantime, Richard Neumaier has met Eugene A. Nida, the director of the American Bible Society, in Germany; he has patiently argued and humbly negotiated, as far as possible under the circumstances. Nida does not want to budge from his position, even criticizing him for trifling matters, such as his obervation that Richard has only used double quotation marks. When Richard Neumaier points out to him that his typewriter unfortunately does not have single quotation marks, Nida even has the presumption to demand he should just add them by hand. Neumaier is understandably extremely disappointed, but he restrains himself so as not to endanger his work.

Wilhelm himself is slowly losing patience. By now he is declining the offer of texts available (from copies sent from the States) to the pastors for sermon preparation and for Sunday school work translated and completed without any further cultural adaptation. He is requesting theological material suited to the needs of the islanders and their culture: "I am sorry, but I just can't go along with this business any longer."

Moreover, it becomes more and more evident that it would be better to have the Liebenzell Mission again take sole responsibility for its sphere of influence. This happens as of January 1955.

Harold Hanlin, the American field director, agrees to this plan, but afterwards intensifies his efforts to push for a translation of the New Testament according to his own ideas. Wilhelm, who has inevitably to negotiate with him, is more and more taken aback. He and, of course, Richard Neumaier both realize more and more that Hanlin is not only simply taking over whole passages from Neumaier's translation, but that he is also introducing phrases that are just not how islanders express themselves. There are other strange peculiarities as well.

One of the special characteristics of Richard Neumaier's translation is that it contains parallel references. These are important for pastors, but also for church elders and Sunday school helpers in their preparation. It is one of the reasons why Wilhelm and the pastors want to have this translation. But for completely obscure reasons the American Bible Society insists on printing translations without parallel references.

Meanwhile, these quarrels have also come to the attention of the leaders at the Württembergische Bibelgesellschaft (Württemberg Bible Society) in Stuttgart, since the Liebenzell Mission has asked them to mediate. Wilhelm is in correspondence about the matter with Prelate Schlatter. But he doesn't believe that he will be successful: "To be involved in working has always been easier for me than in negotiating."

Soon after, Wilhelm is just about losing patience. This is evident from a letter dated September 9, 1955, to Richard Neumaier: "Now it's time to pile on the pressure. We do not want the matter to be shelved yet again. Where negotiations do not come to anything, we will simply have to act."

In the meantime he has done something meant to prove that the demand for printing the Testament is not just coming from the Mission, but that the churches themselves think it is time to see their own Bible text, to read it in a translated version formulated by one of their own missionaries. He launches a questionnaire to poll the church members as to whether they wanted Richard Neumaier's version of the New Testament or the one by Harold Hanlin, which is still in its development stage. The result is an almost one hundred percent vote for Richard Neumaier's version.

How difficult it is for some pastors to make their decision can be seen by the fact that the questionnaire is only being returned after much hesitation. Wilhelm decides to help the pastors "get a move on" by freezing their salary "until the ballots are in." Many among them are afraid of annoying Harold Hanlin with their vote for Richard Neumaier's Testament, fearing that he might take them to task. Strange things are happening in this connection. One of the pastors decides to vote for both New Testaments, others have their church elders cast a vote so their own name wouldn't appear.

In August that year a notable encounter takes place. Wilhelm is visiting Harold Hanlin to introduce a new coworker who has arrived on Chuuk in the meantime. We will get acquainted with him right away. What happened at the end of that visit reads as follows: "When it was time to leave, Dr. Hanlin held me back, and he looked all jaundiced about the face. He read me parts of a letter sent by Dr. Nida, containing approximately the following: 'To my great amazement I had to read in a letter from Dr. Schlatter that the Liebenzell Mission wants to print the New Testament for their area.'" Hanlin openly blames Wilhelm for this deci-

sion. The latter, though, has no knowledge of it at all and is totally surprised.

But let us, for a moment, return to the first half of the year.

A Tragedy on the Ocean

In April and May 1955 Wilhelm is once again traveling to the Hall
and Mortlock Islands.

"There is work here in abundance. It is just like a farmer who only has
time once a year to get to his fields. He will probably find a lot of weeds
that have sprung up in the meantime. On the other hand, he also sees that,
here and there, the seed has not been choked off but is ripening in spite of
the weeds. It's like that here."

The church on the Hall Islands has doubled in size during the last
eighteen years. On Nómwiin, the chief, who is a Christian, is having a
very good influence. But on Fanaanú, things look very bad. Apel, the
pastor, has started to drink. The pastor of Ruwó, likewise, is not of much
use.

In the early hours of May 5, a terrible accident happens in the open
sea off the Mortlocks. Six islanders lose their lives. Since Wilhelm, too,
almost paid with his life that night, we want to quote the words he wrote
about it in his story entitled "Through the Breakers," published in 1965:

"In the afternoon, about 2 o'clock, we left the island of Nómwuluuk.
The sea was rough, but the people thought we could easily risk it. Four
canoes already were in the reef waters. On one of them my luggage was
stored. I actually wanted to go with Manur because I knew he was a good
and experienced skipper. But Iyoosef, the Son of our deceased preacher,
said, 'You go with us.' So the young and just recently commissioned
preacher Likireng climbed into Manur's canoe. It left right away. We
rowed close behind them and through the small passage in the reef
reached the open sea. Before the sail was hoisted, I prayed. We com-
mended ourselves to Him whose way is also on the sea and who keeps us.

"As expected, Manur's canoe made better headway through the rough
sea than ours; for after a short while they were ahead of us by several sea
miles. Our progress was very laboured. It was already nightfall and we
were still far out in the waters of the island of Anuwas, quite a way off
shore. The people reckoned on having bright moonlight that night, but
soon heavy clouds approached. It got dark. The wind increased steadily.
For a few minutes the clouds broke up. The moon was shining on the
white sail of Manur's boat. That was the last greeting.

"A severe night followed. The sail had to be reefed because of the strong storm. The rolling waves wore white crowns of foam. The storm ripped and slapped into the sail. Two men wearing diving goggles had to constantly bale water. Suddenly one of them collapsed; he was seasick and exhausted. Another one took over from him. Apart from me, we now had only three active men. The young skipper said to me, 'If the outrigger gets pressed deep into the water by the waves, you come over to my side; but if it is lifted out of the sea into the air, you must quickly go back again to the other side. We now have to really take care that the canoe is not going to be turned over, otherwise we are lost.'

"Thus we plunged through the gruesome, rainy night into the unknown. The canoe was like a horse in panic. We shot up the waves at an angle, were momentarily suspended on the height, and then went over the crest of the wave down again on the other side.

"It may have been midnight, when the skipper suddenly struck sail completely and said, 'We've had it, we're finished!' Freezing, the wet, brown men crouched in the canoe; we drifted.

"After about one hour I encouraged them to try again. At once they did their utmost. Slowly the hours ticked away. The night stretched endlessly. Frightened, we waited for dawn. If we had not been able to see any land then, we would not have had any idea of our whereabouts. My eyes were hurting from staring strenuously into the dark.

"Finally day broke. How thankful we were when the black wall we saw turned out, not to be a cloud, but the actual land we had longed to see!

"But where was Manur's boat? We looked in all directions but couldn't see it anywhere. When we came ashore, the others, who had been way ahead of us, asked us about Manur's boat. On the other islands, too, we searched in vain. A Navy plane, called via radiotelephone, came from Guam and, flying low, searched the sea around the Mortlock Islands. In vain. Days later, they found some pieces of a canoe that had drifted on to an uninhabited reef islet. Six men had been swallowed up by the sea that night, close to where we were, without our being able to see them. How graciously and miraculously the Lord had watched over our own lives!"

It is not clear why Iyoosef had insisted on having the missionary in his boat. A possible explanation would be that islanders reckon with God's automatic special protection for an exceptionally faithful Christian, a pastor, or a missionary. They then conclude that nothing can happen to a boat with somebody like that on board. The events of that night seem to confirm this. Wilhelm, however, sees things a bit differently: "Certainly, the Lord could also have kept me on the canoe that was shattered in the sea; but sometimes He uses other people to guide us according to His will."

Later, Wilhelm was to hear the accusation that he could have prevented the accident by making the trip in the "Jugendbund EC." But that would have been a much bigger mistake, because the motorboat, though seaworthy, is not suitable for the open sea.

Legends

In the course of time, events like this lead people to ascribe supernatural powers to the missionary. More and more he is regarded as *manaman* or *iiman*. Islanders expect miraculous attributes especially in everything he says, by virtue of his authority. People are convinced he can cause things to happen by simply talking about them. This notion produces strange fancies: rumours and stories get spread about him.

Thus, he supposedly looks at a goat one day for some time and then says in passing that it probably won't last much longer. The next day, the goat is dead. The word of the missionary must have caused it, the islanders conclude.

To Wilhelm himself it was clear when he looked at the animal that it was sick and that it probably wouldn't live much longer.

Another legend tells of a service held by Wilhelm one day. A drunk is said to have appeared and caused quite a disturbance. Wilhelm supposedly rebukes him, demanding that he leave the church. But since the drunk does not stop his vulgar behavior, Wilhelm reportedly grabs him and throws him out the window. There he lies dead. After the service the missionary prays over him, whereupon the culprit comes back to life again.

Even today, such rumours and legends concerning his person can still be heard on Chuuk.

One of the most absurd stories he ever heard about himself and his fellow workers, leaving him speechless, comes to his notice one day on Sowuk: Wilhelm is said to have perished out on the ocean; Anneliese Stüber – later on a teacher at the girls' school and co-translator of the Old Testament into Chuukese – has reportedly become a Roman Catholic and died shortly afterwards.

For Elisabeth, the rumour that soon reached her about her husband having drowned during that voyage from Nómwuluuk to Ettaal, is understandably devastating. But soon she learns from a district official that a radio communication has come in from the Mortlock Islands, stating that her husband is alive and well.

During her husband's absence, Elisabeth takes care of the work on Toon as well as bringing up her sons. Ernst, meanwhile, is eight years old and has to be taught school classes. What it means for her at those times when her husband suddenly decides, while actually on his travels, to change his itinerary or extend it for the benefit of an island congregation is best shown by the following story.

On Sowuk

In August 1955, Wilhelm is aboard a freighter called "Roque." Once again, he wants to visit the islands west of Chuuk, where Christianity is still in its infancy. On Sowuk there is a small congregation of about thirty Christians, and Tatewus, their pastor, has motivated them to build a small but still spacious enough church.

For Wilhelm, as he writes to Richard Neumaier, it is "a pleasure to proclaim the gospel to the congregation." He gets the impression that he should remain there longer than originally planned. "In a canoe I went out to the ship at night time, paid my fare, bought some food, got my suit-case, and wrote a greeting to my wife, telling her that I would not be back for an unknown length of time."

What a patient and reasonable wife Elisabeth must be, if her husband can simply decide things like that on the spur of the moment!

When Tatewus realizes Wilhelm is staying, his whole face lights up in the glow of his lantern, goes and gets a mat from his hut and stretches it out on the floorboards of a smaller hut next to his cooking place. The dogs lying under these floorboards are furiously barking at the intruder. Someone brings him something like a pillow. His mosquito net he always has with him, and he covers himself with his rubber coat. The first night, though, he cannot sleep very well. He is surrounded by a strong smell of a pigsty. Next morning, he discovers it and its inmates, right next to his sleeping quarters.

While he is once more sleepily turning over on his side, he notices a peculiar noise. The men of the congregation are reaching under the rafters of the hut, pulling out pieces of clothing. These are their trousers that they usually pull on over their loincloths when they go to church services. They are Christians, like the missionary. He always wears trousers. Since they want to be like him, they feel a strong need to wear them also, at least in church. Between church services they are kept in some kind of cloakroom close to the church. This, then, is where Wilhelm has spent the night.

Since he can only sleep rather badly on the uneven floor, and the sand fleas are plaguing him there, he asks Tatewus for a few pieces of wood. He wants to make himself a stringboard. This is a bed-sized frame with string stretched over the length and breadth of it. This way, he manages to weave a kind of mattress. Wilhelm calls his creation an "island comfort deluxe."

The church on Sowuk has only been in existence for five years. When Wilhelm preaches, he must speak slowly and enunciate his words clearly, for the languages of Sowuk and of Chuuk differ from one another about like the German dialects spoken in Swabia and in Berlin (or Oxford English from the dialect of the southern American states). Anything at all has to be done in a very simple manner. Those who want to become Christians first have to be taught by him how to pray. So he speaks one sentence, and they repeat it after him.

Pwolowót lies about fifty miles (80 km) north of Sowuk. Its inhabitants are regarded as expert canoe builders and seafarers. For some time a young pastor has been living on the island. His name is Ayiten and he hails from Paata, a neighbouring island to Toon. When Wilhelm comes from Sowuk to Pwolowót, he is surprised at the work Ayiten has already achieved. The places where sacrifices were offered to the spirits have gone, and the people no longer feel so bound to observe taboos in order to protect themselves from disaster. They also want to live as Christians, just as it is the rule on the other islands.

Ayiten has received support from chief Romolow who has decided to live a life according to the Bible without compromise. Under his leadership, the congregation has grown to a hundred and sixty Christians. But there are also trials and testings.

Ayiten's seven-year old son dies suddenly, even though the whole church prayed earnestly for him. Again, the islanders cannot understand why God would deal in this manner with a faithful servant of His. They see it as repaying good with evil.

This is also a hard blow to Romolow's family. Wurák, his oldest son, contracts leprosy and has to be taken to the Mariana Islands for treatment and, after that, to the leprosy station on Pohnpei. Later, Wilhelm visits him at the hospital on Chuuk: "It was hard for me to visit this strong and now leprous islander in the hospital and hear his father, who sat on the floor in front of the bed, say, 'Look, my firstborn has leprosy!'"

For Romolow's family, Wurák's sickness has a good ending, even though it is not until a long time later. In 1959, he leaves hospital, pronounced healed.

The Opening of the Girls' School

According to Wilhelm and Elisabeth's plans, it is to begin functioning as of September 1955. In the course of construction, Wilhelm has to acknowledge the fact that it would be closer to January 1956: "If I don't work at the school, the others don't work either or precious little." But in December it is ready for the most part. There are only a few construction jobs that still need to be done.

Wilhelm and Elisabeth greet the arrival of Erwin and Dora Pegel, who will be responsible for the church work, with great relief: "We are very grateful that finally, after an interval of eighteen years, a young German missionary was able to come here again. After the war, a variety of great men have visited us, giving us good advice, but nobody wanted to stay and help to gather in the harvest. No farmer is thrilled about high-ranking visitors during harvest time, as he has to take care of them and they keep him from his work. But he rejoices when during the harvest someone comes to fill the ranks of the harvest workers and really puts his hands to the work."

For the time being, Erwin and Dora Pegel will be stationed on Nómwiin in the Hall Islands and afterwards on Woneyopw in the Mortlocks.

In his last newsletter of the year – dated December 31 – he speaks of wanderings in the wilderness and of the sinking Peter. This is evidence of how much strength the fight for the New Testament and the construction work has taken out of him. The girls' school is virtually ready. School classes can indeed start in the New Year. But one look into the mission station's cash box reveals an alarming fact: It is completely empty. Wilhelm even has to start the New Year with debts, and last-minute jobs to complete the new building have to be put on hold for now.

In this situation he does something he would never do under normal circumstances, though it is a normal thing among the islanders. He promises the cashier of the company on Wééné that delivered the cement that he would pay his debt in January down to the last penny. Yet he has no idea where to get the money for it. The result is a surprising experience for him.

In his troubles he relies totally on God's word in Joshua 1:5, "[…] I will never leave you nor forsake you." When the due date for the payment arrives, the money is there, too. From Milwaukee in the States he receives fifty dollars, especially designated for cement, even though the donor cannot know that Wilhelm has to pay for cement. From the American Air Force on Guam comes a substantial amount, from Switzerland the lion's share, and from the Liebenzell Mission 300 dollars. Wilhelm is rid of his burden of debt at one go, and this fact reminds him of John 11:40, "Did I not tell you that if you believed, you would see the glory of God?"

The girls from the churches of Fááyichuk can hardly wait. Hardly anyone from their villages has ever seen such a beautiful boarding home as they will have at the school.

One problem is posed by the question of when to celebrate the school's dedication day. It is not possible to have it at the beginning of classes, since setting up a beautiful program necessitates the collaboration of the girl students. Besides, how could a great banquet be provided in such a short time? The suggestion of celebrating the occasion at the same time as Pentecost is rejected by the pastors, who point out that it could be raining at that time; and those responsible for the food mention the fact that breadfruit would not be ripe by then. Finally, Elisabeth is asked for her advice. Her argument goes:

"At Pentecost, many friends of the Mission come together in Bad Liebenzell who have especially donated gifts and prayed for the construction of the girls' school. Moreover, it would be such a joy to the Mission leadership if they could pass on our thanks for all the 'Drops of Blessing' that have come from far across the oceans to us."

That makes sense. It is decided that at Pentecost the island Christians should celebrate a festival together with the home church in Germany.

Preparations are tackled almost euphorically. Elisabeth reports, "Time and again I had to put the brakes on and admonish them to keep things simple."

A choir is practicing songs. Over fifty chiefs and other dignitaries receive a written invitation for the church service and the banquet.

During the days preceding Pentecost, the forty-six girl students who have been taking classes since January, are busy cleaning and decorating the whole Mission campus. Some men are spending two days on the "Jugendbund EC" by the outer reef to catch fish for the festival. Their efforts result in a catch of over five hundred fish.

It is the day before the celebration. Wilhelm and Elisabeth are finding the hustle and bustle similar to the Saturday before Pentecost in Bad Liebenzell. A radiant sun is rising after a heavy tropic rain filled all the water tanks during the night. The day has hardly begun when all the cooks arrive to cook the food in their big pans. Motorboats are docking at the pier, bringing workers, then casting off again. The "Jugendbund EC" is picking up people all day long from the islands around Toon. In the afternoon, a siren sounds from the boat announcing the arrival of the governor and a delegation of twenty Americans.

On Dedication Day the church is far too small for so many guests. Those who can't find a place inside are camping outside on the lawn-covered slope, from where they have a good view of the church's interior.

Speeches, greetings, songs, and thanksgivings seem to be endless. Even Dr. Hanlin is present and speaks about the importance and necessity of training and education for the island youth in government and mission schools.

One of the islanders gets carried away by the new school building and remarks, "If one of us could build such a beautiful house on Chuuk, he would no longer just walk on two but on three legs!"

Wilhelm's sermon is about the Israelite girl from 2 Kings 5, who had been taken captive during a Syrian military campaign, came into Commander Naaman's household, and had in the end become such a blessing to the leprous Commander and to his family because of her exemplary conduct and her faith in the living God: "Thus, may it also be our desire and, at the same, our petition to God that all the girls passing through our school in the future may be able to be a blessing to others."

Afterwards, the banquet is served in the schoolhouse for the American officials, the political chiefs, and the pastors. On this occasion, Wilhelm once again thanks everyone for their contribution to the building of the school. The girl students in their snow-white dresses, with red ribbons in their shiny black hair, entertain the festive crowd with songs, busily playing on their guitars and ukuleles.

About School Experiences and Chickens

The task of teaching is shared by Ruut, the skilled wife of Rev. Kono, Tapeya, the daughter of Rev. Noor, and Dora Pegel. Elisabeth Kärcher is the temporary principal of the school. Occasionally, Wilhelm also teaches a class.

Since Elisabeth has to home-school her two sons as well, she keeps them busy with written assignments, while she herself is teaching her class at the girls' school. One day, she returns from there to the apartment to look for Ernst and Helmut. They have both disappeared. A short while later, she discovers her offspring down at the pier swimming, instead of doing their homework.

What she experiences among the islanders at Christmas is very interesting. In those days the Christians on Chuuk do not give presents among family members but only in church. The missionaries get presents, too, of course, sometimes more than they would like. After their first Christmas celebration on Nómwiin, Erwin and Dora Pegel thus see themselves confronted with forty live chickens.

Naturally, the girl students focus their giving rather more on the children of the missionaries. Ernst and Helmut are almost beside themselves. Everything possible is heaped up in front of them: soap, chewing gum, handcrafted bags, eggs, and – well – chickens!

Plans for a Boys' School

Micronesia, meanwhile, is completely given over to entering the modern era. This includes the creation of a comprehensive educational system to enable future generations to take the destiny of their islands into their own hands.

At the mission conference for all of Micronesia, taking place on Toon in the middle of 1956, the question of a school for boys is also discussed; including, above all, a suitable location. They do not arrive at a final decision just then.

Traveling Ministry – Still by Outrigger Canoe

In September 1956, Wilhelm is once again on Pwolowót. He has covered the distance from Sowuk by outrigger canoe in almost thirty hours. On the following morning he preaches about the arrival of the apostle Paul in Rome.

Some of the children, who do not often get to see foreigners, are still afraid of him. To counteract this, he uses a simple method. His wife has given him candy, and it gets results. Among the children still afraid of him the good news is spreading rapidly that he does not in fact eat anyone but rather distributes tasty goodies.

He has brought along the galley proofs of the biblical stories translated by Richard Neumaier that are soon to be available in book form. The beautiful pictures they contain prove to be a great attraction.

Tim and again people ask Wilhelm whether it wouldn't be possible to station a missionary on Pwolowót also. That is the intention, but Wilhelm cannot make any firm promise. Not until the 1970s is this desire of the church granted. At that time, Klaus W. Müller, Wilhelm's nephew and godson, and his wife Ulrike are going to settle on the island.

On September 15, 1956, about noon, Wilhelm is once again sitting on an ocean-going canoe. He wants to go back to Chuuk with Ikepi, an experienced skipper and boat builder. With favorable winds and weather this takes two days and two nights.

The voyage to Chuuk with the canoe takes them across almost 200 miles (over 300 km) of open sea. They reckon with about 50 hours of traveling. "It is terribly lonely on the ocean if you sail around in a simple hollowed out tree trunk." There is no proper opportunity to sleep. During the second night, already by midnight, Wilhelm is staring towards the east, waiting for the sunrise. He knows from Ikepi that they should be able to see at least the highest peaks of the Chuukese mountains if he has maintained the right course and has not drifted away from it because of the currents. He does not want to miss that moment.

When it gets a bit lighter in the east, Ikepi asks him whether he can see anything. "If I am not mistaken I can see the peak of the Winipwéét, the mountain on Toon." Ikepi nods in acknowledgement: "Then it really is Chuuk!"

They wake up the other men who are immediately wide awake. Now Ikepi can lie down and sleep. A younger man takes over the place of the skipper for the rest of the trip. After a heavy rain squall has fallen, thus giving them their morning shower, they all sing *Sipwe fókkun kinissow ngeni Samach Koot wóón nááng* ..., "We thank you, God our Father in heaven ...!"

In the afternoon at two o'clock, they enter the bay by Amwachang on Toon. They blow the conch shell, and right away Ernst and Helmut know that their father will be there any moment. Full of admiration they look at the vessel in which he had been traveling such a long time.

The Burden Threatens to Become too Heavy

On November 26, he is writing another letter to Richard Neumaier. This time, too, the issue is the New Testament. It is driving him to despair: "This matter is almost breaking my back," he writes. Wilhelm gets the impression that American colleagues only see him as a stubborn and difficult fellow worker, as a troublemaker. He fears they are intriguing against him. His report is indeed amazing: He tells of a letter from the Liebenzell Mission, proving that there is a plan to relocate him to Palau. This hits him so hard that he is seriously considering going there voluntarily, or perhaps to Pwolowót or to any of the Mortlock Islands; as long as it is far away from everything that is such a burden. "After all, I can spend my last ten years transferred to some hardship post. That will probably not do any harm to my inner man."

These must have been hard weeks for him and Elisabeth. The only gratifying factor in these circumstances is the long-awaited news that the New Testament has now definitely gone to the printers.

Public Acknowledgment

The respect that is meanwhile being shown to Wilhelm and Elisabeth for their work to support the islanders and the authorities is evident from a decree issued by the director of the Wééné trading company, just when Wilhelm is visiting the Hall Islands shortly before Christmas of 1956: the company's boat that the missionary is depending on during his trips to the Outer Islands is to stay on the Hall Islands as long as it takes him to complete his activities there. Even after a week's stay on Nómwiin has passed, the captain points to this order, saying: "I've got to wait here until you have finished all your work."

Affliction as Judgment and Grace

On January 11, 1957, a severe typhoon from the west is raging over the islands around Chuuk. Already in the morning, during the early devotional at the church of Chukiyénú, people can hardly communicate because of the rain splattering loudly on the roof. The first trees are crashing to the ground. The motorboat "Jugendbund EC" is tugging so strongly at its mooring ropes that the timbers it is tied to are coming out of the ground.

In the village of Fóósón the storm gets hold of one house after another, tears the roof off its corner posts and drops it crashing to the ground some distance away. One man asks the missionary for a rope so he can lash his hut to the ground. But it is useless. The storm sweeps it with all its scanty furnishings to the foot of the mountain.

Two young islanders outside the lagoon in their motorboat recognize too late that they are getting into a typhoon, and capsize in the breakers. They manage at the last moment to rip out the boat's floorboards and use them as swimming aids. They are drifting out into the night. There is hardly any hope for them, as they must reckon any moment with being attacked by sharks. Clinging to their boards they live through hours of terror, until a police patrol boat finds them alive the next day.

At the beginning of February, the "Jugendbund EC" gets into a severe northern storm. In the great surfing waves, the wire cable operating the steering breaks. This puts its crew in grave danger as the boat is drifting in the immediate vicinity of an island reef; without its steering controls it risks being thrown on to the reef by the breakers. To repair the damage, even in a makeshift manner, is dangerous for two reasons: The breakers make any steady work impossible, and in order to reach the cable, the deck of the boat will have to be ripped open. So it is drifting, seemingly unstoppable, towards the reef. But shortly before crashing into it, Wilhelm is able to temporarily repair the broken cable with his torn hands. The helm is responding again.

The Hall Islands, too, that have already been afflicted by a typhoon a few months back, are suffering heavy damage. The house Wilhelm had built on Nómwiin twenty years before collapses, and almost all breadfruit trees are lying on the ground; the rain has so softened up the soil that their roots have lost their grip.

In a short while, the whole island is completely flooded. Gardens and plants are destroyed in the salt water. People are standing in the water up to their knees, holding their children on their arms and waiting for the island to sink. But the church remains standing.

On Nómwuluuk and Sowuk, too, the typhoon has caused heavy damage, carrying pigs, chickens, and goats out to sea and rendering all the canoes useless.

Three typhoons have occurred in only three months. Wilhelm gets the impression that the whole Pacific Ocean is in chaos. The islanders' faith is highly challenged by such a typhoon. When this kind of stormy weather has broken upon them from the west in earlier times it has been seen as punishment by the deceased for wrong behaviour by the living. These ideas are now surfacing again regularly, even among Christians. They are afraid and consider whether it would not be better to bring an offering to the ancestral spirits, to placate them. Wilhelm, however, speaks of affliction as judgment and grace.

Such words are hard to understand for the islanders under the given circumstances, especially any talk of grace. But shortly after, they experience God's grace as Wilhelm receives a cheque for two hundred dollars from a church in Chicago, meant for the victims of the typhoon and to be paid out by him to them.

A High-Ranking Visitor

In the spring of 1957, a high-ranking official from the German embassy in Manila announces his visit to Toon. Dr. von Schweidnitz is spending a number of days in Philadelphia to inform himself of the work of the

German missionaries. He and his wife are committed Christians, and his report turns out to be exceedingly positive. Wilhelm is of the view that the letter he receives soon afterwards is worth publishing in the "Mitteilungen der Liebenzeller Mission" (the news bulletin of the Liebenzell Mission). He presents his suggestion to the responsible mission inspector. That gentleman, however, disagrees and points out that one must remain humble. Wilhelm feels considerably hurt by this refusal. In no way does he deserve such an attitude, given the modesty that has always characterized him. We will, therefore, reproduce the letter here in somewhat shortened form:

Embassy of the Federal Republic of Germany
MANILA Pol 318   *Manila, May 6, 1957*

The Mission Inspector of the Liebenzell Mission
Rev. Heinrich Hertel
Bad Liebenzell/Württ.

   Dear Reverend,
   I still have to thank you for your letter of March 9, which I received shortly before I started my journey to Micronesia on March 20. I returned from there on April 10, having spent a really interesting time on the islands. [...]
   On TRUK[26] I spent one week with the Kaercher Family in TOON and also met Mr. Pegel during this time, who had come over from Mortlock.
   I am filled with sincere admiration for the work of reconstruction the missionaries have performed on the islands after the time of war, which was also for them so severe and filled with losses. Apart from the blessing of the missionaries' pastoral work, I was also able to see for myself that the achievements of the schools are being highly appreciated and acknowledged, both by the national population as well as the American Administration. Likewise, in my report to the [German] Foreign Office, I have expressed my opinion that a notable achievement has been accomplished and is still going on here, with the most modest means and under most difficult circumstances; this is serving to strengthen and promote the reputation of German culture in the Pacific region. I am furthermore endeavouring to procure some teaching material for the mission schools free of charge. [...]

---

[26] former spelling of Chuuk

With my best wishes for the further work of rich blessing your Mission is doing on the Pacific islands, I am, dear Reverend,

Yours respectfully,
(sgd.) Dr. von Schweidnitz

No Privileges

For his trip to Pwolowót and Sowuk in June, Wilhelm is again using the government ship. Though he has been promised a cabin, nothing has come of it. What he does get is a place on the upper deck, far aft near the lifeboats. Here he establishes himself for ten days under the open skies, together with other men and women. The seas are at times so rough that he cannot stand up freely. He has to secure his bed with ropes. He does have some sort of tarpaulin which he manages to drape over a cable so that to some extent he stays dry, but under him the water is sweeping through in a broad stream, from one side to the other. Most unfortunate is that he has to face into the wind: since he is located at the stern of the ship he has constantly to breathe in the acrid smoke from the funnel.

He also finds out that times have changed on Chuuk, too, even for him who is known by everyone and about whose welfare and mission work everybody has heard. Younger islanders, with jobs in the government, have cabins with washing facilities as a matter of course. Wilhelm has to make do as a passenger out on deck, something that would have been unthinkable twenty years ago. But he is glad to be able to be on board at all. He is also allowed to eat in the canteen and stay there during the day. It is more comfortable than on deck; he actually only has to spend night-time on deck.

Ikepi

For all this, he is doing very well on Sowuk, where Ikepi, the old sea-farer, has had a nice house built for him. That had also been done in the hope that the church on Sowuk would still get its own missionary.

In this connection, one must realise that the islanders have a whole number of advantages if a missionary is stationed in close proximity. He teaches school classes, and people turn to him or his wife when they are sick and need medication. Most of the time he has radio contact to the authorities so that he can help in emergencies. Moreover, the islanders can usually count on the missionary's support if need be. This was especially significant in the days of the explorers and at the beginning of the colonial era. Missionaries were often the only ones to confront the ships' crews who came to fill up their stores of food and water on the islands, frequently behaving rudely and sexually harrassing the women.

Ikepi is one of the best canoe builders and skippers in the region. In earlier days, when he was not yet a Christian, he was regarded as an expert on boats and weather magic. The knowledge relating to this he had received from his father. He cannot read or write, but he is one of the most attentive listeners in the services and never misses them. Sometimes he is wondering about the politicians in the countries of Europe, America, and Asia. He ponders the fact that in earlier times they themselves, the Micronesians, had fought many wars against each other. But that had stopped when the gospel reached the islands. Now he is wondering why the Europeans, Americans, and Asians have not also understood this and become *miriit*, that is, reasonable.

Spirit Figures:
Ikepi's weather magic

Reading Material

On July 2, 1957, the boxes arrive on Chuuk, containing the New Testaments and the stories taken from the Old Testament (*Wuruwo mii pin*). For weeks, Wilhelm had actually been "lying in wait," not missing any ship arriving at Wééné. Time and again he was disappointed, and time and again he had to put the pastors off when they kept on badgering him with the question, "When will the books arrive?"

One day, he travels from Toon to Wééné to go shopping. Already at the harbour an islander calls out to him, "You have got many, many boxes. Your name is on them!"

What it means for the Christians on Chuuk to be able to read the New Testament in their own language can only be appreciated when one witnesses what is happening now. Right on arrival at the pier on Toon, the first box has to be opened. Everyone wants to see whether they have actually been able in Germany to produce a book in his or her own language. Wupwiini, the chief of Toon, who has likewise already been waiting for "the books" for a long time, stands – with oversized sunglasses on his nose – in the midst of his people and reads, and reads, and reads.

Wilhelm, too, is full of joy: "Now I would like to start immediately on a roundtrip and read the New Testament with all the preachers on the remote islands." How much the islanders have been waiting for this can be seen by the fact that 2,000 copies of the New Testament and all of the

1,000 copies of the Bible Stories from the Old Testament are sold within one month. Wilhelm has some interesting experiences in all of this.

In December of 1957, he is on Pwolowót. There he reads slowly from the Gospel of Matthew every afternoon with a group of about twenty people, aged ten to forty years. He notices again and again that the "new" New Testament is encouraging the islanders to read the Bible texts with different and better understanding than so far; the "old" New Testament had simply been too hard to understand for them. His "Bible class," as he calls it, is also regularly attended by a boy called Erinis ("Ernst"), one of the sons of the chief.

One day (it is already dark) his mother comes to Wilhelm with a dollar in her hand and says. "My Erinis is lying in the hut and crying because he doesn't have a New Testament." The boy desperately wants to have a book that belongs to him alone and that he can read for himself.

Another time, while Wilhelm is writing the draft of a newsletter, he sees a man about fifty yards (50 m) away in the island community house, busily twisting a rope on his thigh out of coconut palm fibers. Little John, twelve years old, is sitting next to him reading to him an Old Testament story from *Wuruwo mii pin*.

It is now becoming evident that it was not wrong to pursue the publication of the New Testament and the Biblical Stories with such vigour. Without them, the pastors would have had to keep on making do with compromise solutions, as Harold Hanlin's Testament is still not ready; in fact, the American Bible Society even advised him not to have it printed at this time.

Reading Aids

One difficulty for older islanders who want to read lies in their defective vision due to their age. Most of them need glasses. But on the islands they neither have ophthalmologists nor opticians to quickly remedy things. One definite solution to the problem is supplied by discarded glasses collected by German friends of the Mission and sent to Chuuk. Whenever Wilhelm announces that another consignment of glasses is on the way or has already arrived, the news spreads like wildfire from village to village and island to island. Whoever needs glasses is allowed to dig in the box and try them on. For the interested people who come first, the choice is considerable. They can select from among three hundred models. There they sit and take their pick, discuss, test, put a text close to their eyes and then again farther away with outstretched arms. And many do indeed find a pair of glasses which help them read more easily.

A Songbook with Notes

According to Wilhelm's thinking it is also time for the islanders to get a proper songbook again. Most of them only have an older version that by now is in tatters. The new book is to contain music, not just set as melodies but for voices in harmony. The islanders are used to improvise singing in harmony. But if instruments are to be added for accompaniment, the players will need music. This proves especially necessary at school.

The girl students are interested primarily in the harmonium. Altogether they have twelve small Japanese instruments. In their zeal to play the keyboard, the girls outdo each other. Wilhelm reports: "They learn more easily than I did at Liebenzell. We already have about fifteen girls who can accompany the hymn singing at church on Sundays. These girls first have to copy the song they want to play at the Sunday service [with each musical note] on a piece of paper." If they had a printed songbook, none of this would be necessary."

Anniversary

On July 20, 1957, the Hall Islands of Nómwiin, Fanaanú and Ruwó are celebrating their twentieth anniversary (often called a "jubilee" from the German term Jubiläum). That is how long ago their inhabitants became Christians, almost without exception. This is not to be taken for granted, as the congregational work during all these years had mainly been left in the hands of indigenous pastors. A missionary had only been present for a few years .

People flock from the islands to Nómwiin to celebrate the anniversary. Almost the whole congregation of Fanaanú is spending all week there. The "jubilee" service lasts four hours. At the following banquet the guests consume ten big hawksbill turtles found on the uninhabited sand islands close by.

Wilhelm reports on the very beginnings of church work there; and a number of speakers talk about how they themselves had become Christians. One of these testimonies is remarkable. Head chief Oto ("Otto") tells how at first he was quickly convinced that Christianity would be good for the younger generation, yet he couldn't see it for himself and the older ones. But at some time the story of the event near the city of Damascus, in the course of which Saul had become Paul (Acts 9), had "bitten his insides," as he says in his language; that's when he realized that he also had to become a Christian.

New Difficulties

During this time, news reaches the Mission about a decree from the American authorities, ordering not only that new workers from the Mission arriving in Micronesia must have been granted American nationality, but also all other non-Americans working already there, including Wilhelm und Elisabeth. That is a demand that seems to them excessive. Should they really, at their age, have to change their citizenship? So then, they begin to think about possible successors, though they do so hesitantly.

But first, the churches from the whole area, including those under the care of the American mission, approach Wilhelm with a project that he wants to start right away and finish by 1963: a school for theologians. For logistical reasons, such as the supply of necessary material, this is to be built on Wééné. This is where the harbour and the airport, the authorities, the post office, and the hospital are all located, and all islanders come here first, whenever they have to travel from the Outer Islands to Chuuk. The school is necessary for the simple reason that soon there will be a lack of new pastors, as the older ones, who had been trained before the Second World War, are gradually reaching retirement age.

Secretly, Wilhelm had started already some time ago to put moneys aside for such a project. This is something like a "hidden fund" for a good and sensible purpose. He fills it with the profits from the sale of the New Testaments and Bible stories with the intention that the island congregations themselves will finance the school. An ingenious idea. It is a disappointment to him that the Liebenzell Mission leadership does not quite share this view. He is of the opinion that, if the Roman Catholic Mission can maintain five schools, two schools cannot be too much for the Liebenzell Mission.

This will mean that the work on Chuuk needs another missionary couple for the itinerant ministry. He sends the Mission an application for this, even though he doubts whether it will be successful. He also urges them to give more decision-making powers to the leadership of the American branch of Liebenzell Mission in Schooley's Mountain, in order to keep bureaucratic obstacles in the future to a minimum, and to simplify and accelerate decisions. These suggestions get him a reputation for not being patient enough. He is even accused of always wanting to throw in the towel a bit too early.

However, a short while later there is evidence of how justified his demands are. At the beginning of 1958, Harold Hanlin and the churches under his leadership are asking for a final decision concerning the opening of the school planned by Wilhelm. For over a year they have been waiting patiently. But Wilhelm cannot deliver such a decision; his hands are bound because of the "miserable business" waiting for an answer from Germany. Finally, Harold Hanlin resigns from his cooperation with Liebenzell. And, as is so often the case, an affirmative answer does come from Germany, but it comes two months too late. A huge disappointment for Wilhelm and Elisabeth: "This school would have connected East and West Chuuk with each other on the island of Wééné; but now it's too late."

There is nothing left for them than to build and run the school under their own direction on Toon. In the correspondence regarding this project it is called the boys' school, complementary to the girls' school, which has already been in existence and running successfully for two years.

Under the conditions prevailing on a mission field it may indeed happen that the responsible missionaries orientate their decisions and expectations too strongly according to the circumstances they have to struggle with. This can be seen by the disappointment Wilhelm feels about the delays he experiences with the publication of the songbook. For two years he has to put off the churches time and again. He himself cannot understand why this has to be so, seeing that the printing house and the publisher in Germany are making intensive efforts to arrange the book as best they can, typographically as well as musically. That just takes time. Therefore, it looks indeed like a lack of self-control on Wilhelm's part when he asks Richard Neumaier to send him all the material for the songbook by airmail to Chuuk, so he can see to it "immediately himself."

Besides, not all the delays frustrating Wilhelm are because of the rather ponderous workings of the particular Mission committees. He has already ordered a new delivery of the Biblical Stories from the Old Testament some while back. This also takes unduly long. One day, he learns that the previous December a storeroom had burnt out on the "Alaska Bear," a ship going from San Francisco to Guam. This could have explained the delay.

Prolonged inquiries finally reveal that the boxes with the books have been left behind at a warehouse in San Francisco, sitting there since November 1957. The Norddeutscher Lloyd agent in San Francisco even wants to know when Wilhelm is planning to finally come and get his boxes. It is hard to swallow: A recipient, waiting on a South Sea island thousands of miles away from San Francisco is being asked why his goods are of so little interest to him!

While the Cat's Away, the Mice Will Play

At the start of the Easter holidays, when he doesn't have to teach any classes, Wilhelm is once again off to the Hall Islands. When he enters the missionary residence on Nómwiin, he gets a surprise. It is being lived in, and the squatters cannot simply be asked to leave the house just because the missionary needs it himself. They are unresponsive to any offer and have to be caught. They are rats, apparently populating the house in great numbers! Wilhelm must have expected something like this because he has brought along an experienced "pied piper" on his trip, of proven courage and skill – a cat! The first night alone it hunts down thirteen of the unwelcome squatters. But it will not eat even one of the rats; instead, it deposits them neatly and tidily under Wilhelm's bed. The following night, it only has to catch four more. From then on, the missionary's house is completely free of squatters.

The Children

There is obviously good news from his daughters in Germany. Meanwhile, their two brothers, Ernst and Helmut, have adapted themselves totally to life in the South Seas. They have forgotten all about Germany. Everything revolves around boats, motors, catching fish, and swimming in the ocean. Their mother, who is teaching them as well as working at the girls' school, occasionally has a really difficult time with them. In their quest for adventure the two boys are of the opinion that school is something that hinders actual living and should, therefore be subordinated to it. "They are convinced that they have already learned everything they need for life in the South Seas."

Construction of the Boys' School

In May, the current governor visits Philadelphia. He is so impressed by the work of the German missionaries that he has decided to take a U.N. delegation, which he expects to come to Chuuk within the next while, to Toon as well. It appears that the local authorities already consider the girls' school a showcase model. The leader of the delegation, an Englishman, comments that he had never seen such a beautiful clean school on Chuuk until now. The registration document that the High Commissioner for the Trust Territory needs to issue for the school is handed to Wilhelm on the very same day.

Conspicuously, there is hardly any news available about what is happening on Toon for the last six months of 1958. It seems Wilhelm could not find the time to write letters or reports. Only relatively late in the following year is it obvious what has kept him from doing so: the construction of the boys' school.

Originally it was planned to build the school in the village of Fóósón, so it wouldn't be too close to the girls' school. But then the opportunity presented itself to buy a piece of land that includes a taro field and a creek.

The ground has to be cleared. Some of the prospective students are helping Wilhelm with this. Their fathers, church members, are dragging basalt stones down the mountain and coral blocks up from the lagoon, and the boat "Jugendbund EC" is going every morning after the chapel service to the neighboring island of Romónum to get sand.

Elisabeth is building a pathway, together with her girl students, so that the boys do not constantly have to sink into the mud while transporting building material.

Occasionally, workers appear whom Wilhelm would rather not see there. This is because the government is supporting the building of the boys' school with food supplies, attracting many a "worker" who only comes for the food. "It often was a great exercise of my patience, and it taught me a lot about myself."

On April 11, 1959, he is sitting exhausted in his new study in the boys' school building that has just been completed and which is to be dedicated on April 26. Weeks of heavy work are behind him. Together with a group of future pupils from Pwolowót, Sowuk, Nómwiin, Fanaanú, Mwirilé and the Mortlock Islands, he has finished construction of the building. Only tables and benches are still missing and what's more, Wilhelm has to make these himself. A total of fifty-seven pupils are expected at the beginning of the school year.

Erwin Pegel has been busy helping him with the construction; he made the truss-beam constructions and the framework for pouring the concrete.

Building the boys' school went much better than the girls' school. This is due to the experience gathered, and the financial situation also is no longer so tight. On the ground floor there are two simple and spacious classrooms, open on both sides, which means without windows. Next to these are storage rooms, a workshop, washroom, and an office. On the upper level is the missionary apartment including a kitchen and four rooms, followed by a thirty-three by thirty-three feet (10 by 10 m) dorm for the students. The apartment and the dorm can be reached via separate outside staircases.

At the dedication, Wilhelm talks about life and building. At some point a beginning has to be made when everything is cleared and cleaned. Then steady progress in construction must follow, even if circumstances are difficult because of the heat, and thirst and hunger. Only after that can one receive the crown of life (2 Timothy 4:7–8).

Students of the Philadelphia Boy's School

Wilhelm alone cannot teach the almost sixty students. To assist him he has employed Apel and Koyichi, graduates from a school for future pastors on Pohnpei. He is still firmly counting on getting a teacher from the United States.

First Graduation Festivities at the Girls' School

A few days later, on April 14, the school celebrates the graduation of fifty-two girls: all have passed their courses and receive their diplomas. There are elaborate festivities.

On the program, among other items, it mentions music by George Frideric Handel, performed by Elisabeth on the harmonium. The "Largo" is even played by a student called Imiye, a niece of Wupwiini's.

By this time, sixty girls from Chuuk alone have registered for the new course. If the demand for places at the school continues as high, Wilhelm and Elisabeth will have to see how they can create more room at the girls' school.

Meanwhile, a new teacher has announced her arrival in the near future. Besides Anneliese Stüber, who has been working at the girls' school for some time now, Esther Hahn will soon take up her teaching assignment there.

Graduation of the first alumnae at the Philadelphia Girls' School in 1959

Announcement of a New Separation

Five years have now passed since Elisabeth's second departure from Germany in 1954. That is how long since Hannelore, by now eighteen years old, Waltraud and Anneliese, now sixteen and fourteen years old respectively, have not seen their mother. Ernst and Helmut, in the meantime twelve and ten years old, have graduated from elementary school and are due to attend a secondary school. Accordingly, Elisabeth is preparing for the trip home to Germany. For her, this means farewell forever. Her husband will remain on Chuuk for another four years.

Ernst and Helmut are not very enthusiastic about the prospect of going back to Germany. Their father comments, "You can't see them getting ready." They wish things could always stay as they are now. Ernst finds it especially hard to say good-bye to a friend on the island with whom he often went out deep sea fishing. Helmut, while looking forward to the flight to Guam, is still very conscious of the fact that he may not see his father again for a long time.

On May 12, 1959, all three of them leave Toon. On June 16, their ship is to leave from Kobe in Japan, arriving in Genoa, Italy, on July 21. From there they want to visit Rosa Mäder in Berne, Switzerland, and then proceed to Waltenhofen in Germany. Elisabeth's parents are both still alive, and it is at their home that they will also meet up with Hannelore, Waltraud, and Anneliese.

Elisabeth is worried about the years her husband will have to live and manage alone again as he did long ago on Lúkúnooch. So that he won't have to take care of his food and laundry as well as his usual big workload, she teaches two boys from the school, one to cook for him and another to do his laundry. Wilhelm voices his fear "that this may go a bit wrong the first few times." But he is hoping for the best.

There is little recorded about this time of departures and farewells; the work seems not to have permitted it. One thing, however, Elisabeth wants to really make sure about: before she takes off on her trip, she packs a suitcase with clothes for her husband. She impresses upon him that in four years' time, when he is due to return from Chuuk for good, she wants to see him arrive in Germany in no other clothes than these. This is because she fears that the clothing he is wearing now and in the coming years will be so faded from washing and that he will wear them so often, reverting to his unassuming nature that characterized him when he was a bachelor, that they will be mere shreds.

With the outfits reserved and ready in the suitcase, she expects him to make it to Germany dressed properly; then she won't have to be ashamed of his appearance.

13

Alone on Chuuk
(1959–1963)

A Question of Independence

For Wilhelm and the Chuukese congregations much more is at stake with the founding of the so-called boys' school than the girls' school. Their idea is that it will create the conditions for the future independence of the indigenous church on Chuuk. Independence presupposes competent leadership personalities who have a much wider horizon of knowledge than the average islander. Wilhelm is firmly counting on finding several among the students, here and now, being trained by him and his coworkers at the moment, who will later take on the pastoral functions.

He himself has a positive outlook on this development: "Striving for independence is quite natural if the outcomes are pursued in the right spirit, and we do not want to stand in its way."

However for the moment it means, for the boys' school, that they will have to provide food and lodging for about one hundred and fifty people. With three meals a day, that is quite a lot to manage.

Students, Beer, Cigarettes, and Other Disciplinary Problems

Children on South Sea islands experience a totally different nurture in their early childhood than children in Europe or in North America. Until they are about six years old, island children live a life of very great freedom. They roam about, come home when they are hungry, and are mostly together with playmates of the same age or with older siblings. This is especially true of the boys. For girls, it is a bit different.

Chuuk islanders trace their descent matrilineally, i.e. through the genealogical line of the mother; women thus have a special position. They are the ones through whose lineage land is inherited. As children, therefore, girls receive clearly more attention from parents and relatives than boys. Though they have to take on family responsibilities earlier than boys, they are being cared for and protected until they get married. Unlike the boys, this makes young women at the age of sixteen seem to be already mature adults.

The social position of the boys is not nearly as well established as that of the girls. They are regarded as having little common sense, and yet they are left to themselves for a long time. As a consequence they show little maturity even as young adults; they like to form gangs roaming the islands, engaging in drinking bouts, instigating fights and other mischief. Some of them remain in a state of immaturity for a very long time until the parents decide that their son needs to marry in order to come to learn about life. Once he has to take care of a wife and children, it is hoped that he will become *miriit*, i.e. "sensible." One can well imagine what a marriage contracted under such conditions must often look like.

From now on, not only does Wilhelm have to teach such a group but also take care of them – round the clock. He is responsible for them, and they have to obey him; for among the islanders it is normal for those in parental authority to relinquish their duties to the school director taking their sons and daughters under his wing.

Wilhelm is not alone in this. Several national young men are working as teachers at the school; but the troubles caused by the students are occasionally due to these teachers.

Among his students are some "difficult guys," as he calls them. There is, for example, Timoti, the brother of Wurák. On his home island of Pwolowót he was known as one of the best students.

Timoti is suffering from scoliosis (curvature of the spine). As a child he had played on a tree trunk floating near the island in shallow waters. When a wave took hold of this tree trunk and threw it on the beach, Timoti was seriously injured.

The boy is loved by all, and his teachers are of the opinion that now he could take over the chapel services at school. There are plans to send him to a school on Pohnpei where he could be trained as a pastor.

But what does Timoti do one day? Together with a bunch of other boys he organizes a drinking orgy, while Wilhelm is busy on Wééné.

Alcohol is strictly forbidden in the schools on the islands. The same goes for smoking. The reasons are obvious. It is expensive to run a school. So the students should not drink away the little money their relatives collect for them, or let it go up in smoke. The prohibition on alcohol, though, exists for another reason also.

In this island society it is not acceptable for someone to want to be better than other people. *Mósónósón* – humility – is a highly prized virtue. Children are taught this from early on. They therefore internalize the compulsion to be submissive. They are ashamed if they draw attention to themselves, whether in positive or negative matters. But sometimes men want to show what they are made of. For islanders who have been brought up to restrain themselves, this is rather difficult. Therefore, in order to lose their inhibitions, they get drunk. When they are drunk, they feel *péchékkún* and *pwara*, "strong" and "courageous."

This is also a great temptation for Wilhelm's students. Once they lose their inhibitions, things quickly turn to rough behaviour, brawling, and even killing.

The same problem constantly occurs also among the adults in the congregations, so it has to be controlled and contained. Those who are guilty of such conduct experience loss of face before their congregation. Church elders getting drunk and then involved in violence have to lay down their office for a while.

In order to keep matters under control, the school director has no choice but to resort to drastic measures. Those who consume alcohol or are caught smoking, are expelled from school.

Wilhelm assumes, of course, that those "foolish boys" around Timoti did not plan to annoy him. But now he is facing a difficult situation. The matter is out in the open; everybody knows about it. According to school rules it is an offence whose consequence is immediate expulsion from the school. The reasons for this are known.

Wilhelm is extremely disappointed, but he hesitates because he doesn't quite know what to do. The boys in question are really showing remorse. For days he struggles with himself, and finally he doesn't have the heart to throw them out. Until now they had been well behaved. So he lets them "stew" for a few days before telling them of his decision. He wants to see whether their remorse is real repentance.

Unfortunately, it is not known what his final decision was.

A number of students are already eighteen years and older. Some of them make a sport of sneaking off to the village at night to go after the girls there. That causes unrest among the villagers. For Wilhelm, this could lead to an extremely unpleasant situation. If a girl gets pregnant, he will get the blame, because the students' fathers, especially the ones from the Outer Islands, have delegated their authority to him. It would be even worse if the male students were to fool around in the dorm of the girls' school.

In order to prevent this, drastic measures cannot be avoided. Wilhelm has to signal a deterrent as early as possible; he has to punish the first one guilty of such a thing by expelling him instantly if he doesn't want to have disciplinary chaos on his hands in no time at all. This occurs right from the first year of the school; fourteen boys are expelled because they refuse to abide by the school rules; they either roam around at night, steal things, bother the girls, or commit other mischief. Understandably, such things leave their marks on him. Expelling a student may well prove disastrous in another area.

Take the case where one of the delinquents is the son of a high-ranking figure or family from one of the Outer Islands. If somebody of this standing has to leave school, it amounts to an almost unbearable shame, not so much for him alone but for the whole family group; they will be the talk of the village. Gossip about it could possibly go on for weeks. The missionary stationed on such an outer island could find his position compromised because of it. It is not unknown for a family group entangled in an affair like this to start stirring up public opinion against him in order to revenge themselves for their loss of face because one of their offspring has been expelled.

One day, Wilhelm has an experience that shows him how right his decision was to build the school not on Wééné, the seat of the government, but on Toon.

The church of Mwáán on Wééné is celebrating an anniversary over these days, to which Wilhelm is invited. He goes to the festivities with his students, where they will perform as a choir.

On Wééné, meanwhile, a bar with beer has been set up, and other attractions are also being offered. Things are going on there that Wilhelm would not want his students to be involved in. He certainly knows about the adventurous spirit of young people, but it is also clear to him what could happen to young islanders if they got hold of alcohol. An added problem is posed by numerous places where people gamble for money all night long. This is where, during weekends, some men can gamble away many a government salary which they should have spent on the needs of their extended families.

Such a problem does not exist on Toon, for the chiefs have decided that no liquor may be brought on to their island. Their reasoning is that they don't see why money should be squandered in drinking bouts when it is so badly needed for much more important things. The chiefs' decision, as sensible as it is, brings Wilhelm into a difficult situation. Some delegates of the parliament of Chuuk are spreading the slanderous suspicion that he himself had a strong hand in the making of this decision.

Initially, he always tries to be patient with all his students who draw attention to themselves by their deviant behavior. This is often easier said than done; there are some among them who have already been expelled from a government school as troublemakers. Sometimes Wilhelm oversteps the mark when something is happening again. If he is under stress he can hit the roof and lose his cool; for example he may slap someone in the face because he has disturbed the singing. Once he expelled a student from school because he tried to hand a note to a girl during prayer time. The repercussions of such acts are often so devastating because all the relatives of the punished student feel so exposed and insulted.

Afterwards, he always regrets such scenes. Meanwhile he also regrets that he has allowed other workers to make him react sharply by urging him to use unnecessary harshness against the islanders.

A similar problem occurs whenever a student fails to graduate from school. He and his relatives would be terribly insulted by this. One cannot treat an islander in this way. At the public graduation ceremony, therefore, he will be handed the same kind of documentary scroll as the others. However, it does not contain a diploma but only a confirmation that he has attended school for three years.

But there are also many delightful experiences Wilhelm has with his students. Some of them keep their exercise books so neatly that it is an aesthetic pleasure for Wilhelm to check them through.

In the afternoons, the boys have to do practical work on the school land. Grass has to be cut, weeds must be dealt with, and firewood must be chopped. The students just love it if they can work with Wilhelm, especially when something has to be built, then they revere him like a father. He makes use of this and encourages it wherever he can: "If a hundred and fifty students stand behind me, that will mean just as many groups of relatives."

On Sundays he takes all his students along to the church services in the villages on Toon, wherever he happens to be preaching. There they form a choir of sixty singers with a mighty voice.

Valets

The two boys whom Elisabeth had apprenticed before her departure to take care of her husband are also a real joy to Wilhelm. Aki from Woneyopw is his cook, Teyifis from Nómwiin does his laundry. The way he feels about his two "valets" can be seen in his following description: "My wife must have somehow given them instructions to always cook up something to eat. And they really keep to that. When it is time, they always make a fire and cook something. If sometimes they don't know what to cook, they will at least boil water for tea or coffee. Then they set the table and serve up whatever might be available in the cupboard. I am getting used to it slowly. It is a good thing to have been equipped with a cast-iron stomach; I am always grateful for that."

Teyifis doesn't find his role as housekeeper very satisfactory. What he is interested in is something totally different. He is one of the best fishermen at the school. He knows how to handle a spear and an elastic band so that turtles seldom get away from him, and he is usually fascinated by anything technical. Within a short time he learns how to handle an outboard motor and maintain the electricity generator. Wilhelm understands Teyifis and his interests very well; he is similarly "wired."

Besides his aversion to kitchen work Teyifis has another problem. Shortly before his graduation he confides in Wilhelm: There is this girl, the daughter of one of the pastors. He would really like to marry her. Could Wilhelm mediate in this? The latter would be overjoyed if the young man's marriage plans could succeed. But the father rejects it. Teyifis is from the Outer Islands. People coming from there are somewhat looked down upon by the inhabitants of the Chuuk Lagoon. Teyifis is, so to speak, a "country bumpkin." The girls on Chuuk would rather not choose someone like him. And yet, the people from the Outer Islands are, as a rule, more industrious, more persevering, more skilled and more modest. For a few days Teyifis suffers unspeakably, but he finally comes to terms with the rejection.

He is hardly back home on Nomwiin when he starts to teach the children there how to read and write. But after a short while he is back again on Toon. Wilhelm needs skilled hands for the practical work there. And Teyifis does not shrink from any job, however hard it is. He proves to be the perfect foreman. From the wages he receives from Wilhelm he pays his younger brother's school fees.

For a long time Wilhelm is wondering what will become of this young man once he himself is no longer on Chuuk. He finally finds a way to provide for his theological training on Pohnpei.

How much loving care Teyifis experienced, and how grateful he feels towards Wilhelm, is expressed in a letter Teyifis sends to him from Pohnpei after discovering that Wilhelm will be returning to Germany. Here an excerpt:

"Now I want to write my thanks to you because we will not see each other again. Many thanks that you loved me from the beginning, when I came to the school, until the end, when I went to Pohnpei. You also fulfilled my request and helped me so that I could attend this school here. I know how you were troubled one time when I was so very sick. You gave

*me medicine. For this I want to thank you, too. Now you are leaving, but I
will never forget your great love to me. I also know how you will rejoice
to hear that I am a good Christian. I want to promise you that I will walk
the narrow path. You have helped me so much when I was at school with
you. God will be with us for all eternity! In love, yours sincerely, Teyifis.*

What a sad and incomprehensible disappointment it must have been,
then, for Wilhelm a few years later to hear about this young man, for
whom he had so much hope. Together with two other students, likewise
former students of the Philadelphia School, Teyifis has to leave Pohnpei
because of a serious offence against the school rules. For his father, a
reliable church elder of the congregation on Nómwiin, this is a hard blow:
Teyifis is now the second son to return home as a failure.

Loneliness

Christmas Eve of 1959 feels lonely for Wilhelm. After the Christmas
celebration, the students from Chuuk have returned to their home islands
for two weeks. Only the students from the Outer Islands are still around.
On Christmas Eve he takes them along to Romónum, an island about
three miles (5 km) away from Toon, to celebrate with the church there.
He describes his experience of that Christmas Eve after the church service, in a touching manner:

"I went back to the house that belongs to the church. There was no
Christmas tree. But I went and got what had remained of the six candles
from the altar in the church and put them on the table. I burned five of
them in memory of my children and one for my wife who were celebrating Christmas in Germany. When they had all burned down and melted, I
went out to the beautiful sandy beach. The ocean was roaring in breakers
at the reef, and the Southern Cross stood high in the sky, as if held there
by a strong hand."

The next day he spends on the island of Éét. There he does get his
Christmas tree after all, and even some presents:

"When the service ended after three hours in the church that was full
to overflowing, everybody got something to eat, packed in a small basket
of palm leaves. For the chiefs and myself they had placed a nicely laid
out table under a breadfruit tree. All of a sudden our former student Tay-
eko came towards me with her children's group. She was carrying a beau-
tifully decorated little mangrove tree in her hand, and each child had a
small present for me in form of lovely shells. The tiny tree was placed in
front of me, the presents put underneath it by the children, and then they
sang a Christmas carol."

At the turn of the year 1959/1960 he builds an additional dorm for the girls' school. This means there is space available for another class.

Besides his work at school, he meets with the pastors once a month. They are very dependent on him. If they want to preach at all competently in their churches they need mental stimulus, since they don't have the opportunity of graduating after wide-ranging studies in theology, nor do they have available to them any proper library in their own language to help them generate ideas. As he meets with them, Wilhelm works through sample texts for the Sunday service. That needs preparation, especially if he is bringing along written support notes that they would find helpful.

Effects of the School

Meanwhile, the Philadelphia school is showing its impact on the church congregations. Wilhelm calls it "an invisible bond" going out and connecting him and his coworkers more firmly with the congregations. The students' parents are also participating with greater interest in their churches. Many girls from the first course are contributing what they have learned in a reliable way.

Gradually it is recognized that this is a school that is benefitting everyone, in the truest sense of the word. Siyales, a pastor from one of the Mortlock Islands, one day hears eighty-six girl-students singing at a congregational festivity in the village of Féwúpé where Wilhelm has taken them. It is quite a spectacular event to hear so many island girls singing. Siyales is deeply stirred by this. Small wonder, then, that he absolutely wants to have just such a school for his island as well.

School as an institution is something completely different for islanders than for children from European-Western societies. For the former, learning means much more than mere access to knowledge. Here at school the island children are learning things and how to deal with them in a way they could never do in the limited world experience of the island situation they come from: They have books about distant countries, maps, slide and film projectors, and many other things. Because of it, islanders go to school with much greater eagerness, as it offers far more to their imagination, their intellectual needs, and their longing for new experiences than anything they could find on their islands and in their villages.

The girls, for example, can satisfy some of their longing for new experiences right in the "washroom" that Wilhelm is building for them. Islanders bathe or wash themselves up to three times daily. At home they may perhaps have a creek or a water hole to do it. But at their school they have a concrete tank filled with forty-five cubic feet (2.5 m^3) of water that they can access directly from their dorm. It is filled by means of a pipe running from a spring close to the building. They only have to have a pail or some other container to be able to pour gloriously cool water over themselves.

However, a school can also cause tensions within a society. In their classes the youngest members learn far more about the big wide world within a short span of time than the older ones will ever know about it. That opens a wide gap between the generations. In addition there is reading and writing – abilities that many older ones, whose word traditionally has carried authority, have never mastered. This creates conflicts of authority.

Such conflicts also come up when the younger ones want to consciously lead a Christian life, no longer accepting the traditions of the original animistic religion, because their scientific knowledge gained at school enables them to differentiate between genuine and false causative connections. In concrete terms: They know, for example, that sicknesses are usually caused by bacteria and not by evil spirits. Therefore, when they get ill, they no longer want to be treated with rituals for exorcising spirits, but with medication like aspirin, penicillin or others. The older ones may see in this a breaking of taboos with dangerous consequences.

Everywhere in the world young people are breaking taboos, not only – of course – because they recognize their lack of validity but also because breaching them is itself a thrill. Three students from Pwolowót prove to be especially bold in this respect. They are using their holidays at home in order to show and apply their newly acquired knowledge.

In the waters around Pwolowót there lives some kind of eel, called *nopwut* by the islanders. Since there is also a magic ritual called *nopwut* in which this eel plays a role, the animal is highly taboo. In practical terms this means that it may not be eaten under any circumstances. People are convinced that someone in the family will get sick, or some other misfortune may befall them, if a person eats this eel.

These three students have learned at school that the connection between "eating *nopwut* and any misfortune" lacks any rational reasoning; in other words it is pure nonsense. Besides, the flesh of this eel tastes very good. When the three boys join the older men in fishing and manage to catch eels they will therefore also eat them, and as boldly as possible. The older ones are horrified; they are especially incensed when the boys give some of it to the children. However, when after a certain time no misfortune or death occurs, admiration replaces anger. This encourages the Philadelphia students to break further taboos.

When the men have been out ocean fishing, they do not from habit go straight back to their homes but segregate themselves for a while in the *wuut*, the communal island house, where they eat and also sleep together. The idea is that on the ocean they had supposedly been in the company of dangerous water spirits, and now they have to get rid of their evil influence before they are allowed to return to their families. It is a kind of ritual cleansing they have to submit to. This, too, the boys choose to ignore. They simply go home, have a bath, and eat with their families. In spite of it, nobody falls sick. Surprisingly, they remain equally successful and always catch as many fish as the others who keep the taboo.

European-Western observers tend to frown when Christian schools teach that it is not necessary to submit to such taboos in a society. Certainly, there is the danger that younger ones will no longer want to obey and acknowledge the authority of their elders. But any authority that rests on keeping senseless rules is not genuine and is already doomed from that point of view. Accordingly, the men from Pwolowót involved in this quickly recognize that within their own culture taboos act as roads to nowhere but mental imprisonment. The three boys' behaviour offers the men enough incentive to choose a positive way-out providing they, too, free themselves of these taboos.

Once the school holidays are over and the boys have to return to Toon, Angéwúr, one of the reputable skippers and boat builders of Polowót, not only takes them to Chuuk in his outrigger canoe but also two new students for whom there is really no space at the Philadelphia school. He perseveres in his opinion that "the more boys go to school here, the better for our church. We have all been impressed during the days these three were with us. They are totally changed." Angéwúr pleads earnestly for the new students to be accepted. Wilhelm doesn't have the heart to refuse his request.

The importance and reputation of the Philadelphia School has actually become so great on the islands that sometimes the strangest reasons are advanced as to why Wilhelm should accept someone as a student. Thus, Wosiko, a former student, appears and introduces her brother Chunewo: "Árákárákár" [that's how 'Herr Kärcher' sounds in their language], Chunewo has no idea that there is such a letter as Galatians in the Bible, and he doesn't even know, of course, where to find it. He can only learn this if he goes to school here." Wilhelm accepts him.

Meanwhile, the effects that modern knowledge can have on the islanders, as it is passed on by the school, become evident in many everyday situations. One day, Wilhelm receives an impressive letter from Eefa, a former student, in which she tells him of her experiences. Since leaving school she has married and now has a child. It frequently cries in the evenings and at night for a long time. Eefa is convinced that it is not sick but simply is disposed to crying. But her mother-in-law has a totally different opinion about the behaviour of her grandchild. She wants to have a magic potion made to act against the nightly crying of the baby. Eefa, who had already been urged during her pregnancy to observe certain rituals, of whose ineffectiveness she was convinced, finds it very difficult to stand up against all this and to insist on following her own convictions.

Her letter shows rather clearly what kind of pressures the young women on Chuuk have to face. Eefa's husband plays no role whatsoever in this matter. According to the islanders' understanding of relationships he is not even related to his children, and thus has no authority over their upbringing. Eefa, therefore, sees herself left alone to deal with the problem. But she does have one significant advantage on her side, which makes it possible for her to get her way. The former student of the Philadelphia School owes this advantage to her education she received there. Eefa is a clerk on Wééné, has been given a job by reason of her diploma, and brings money into the family. That is an unbeatable argument. Her mother-in-law finally gives in to her.

Questions of Admission to the School

The influx of students is constantly increasing, creating more and more problems. Until now, students have been readily admitted because of their motivation and their willingness to submit to the school rules; their intellectual capability is rather secondary to this. This creates a spectrum of talent in the classes that is far too broad: There are too many students who, though willing, are rather slow learners. And since going through the teaching material must be adjusted to suit the less talented as well, these learners will necessarily hinder the progress of the lessons to a greater extent than they should. Teachers are covering the teaching material too slowly. In time, these factors lead to the acknowledgement that there has to be an entrance examination, primarily also to test the English proficiency of the students gained since elementary school. Only those who can understand English sufficiently will be able to understand the textbooks, which are not available in the islanders' own language.

Staff Increases

Time and again, over a span of many years, Wilhelm and Elisabeth have made every effort to gain more staff members to whom they can delegate the work. As of the mid-fifties this situation started to ease up. The scope of this biography is too limited for a more detailed appreciation of the contribution the newcomers made to the work of Wilhelm and Elisabeth Kärcher. For this reason we will merely name them at this point, together with the year of their arrival.

Until 1963, when Wilhelm Kärcher temporarily returned to Germany "for good," the following workers arrived on Chuuk: Erwin and Dora Pegel (1955), Anneliese Stüber (1956), Peter and Inge Ermel (1959), Esther Hahn (1960), and Ernst and Annedore Seng (1960).

Between then and the end of Wilhelm Kärcher's last term on Chuuk (1968–1970) the following were added: Herman and Lois Buehler (1964), Elfriede Schmidt (1965), Roland and Dorothea Rauchholz (1966), Werner and Gertrud Fredrich (1968), Lothar and Gisela Käser (Dienste in Übersee, 1969), Klaus and Ulrike Müller (1970), Siegfried and Gudrun Neumaier (1970), Delyle and Cynthia Ellefson (Christian Service Corps, 1970).

Things Quieten Down

At the end of December 1960, after the various Christmas holidays for the school and in the churches, things quieten down for some days around the tirelessly busy missionary. The students have returned home over the Christmas holidays, and with his new staff members Wilhelm can now delegate the work. In one of his reports from this time for the *"Mitteilungen der Liebenzeller Mission"* (the Mission's information bulletin) we find one of his rare expressions about the burden he feels having to live without his family around: "For me it was a relief when all were gone and things somehow quietened down in the house. But when it gets too quiet, that's no good either. I then feel homesick for my family."

In the New Year, the long awaited boxes with the new songbooks (*Kkéénún namanam*) arrive. How urgently they had been expected can be seen in the fact that quarreling breaks out in some churches because not everyone who wants a hymnbook can get one. This reaches the point where the missionaries give up their copies so that individual islanders won't have to do without. Within two weeks, 1,500 books are sold. Even the wooden boxes in which the books had been transported find their use as "add-on furniture" or medicine cabinets.

The time of tattered songbooks is over. With the hymns set in four-part harmony, the new books are not just suitable for choir singing. Former girl students from Philadelphia, who had learned to play the harmonium, can now easily accompany the congregational singing wherever there is an instrument.

Once Again: a High-Ranking Visitor

In the course of 1961, another official from the Embassy of the Federal Republic of Germany comes to visit Toon. He does not come empty-handed; now, it seems, Germany doesn't mind spending some money on the Philadelphia School. There are wall maps that were urgently needed to make the teaching of geography come alive. This year, the visitor is even bringing big globes. Wilhelm allows the students to unwrap the gifts themselves, and he enjoys the huge thrill the students get out of it. The globes have a diameter of over a foot and a half (0.5 m), which means they are big enough to even find the Caroline Islands and Chuuk on them.

Rage and Blood Feuds

In November 1961, Wilhelm reports on severe clashes in the village of Wiichukunó, which had already broken out much earlier. The quarrel smoulders on, even though the congregation is about to put up a church building. At one point events happen in a rush.

One Sunday Wilhelm is returning from the village of Féwúpé, accompanied by Ernst Seng. They have just finished a service there; it is around three o'clock in the afternoon. In the church of Chukiyénú Sunday school has just started. As the two men are coming from the pier and approach the church entrance they pass by the boat shed. To their amazement they discover almost all of the inhabitants of Wiichukunó hanging about looking furtively, their faces grim and their foreheads furrowed in anger.

Wilhelm addresses the chief first, "Aakos, why are you all sitting around here outside the boat shed and not in church?"

Aakos – the name means August – becomes surly and growls a few unintelligible sentences in response. For an islander this is extremely unusual behaviour, especially towards a person worthy of respect. Anyway, Wilhelm decides not to react to it immediately, but rather to take his things into his apartment. On the way there he meets a man who tells him what happened.

The islanders have a special attitude towards blood. If a quarrel ends with someone being injured, the relatives of the one who is bleeding will angrily express their indignation. If things have gone that far, the one who has caused the injury has to pay, sometimes with such bizarre reasoning as: "If someone is giving blood at the government hospital that is needed for a transfusion, he is being paid for it." This way of thinking is the background to the following scenario.

Aakos and his followers are waiting like highwaymen for a man from Chukiyénú by the name of Pwúúng. During the week he takes care of the Mission's boat. On Sunday morning, someone from Aakos' family who was drunk had bumped into Pwúúng. The latter then blew his top and took revenge for the harm suffered by beating up the one who had jostled him, until he bled. Now Aakos and his people want to take revenge on Pwúúng in their turn. But because he is sitting in church they have to wait until he comes out. You can't have a brawl in church, as that would certainly be too much rage and wrath.

Everybody who knows the reactions of islanders in such matters is aware of what threatens to happen as soon as Sunday school is over. Wilhelm knows it, too. Pwúúng can expect to be beaten to death. Wilhelm, therefore, watches until Pwúúng reaches the church door and then, in a commanding voice, sends him back into the church hall. He himself confronts Aakos and, summoning all his authority, pleads with him to recognize that his plot to retaliate cannot lead to a sensible outcome. And just in case Aakos thinks he must use his cudgel, Wilhelm suggests that he should rather give him, the missionary, the thrashing instead of Pwúúng.

Aakos carries the cudgel already in his hand, a massive thing made of heavy mangrove wood. He does not lift it against Wilhelm, but he shakes with anger and loses all self-control. He vents his entire wrath on Wilhelm by slandering him with the most abusive words he can find.

In the culture and society of the islanders behaving like this is the very last thing one should consider and have the nerve to do. No islander is allowed to act in this way towards any superior – and a foreigner and missionary counts as such almost automatically. Because then the islander must fear that the wrath of the superior will have fatal consequences for himself. In the imagination of the islanders the *manaman* that people ascribe to Wilhelm could make the transgressor sick and even kill him.

The fact that Aakos is ignoring this unwritten law is evidence of how furious he really is. But at least he has enough control to not use his cudgel. And when suddenly old Wupwiini appears next to Wilhelm, the two of them are able to divert the outraged crowd into the *wuut*, the village community hall. Here Wilhelm sits with them for a long time, trying to calm the surging emotions. But events are now going totally awry.

They have managed to regain only a little composure when a brother of the fellow who got himself a bloody nose from Pwúúng appears with a pistol in his hand and starts stirring up the crowd anew. Again Wilhelm has to try and motivate Aakos, summoning every conceivable argument to resolve the conflict differently or let it rest for the time being. After a lot of discussion back and forth, Aakos and his followers set off home. Wilhelm is even able to pray with them beforehand.

He is hardly back at his home when the dispute flares up again with loud yelling in front of the church. This time it is Pwúúng's family on the warpath, armed with machetes, iron bars, and cudgels of mangrove wood; they are snorting with rage, ready to teach Aakos and his people a lesson that they won't forget and that they are assumed to deserve. To prevent a catastrophe Wilhelm courageously bars their way. He is not only successful in keeping the quarrelling sides apart. Kaaw, the ringleader of Pwúúng's "task force," even surrenders his iron bar when Wilhelm asks him to. With many well-chosen words he finally persuades the others to calm down as well. Here, too, he prays with them before they all go home.

Slowly the dust begins to settle over the whole affair. Aakos declares himself willing to let bygones be bygones, if Wilhelm, for his part, fulfills one condition: As punishment for his wrong conduct, Pwúúng should immediately give up his job as a mechanic on the Mission boat.

If Wilhelm would agree to this condition and dismiss Pwúúng, it would be hard on both of them. In the first place, he would rob his capable repairman of his wages that were not very generous anyway; and secondly, at such short notice it would be impossible to find a substitute, let alone train someone to take over this job. Still, Wilhelm agrees because he wants to show Aakos that he can give in. After that, a certain calm sets in.

Several days later, Wilhelm learns from pastors Namiyo and Kono that Aakos is full of remorse that he insulted him, the missionary, at their previous confrontation on that infamous Sunday in such an uncontrolled manner. In reality, Aakos is ashamed in a way that prevents him from personally taking steps towards reconciliation. This reveals one of the totally different ways of handling things in the culture of the islanders. Those wishing to admit some wrong behaviour by going and personally visiting the one they have wronged would just be proving that their audacity is little short of outrageous. In the eyes of the island society, correct behaviour in such a case requires sending a mediator to make things right again.

But Wilhelm is not willing to wait much longer for such a person. After a number of days he lets Aakos know that he would be willing to forgive his rude behaviour. However, neither Aakos nor a mediator comes to see him.

On one of the following Sundays it is Wilhelm's turn to hold the church service in the village of Chukuram. His path leads him past Aakos' dwelling. But Aakos isn't at home. So Wilhelm leaves word that he would like to talk to him on his way back. And sure enough, Aakos is there, and his whole family clan, all gathered in the *wuut*.

Again there are drawn out negotiations and discussions. Finally, they are willing to be reconciled with Pwúúng, but not without preconditions. He would have to come to them and offer his apologies because he had beaten up their clan brother and that was a very bad matter. Afterwards Aakos, privately and quickly, straightens things out between himself and Wilhelm.

That very same evening, Pwúúng and his family are on their way to Wiichukunó, accompanied by Wilhelm, to be sure. In the church they finally bury the hatchet. This also means that Pwúúng can take up his work again on the Mission boat. All's well that ends well?

Incredibly – no way!

As Wilhelm returns the following Monday evening from Wééné, Aakos is again waiting for him with the whole retinue of his relatives. He wants to be reconciled with a young man whom he had beaten up himself in the course of the quarrel with Pwúúng. This is exactly what he does without much ado in Wilhelm's apartment. And now something happens that always happens when islanders want to make an end of quarreling: They exchange gifts. Aakos' wife has already prepared them: a brand new large enamel bowl, fabric for dresses, soap, money, and other useful items. As an indication of his caring part in all of this, Wilhelm adds a pair of trousers, and the gifts are handed over to the young man as a sign of their regret and willingness to make things up.

If anyone believes this to be the end of the story, they are wrong.

Because the quarrel happened in public, on a Sunday and, to cap it all, on the square in front of the church, it also has to be publicly cleared up on a Sunday, after the church service, except not in front of the church but inside it. Wilhelm preaches on John 21:15–17. It is the passage where Jesus asks his disciple Peter three times whether he loved him. After the last hymn is sung, all involved get up from their seats. This is how islanders show their willingness to repent. Aakos and Pwúúng individually ask the church to forgive them for having allowed their wrath to carry them away with such loss of control. And Aakos insists on adding something: He addresses his request even to the newly arrived missionaries,

Ernst and Annedore Seng, reasoning that it has been far too sudden for them as newcomers to experience this whole shameful mess.

With that, the seemingly "never-ending story" finally comes to an end indeed.

Has More Light Really Come?

On certain occasions, Wilhelm cannot help noting also how on Toon rituals of a magic character surface again in Christian churches whenever a special event calls for it. In the village of Wóónipw it is not only the church building that must be enlarged because the congregation has grown to double its size. At the same time, a big *wuut* is being built in another part of the village. Such a traditional community building is, of course, much more closely connected to the long-established culture of the islanders than a church.

Wilhelm notices that the project is being entrusted to a builder from the island of Feefen, even though the village people are quite capable themselves of erecting such a building. When he asks what the reason for this is, he gets an interesting answer.

The builder, as all other inhabitants on Feefen, is indeed a Christian and a church member. But in the past, a building project for such a *wuut* involved a series of rituals, similar to a topping-out ceremony. Only a traditional builder will know these, and the village of Wóónipw, for whatever reason, does not want to do without such rituals. So the builder orders a pig to be caught, suspended with tied legs from a pole, and carried around the construction site. After that, it is to be slaughtered, and its blood to be painted on the roof beams. At the end of this ritual, which is obviously motivated by animistic ideas, they will say a Christian prayer.

Here we see a prime example of a syncretistic mixture of two different forms of religion. It would certainly be wrong to accuse the Christians in Wóónipw of having fallen back into pagan behaviour. Such happenings are not unusual and can be observed the world over, in the past as well as in the present, wherever Christianity has superseded other forms of religion.

People in the ancient Israel of the Old Testament did this constantly. In the (Christian!) vintner villages of Southern Germany it used to be the custom, until a few years ago, to send a posse of men among the vineyards to make a lot of noise by firing heavy guns whenever a hailstorm threatened – a remnant of the pre-Christian Alemannic religion, when people thought it was possible to drive away evil sprits with noise, even spirits causing hail. Besides, there are still Christians who think nothing of taking a divining rod to find water.

So the islanders are acting very normally when they do such things. Still, Wilhelm and Kumo, the pastor of the Wóónipw congregation, are very disturbed by this, and understandably so. When Kumo challenges the church elders involved, they first of all declare that the builder had told them it was a custom practised by the Japanese carpenters who had worked on the island until 1945. Kumo does not want to accept this and demands that all who were involved in it should withdraw from their church functions. But they react angrily. They threaten him with immediately going over to the Roman Catholics if he should force them out of their church positions.

Their extreme reaction can only be understood if one realizes that, in any case, it would involve a bitter loss of face for islanders to have to lay down their church functions; they would lose all dignity and prestige, and their families would lose reputation as well. Conflicts that arise from this are long-lasting and can only be solved with much sensitivity and patience. Kumo tries to do it, even though it involves difficulties for him that are not easily perceived by outsiders.

Pastors are paid by their churches. If anyone among them feels urged by his conscience to point out some wrong to someone in the church, he is running the risk that the person in question will refuse to continue supporting the pastor and his family with life's necessities. Mind you, it is not individuals who refuse but the whole family clan. This puts a certain pressure on pastors to preach in a way that people would like to hear and not the way they really should.

In the case involving Rev. Kumo, the conflict about the animistic sacrificial ceremony – the event involving the pig was that and nothing less – is expanding so rapidly that Wilhelm feels forced to go to Wóónipw to mediate, even though he wanted to stay out of it. The rebellion against Rev. Kumo was threatening to become unbearable.

Wilhelm has barely arrived in the village when an event takes place that changes the whole situation in literally one fell swoop, extinguishing the smouldering conflict before the construction work at the *wuut* is even finished.

When one of the heavy breadfruit trees, needed for the building, is felled, the tree falls on to the village path, killing a man who just happened to be walking there. At that precise moment the conflict comes to an end, for all of Wóónipw is convinced that God himself has intervened, has clearly made known his will, and punished the village for the pagan ritual.

The following Christmas service is attended by over seven hundred people, all finding room in the enlarged church. Wilhelm is just amazed at everyone's sincere participation in the singing, preaching and celebrating.

He remains convinced: More light has come to Chuuk – in spite of such occurrences!

The Year 1962

The first months are filled with construction and renovation jobs. The boat "Jugendbund EC" has to have a new coat of paint, especially under the waterline. So it has to be hauled on land. During the holidays, a few students lend Wilhelm a hand in this. During the afternoons he works on with Pwúúng alone. In the evenings he is busy writing letters.

Towards the end of the year construction work is again necessary. They need storage rooms for food and literature. Songbooks, New Testaments, and catechisms, of which they need quite a stock, can only be kept in good shape in the tropical island climate if they are stored in a dry and well-aired place.

They also have to build a training kitchen, where female students can learn to cook, as well as a small apartment for a lady missionary. Wilhelm himself urgently needs a room where he can assemble the pastors for training courses.

This undertaking is very labour-intensive because, first of all, the old building has to be torn down where the new one is to be erected. But then, no labourers have to be employed to do this. Wilhelm can count on the enthusiasm of his students for construction work. He just needs to tell them once what he is planning to do. On school-free afternoons they simply scramble to get their hands on a hammer, on pliers, and other tools he makes available to them. Then comes his command, "Now let's see what you can do!" and they climb like monkeys, laughing and screaming with delight, on to the building from all sides in order to tear it down. After three hours, the ramshackle thing is dismantled into handy pieces.

Since the new building is to be erected on a slope, a lot of soil has to be dug out first. Even the female students are busy helping. For this work they wouldn't think of wearing some worn-out old clothing but rather their beautiful and colourful dresses. Some even come to the construction site all in white, for they really pay attention to always being prettily dressed, as there are so many young guys around to look at them. However, the thing that just won't do for those dressed in white, is a sudden downpour. All those beauties are then no longer recognizable.

The villagers of Chukiyénú are full of admiration to see how speedily everything is progressing. But for Wilhelm there is a drop of bitterness mixed with the feeling of satisfaction. He surmises that this will be the last building he will plan and construct on Chuuk.

During the early hours of November 12, 1962, typhoon "Karen" causes damage on Guam running into millions. It is one of the severest typhoons ever to sweep across the island. In good time the government moves all airplanes from Guam to Chuuk to make sure they are safe before the storm breaks. There are many dead and injured. After the tropical storm, ninety percent of Guam lies in ruins. Countless families are without a roof over their heads. Even food has to be rationed.

The storm formed as a tropical cyclone in the area of the Mortlock Islands. Near Chuuk it became a severe typhoon, without touching the atoll itself, and then moved on to the northwest.

On Toon there are only a few toppled trees and torn-off tin sheets. What if it had hit the Philadelphia School!?

It gives Wilhelm deep satisfaction to have reached one of his most important goals with the school. Primarily, it was meant to help secure a new generation of pastors for the churches on Chuuk. Meanwhile, six graduates of Philadelphia School are attending the theological seminary on Pohnpei where future pastors for all of Micronesia are being educated.

Farewell from Chuuk, Only Seemingly Forever

Those years, when he is primarily responsible for the Boys' School, time seems to fly by for him: "If the coming years also go by as quickly, the time will very soon come for me to be reunited with my family." This point in time is getting closer as the year 1963 starts.

At the end of January he is fifty-six years old. By now he hasn't seen his wife or his two sons for four years, and his three daughters for ten years. Despite this, the approaching farewell turns out to be more difficult for him than he has been expecting, because it is the farewell to his lifework. He considers Toon itself as his "real" home: "The place, the houses, the pathways, the trees, the boats, the ocean and, above all, the people and children, all were so totally part of my life."

On occasion he speaks about the cloud lifting again, as described in Exodus 40:36–37, signaling that it was time for him to pull up stakes once more. His time on Chuuk is over.

But he does not only think about his heartache. He also sees success and is full of gratitude for the fulfilling time he has had here. His report expressing his thoughts on this ends with the statement: "On the place where the new house is now standing we started in real poverty at that time. I thank the Lord who has allowed me and my wife to serve Him here."

He has set his house in order. The Girls' School is taken care of by Esther Hahn and Anneliese Stüber, the Boys' School by Erwin and Dora Pegel. On Nomwiin in the Hall Islands, Peter and Inge Ermel are working; on Woneyopw in the Mortlocks, Ernst and Annedore Seng.

On March 25, 1963, Wilhelm has already moved out of the Boys' School. The students helping him pack and move are strangely quiet while they are working. In the one room he is still occupying, suitcases and boxes are piling up, together with the first farewell gifts from the islanders.

He feels like one always feels when one's lifework has to be laid aside. He finds it hard to pull up stakes and leave everything: "In between times I got all choked up." Everything he had learned to look upon as home has to be left behind. Wilhelm feels like an old tree that has put down deep roots and that should not be transplanted. Still, he wants to go to Germany. His family is waiting there for him.

Old Ayisawasan from Chukiyénú tries to comfort him: "Let us not weep. You have been here many years, working hard and loving us. You have a good wife in Germany and five children. And you haven't seen them for a long, long time. Now you can go home. So, let us not weep." With that, a few tears do roll down the cheeks of the old gentleman behind his glasses and over his wrinkled face.

The farewell gatherings Wilhelm is holding become meetings in memory of all missionaries who ever worked on Chuuk.

During the night before Palm Sunday 1963, he only sleeps for two hours. Constantly people are coming by who want to take their leave of him personally. They are singing in front of his house almost all night long.

In the morning, at six o'clock, he holds his last church service. He preaches about Jesus' triumphal entry into Jerusalem, the enthusiasm of the crowds for him and, a few days later, their equally loud cry: "Crucify him!" Once again, he points out to his listeners that they should not be that fickle in their lives. This he wants to be understood as his legacy to them.

After the service they all go to the pier. He writes: "Crowded together, the people stand near the boat whose motor is running already. Two other boats lie next to it. On one are the girl students, on the other, totally overloaded, are the pastors wanting to travel to Wééné." The boy students, however, accompany Wilhelm on the "Jugendbund EC."

Everything that is done for the last time is done very consciously, painfully consciously. How often he had left from here in the boat after giving the command, "Cast off the lines!" Now he shouts it consciously for the last time: *"Epichi ewe sáán!"*

While the boat is tuckering out into the bay under a sunny sky, he discovers people lining the beaches everywhere. On the rocks high above the lagoon the Christians from Féwúpé are standing and waving. At the pier on Fóósón, too, a big crowd is waiting. Between the coconut palms on the hillside of Mount Winipwéét mirrors are flashing and signaling farewell greetings.

On Wééné Wilhelm sees to his passport matters; and then the former girl students from Philadelphia, who are now living here, organize a very last and big farewell banquet in his honor. From there they proceed to the airport, where people from all around are flocking together, totally blocking all traffic. There are about one thousand men, women, and children. Many of these started out to Wééné already days ago making sure to be at the scene in time. They are singing and singing.

It takes a whole hour for Wilhelm to shake everyone's hand.

Being two hours late, the airplane of "Air Micronesia" arrives from Pohnpei. Until then, the crowds are standing in the burning afternoon sunshine and waiting until the big bird is airborne and finally vanishes from their sight.

Sitting next to a window in the airplane, he can see the mountains of Chuuk sinking away under its wings. For a brief moment he glimpses once more the island of Toon. Then the aircraft is flying out over the open ocean to the northwest. The date is April 7, 1963.

Once the airplane reaches its cruising altitude, his tension eases a bit, and he drinks the coffee served by the flight attendant. He is overcome by tiredness. Reclining his seat he sinks into it and sleeps. He would love it if he could just stay like this without interruption all the way to Eutingen. But on Guam several matters await his attention, and on Yap and Palau he has been asked to inspect the work of the Liebenzell Mission for one week each.

It is twilight as the plane lands on Guam. The first thing he discovers here is that he is once again in a civilized country. He has to present his passport. In all the years on Chuuk nobody was interested in anything such as a passport. And the official checking him promptly discovers a missing document: "You don't have a visa for Guam!" He should have applied for one, since he is a German and Guam is a U.S. American Territory.

When the immigration official asks him how long he had been on Chuuk, he replies, "Twenty-six years." That makes the official suspicious. But finally he lets him enter under the condition that he must obtain a visa before his return from Yap and Palau within the next weeks. Because on Guam itself you cannot get a visa for Guam.

At the airport he is picked up by Rev. Wilhelm Fey and his wife, several alumnae and Kikiwo, a younger man who had taught together with him at the Philadelphia School. He does not find it easy at all to report on Chuuk at the evening service of the Palauan church. He describes his emotions with the words: "It was like taking the bandage off a fresh wound."

Of Guam itself he has a problematic impression when he thinks about all the young people who will be coming here more and more from the islands of Micronesia in order to find work or further education. Guam is an important military base, a kind of aircraft carrier with all the trimmings: barracks, military hospitals, but also entertainment places for the soldiers, some of them of a rather doubtful quality. He fears the worst for his students. Guam appears to him something like Sodom for Lot and his family.

An Excursion to Yap and Palau

On April 9, at nine o'clock in the morning, his plane takes him from Guam to Yap, where it lands three hours later. In those days, the western Micronesian island groups of Yap und Palau were still serviced by propeller machines.

The mission station of "Salem" on Yap impresses him because of its beautiful location. He thinks it must even be the most beautiful of all of Micronesia – after Toon, of course – for on Toon things are most peaceful. On Yap cars rumble and motorbikes roar by, day and night, past the Mission house where he is staying.

The Mission's work on Yap has only been started relatively late and is by no means as advanced as elsewhere in Micronesia. During church services in the villages he notices that people are chewing betel nut. The islanders of Chuuk do not know this custom. Here on Yap only the very young children have snow-white teeth. The whole mouth cavity of all others is colored dark red and smeary with black teeth, all looking most unappetizing.

There are still people here who had once learned German during the colonial era of the German Empire, and who remember certain phrases. An old man, whom Wilhelm is visiting with missionaries Adam Müller and Edmund Kalau in his hut, suddenly gets up, stands at attention and shouts: *"Das Gewehr über!"* (Shoulder arms!). Then he starts to sing the German national anthem in a thin, shaky voice – the first verse, of course.[27]

On Palau he visits "Emmaus" and "Bethania," the two schools in Koror und Ngarard, maintained there by the Liebenzell Mission for the Palauan churches.

He has to wait for his return flight, and that becomes a test of patience. The plane that was to take him back to Guam is not coming. It is delayed on Yap because of engine trouble. The required spare part must first be flown in from Guam. He is waiting for two days already, constantly searching the sky and imagining that he can hear the droning of aircraft engines from time to time. Nothing. When it finally arrives in the evening of the third day, it is too late for a return flight. For him, this means that he can no longer catch the flight he has booked from Guam via Manila and Hong Kong to Frankfurt.

The Long Way Home

As he boards the plane to Europe in Guam a few days later, on April 25, 1963, a depressing feeling of emptiness starts to spread in his heart. Each person and thing must be left behind. It is terrible.

On the plane he is surrounded by soldiers. He is one of the few passengers in civilian clothes. His flight goes via Saigon in Vietnam, and they are at war there. During his seven-hour stopover he does go on a short sightseeing tour, but otherwise he stays at the airport because of communication difficulties. In Saigon French is spoken. Hardly anybody can understand English.

Late afternoon, a propeller machine takes him on to Bangkok. He misses the quiet flight he had in the modern jet whose engines produce much less noise. From New Delhi in India onwards he has another jet that

---

[27] The first verse, starting "Deutschland, Deutschland über alles" has been outlawed since the end of WW II; Germany has since started its national anthem with the third stanza.

"can transport over one hundred passengers," as he notices with amazement.

In Teheran he experiences once again, after ten years, "what cold air feels like." In the airport departure lounge he discovers a little boy dressed in a sweater and leather pants. He must surely be able to speak German. So he talks to him – and promptly gets a reply in the Swabian dialect of Lake of Constance. Shortly after, he also gets acquainted with the parents and the boy's little sister. "Now we can't be very far from home anymore!"

After an endlessly long flight via Beirut, Istanbul, then Greece and the Balkans he soon recognizes from the green meadows and well-groomed fields he can see from the plane window that he will soon be flying over Germany.

In Munich all passengers have to leave the airplane to go through passport control. Now he is in his own country but he sticks out. After leafing through Wilhelm's passport with obvious interest, the immigration officer looks him over. He wants to know where this peculiar passenger might be coming from. "From Micronesia," he answers. The official does not know what to make of that. Again he scrutinizes him, especially his hat, which is decorated with a wreath of shells.

In Frankfurt, too, he sticks out. This time because of his trousers. Unfortunately he has torn them on the plane and then patched them himself, in a makeshift way, as best he could.

14

The Time in Germany

Until the Second Departure

(1963–1968)

Return to an Estranged Family

So then, he is back again in Germany – after a ten-year absence. One would think he would be unreservedly glad and happy about it. But it is not so easy.

In Frankfurt among his daughters he only manages to address Hannelore by her proper name. Elisabeth has to reintroduce the two others to him. These young ladies, taking a certain pride in themselves, notice right away that Wilhelm is not dressed according to the latest fashion worn in Germany at the time. Well, how could he be? Hannelore finds his clothes odd, especially his shoes. They are ridiculous! In this country you don't wear that kind any longer.

Elisabeth had already found it difficult in 1954 when she had returned to Germany with Ernst and Helmut. Anneliese described the situation as follows:

"Mother arrived with our brothers by train. We girls stood on the platform to pick them up. Mother had become a stranger to us and it took some time until a relationship of mutual trust had been established again. She had to summon a lot of patience and love. After such a long time in an area with a totally different lifestyle it had not been easy for her to find her bearings again in Germany with five children, and especially without a husband. Financially things had always been a bit tight, but my mother knew how to make a feast out of small things, and we as children were able to find joy in the little we had" (1996:64).

Wilhelm returns to his family that is expecting him with great joy. But he has to cope with the fact that he hasn't seen them for a long time and that he has become a stranger to them – to his wife and two sons in four years, to his daughters in all of ten years. One has to think about what that means. Anneliese, the youngest of the girls, was eight years old when she said good-bye to her father in 1953. Now she is eighteen and her sisters are twenty-one and twenty-two years old respectively. They have become young women. In the decisive years of growing up into adults they had to do without their father as a male role model, a circumstance that can impair the normal development of one's personality. Just how strenuous, tense, and strange living together with their father was during the initial period after Wilhelm's return is again concisely but impressively described by Anneliese:

"There was great excitement as finally the day arrived when we were to go and pick him up at the airport. For us as girls it was again a strange feeling. [...] During those ten years, and in spite of letters and pictures, our father had become totally estranged from us. Neither did he recognize us anymore. He constantly confused me with my sister who looked very much like me.

"A period started yet again in which a new relationship of trust had to be built up with much love and patience. At the beginning it almost seemed impossible. For my father we were still the little girls" (1996:65). But the hurts do not last long: "Despite everything, we were happy to have our parents back again, to be together as a family, just as was the case with our schoolmates. Slowly but surely, with God's help, family life developed again, where one person loved the others, trusted them, and accepted them the way they were. The wounds healed and the strangeness disappeared" (1996:65).

The Kärcher Family in 1963 (left to right):
Wilhelm, Waltraud, Helmut, Hannelore, Ernst, Anneliese, Elisabeth

But first, the drive by car from Frankfurt to Bad Liebenzell is one single joyful event. Wilhelm can't help being amazed – at the traffic on the Autobahn he thinks is one mad rush; about the cleanliness wherever he looks, because nowhere are there leaves to be seen and no grass is growing on the pathways, unlike everywhere on Chuuk; amazed at the glorious woods, the houses with their tiled roofs, the Black Forest in its spring-blossom glory. Germany had changed enormously in the ten years of his absence.

Return to an Estranged Professional World

The world of his life he has left behind had been full of warmth – in terms of climate as well as human relations. This has changed, at least as far as the climate goes. The air he breathes is cold; everything he touches is cold.

Those who, like him, have lived many long years of their lives in a strange society and have learned to appreciate and love its totally different mentality and its people, will have conflicting emotions as they finally return from that foreign world where they have let down their roots. The most difficult part in such a return is always the fact that one has become in certain respects a homeless person. You suddenly realize that the world in which you have grown up is no longer as you remember it, and that you have become a completely different person in an alien world.

Wilhelm, too, has to cope with the fact that he is no longer totally at home anywhere. The reasons for this are many.

For the missionary "on the field" or "out there" an exceptional situation pertains. There are many people who know him, think of him, pray for him, and donate money so that he can do his work. He regularly writes reports, perhaps even books that have a wider print circulation. People write letters to him and ask how he is doing. All this changes drastically as soon as he leaves his field of ministry. Not that he becomes a total "nobody," but it is amazing how quickly it happens that only a few people still know him and ask about him. There are many missionaries on whom such a situation weighs heavily.

In addition there is another difficulty. "Out there" he did not merely have the opportunity to develop all kinds of ideas and take the initiative according to his personality; and, moreover, it was not only opportunities that opened up to him, but it was taken for granted that one could expect him to come up with ideas and take the initiative. Nobody would step in his way, nobody would give him the feeling of transgressing on his territory and poaching in another's hunting grounds. Back from "out there" he has to discover that he can easily get under someone's feet by taking the initiative, and that he experiences rejection when he acts on something. He has to deal with the accusation that he is acting on his own authority, that his ideas and opinions are impossible, old-fashioned, and out-of-date.

He, however, has learned "out there" to see many things differently. He has gained discernment that one can lead one's life according to other principles, can deal with people in a completely different way, can solve problems altogether differently and better than is done by those who have never looked beyond the end of their own noses in their own society and culture.

This is exactly the situation Wilhelm finds himself in from now on. He can only barely cope with it, especially at the beginning; and it leaves its mark also on his family eager to help him to familiarize himself again with a changed German society.

For several years he acts as "Keeper of the Holy Hill" in Bad Liebenzell. In his sphere of work he is responsible for the technical area, supervising the workshops and assigning the weekly practical workload to the students. However, they do not always treat him kindly. It may be that the first signs of the so-called revolution of 1968 that is gripping Germany at that time, are also making themselves felt. Much more serious is that Wilhelm with his opinions, his understanding of technical processes, and his whole behaviour is regarded as antiquated. The young trade professionals among the seminarians are far superior to him in their working techniques and in management issues. And small wonder: How could a missionary, who has lived most of his life in the extreme remoteness of the South Seas, know, understand, and master all the changes and innovations that have since taken place in Europe?

He tries to come to terms with his lot, but it is stressful for him. At night, when he returns to Eutingen, he is dissatisfied with his day's work. Sometimes he is in despair. But in spite of it he doesn't lose his agreeable sense for comical ideas. One day, he announces to a younger worker that he would reward anyone handsomely who could manage to get him out of his job as "Keeper of the Hill."

He is in his element when he is doing deputation work, holding Bible classes and giving lectures on his ministry in the islands. He willingly works alongside others in the Fellowship districts of Pforzheim and Mühlhausen, taking on preaching assignments when someone drops out. Whenever he speaks people listen with interest. He can tell stories in an unusually vivid way without appearing talkative. Children, too, are curious to hear what he has to tell them.

Back to Chuuk Once Again?

From 1963 onwards there is no report from Wilhelm's pen in the *"Mitteilungen der Liebenzeller Mission."* But suddenly, in issue No. 7/1968, he speaks up again in a word of farewell. It starts with verse 25 of Psalm 37: "I was young and now I am old, yet I have never seen the righteous forsaken or their children begging bread." The reason for this farewell message: The Mission had asked him whether he would be willing to go back to Chuuk once more, to help settle various problems that have surfaced in the meantime concerning the indigenization and independence of the national church organization.

Developments in Micronesia in the 1960s have moved the islands giant steps away from the colonial era towards modern democratic conditions. The churches on the islands and their leaders have also been pressing for independence and structural changes; they are thinking it is time to lessen the impact missionaries still have in their decision-making, regarding their involvement as patronizing.

The concrete issues had to do with the congregations wanting to unite under one church organization with its own rules, giving itself a constitution binding on all its members and workers.

Certainly the churches and their pastors conduct themselves loyally in the demands they put forward. They do want partnership in cooperation and that is, in principle, a justified demand. On the other hand, it cannot be denied that in this process they also run the risk of throwing out the baby with the bath water. The younger missionaries and workers of the church on Chuuk, who have stepped into Wilhelm and Elisabeth Kärcher's place, are willing to accept this cooperative partnership. But they do not want to do it without biblical structures for the leadership of a Christian church and other ethical principles they consider indispensable. It is in these issues that very different viewpoints surface, for the islanders do not separate politics and religion, a pastor's office and the position of the political title bearer, the chief, the *samwoon*, in the way that Europeans do or expect. That means that, for the islanders, a pastor with a spiritual mandate automatically also has a claim to a political mandate.

From this difference in opinion regarding societal mechanisms arise tensions with the missionaries, whose own view of things, of course, also has its justification. The only problem is that they are all too young to possess the status within the island society that is needed to lend the necessary weight to their judgment and decisions. At present this kind of status is found only in one person: Wilhelm Kärcher. For the islanders, he is such a *samwoon*. All would listen to him, and no one would contradict him without an absolutely compelling reason for doing so.

It is in this capacity that he should once more – and for a limited time – go to Chuuk, according to the will of the islanders, the missionaries, and the Mission leadership, in order to help solve the present problems. One of the most pressing problems has something to do with possession of land.

In the course of the history of Christianization on the islands, certain family clans had made property available to their church or the Mission so that churches or missionary housing could be built. This happened in part through a proper purchase, but perhaps also in the form of a dona-tion. Since the island society originally had no knowledge of written doc-umentation, because they rather dealt in word-of-mouth agreements, there existed no bills of sale, let alone land registries, for such transactions until far into colonial and post-war times. The borders were perhaps marked by a creek, a big rock, or simply by trees. Regular boundary landmarks, in the sense of European-Western customs, were unknown. This often led to violent disputes that could flare up even generations later. Time and again, potential heirs wanted additional financial remuneration or even demanded the return of "donated" land.

The problem of missionaries working on Chuuk during the sixties is difficult in a threefold sense. No one knows the history of such property negotiations from their own experience, and no one really knows which way the property boundaries are located. The biggest difficulties are with the older islanders, who do know the facts but want to stay out of the disputes because they are either related to the fighting parties or because they shy away from getting between the battle lines.

This state of affairs, interestingly, leads to a Solomonic solution, and nei-ther the missionaries nor the islanders have a problem accepting it: The only one who possesses the necessary authority and the corresponding knowledge, is Wilhelm Kärcher. Let him come and set the boundary stones, and thus clear up the property situation in a judicially acceptable way.

On the one hand, the call from Chuuk, to help in the work there once again for one or two years, comes as a "godsend" for Wilhelm; but on the other hand, he is very much aware of the fact that by now he is sixty-one years old and will not be able to cope with the physical and psychological stress awaiting him on Chuuk as he used to.

The Crossing of Two Biographies

During the last two years before his third departure, Wilhelm is often on the road again to report to churches and Fellowships on his mission field and on what he can expect there upon his next arrival. The school, which has become one of his most significant legacies, has a special place value in his slide-lectures. In earlier days he always referred to it as the School for Girls and the School for Boys. Now he calls it the "Philadelphia School," for in the meantime boys and girls are taught there coeducationally. That is not quite what was envisioned according to the original rules of the islanders, but times have changed. The government no longer practices segregation of the sexes, and teaching in mixed classes has a decided advantage: It saves on teachers. Employing teachers involves considerable costs, and it is difficult to find suitable people to work on the islands of the South Sea.

Since 1964, the Philadelphia School is being led by Herman and Lois Buehler and conducted as a Junior High School, the equivalent of a middle school (*Realschule*) in Germany. Within a few years they will be going on home ministry assignment; before then the Mission will have to find somebody to take their place.

In February 1966, Wilhelm gives a lecture on Chuuk in the hall of the Liebenzell Fellowship in Freiburg im Breisgau. I myself, the author of this study, am among the audience. Again and again the speaker mentions that a teacher is needed, and that he knows that there is one person among those attending that evening, who has trained as a teacher.

I prick up my ears. Does he really mean me? He really does! How can he know that I have become a teacher? I decide to talk to him after the meeting.

For some time now, my wife and I had been talking about doing "something like this," and we decided to take the opportunity if it should be offered.

When I put my question to Wilhelm about his idea of what our work on Chuuk should look like, it becomes evident that he already has a plan in mind: "You only need to apply to *'Dienste in Übersee'* (Overseas Services, at that time a well-known voluntary overseas service of the Protestant Church in Germany). At the same time, the Church of Chuuk will request you via Liebenzell Mission for their school. And once you are accepted you can promptly depart for the field."

No sooner said than done. It was to take about another three years before the plan became reality. In any case, with our conversation in Freiburg, my own life path and that of my family, crosses that of Wilhelm Friedrich Kärcher; the consequences are unexpected and positive, as we shall see.

15

The Last Two Years in Chuuk
(1968–1970)

Words of Farewell, Once Again

His last farewell took place at the Pentecost MissionFest of 1968 in Bad Liebenzell. In his message he points out, among other things, that he is really too old already for the task ahead of him: "If no one else is willing or able to go, then it is simply left to grandfathers to go!"

These words, announced by Wilhelm into the gathered crowd, are heard by a young man who had recently finished his training at the Seminary of the Liebenzell Mission, in preparation for missionary service. He had actually decided to go to New Guinea, having refused an unofficial offer several weeks before to go to Japan as a missionary. Wilhelm, too, has known this young man all his life. It is Klaus Wilhelm Müller, youngest son of his sister Frieda, in other words, his nephew. His uncle Wilhelm is also his godfather.

What Wilhelm doesn't know, and therefore can definitely not be attributed to his initiative, is this: Two years later, both of them are to meet again on Chuuk – as coworkers and colleagues.

On June 10, 1968, Wilhelm takes the plane again from Stuttgart via Guam to Chuuk.

Back on Toon

At the Chuukiyénú dock he is welcomed back by the singing islanders. Wupwiini is already waiting for him to tell him that he has been critically ill and has been praying constantly to get well again so he could experience the return of the missionary, "his" missionary. Only if he, Wilhelm, were on the island, could he die in peace, for then it would be Wilhelm who would bury him.

Wupwiini's wish was not to be completely fulfilled as he had thought at Wilhelm's arrival. He only dies in the 1980s, when Wilhelm has been back a long time, and for good, in Germany.

The pastors, too, are celebrating the return of "their" missionary, sometimes in touching words. One of them, Wuwanter from Wútéét Island, reminds them in his welcoming address, that Wilhelm once gave him a pair of trousers, a piece of clothing that had really always been a painful reminder to him of Wilhelm. From time to time, therefore, he had thought about burning them. But now that Wilhelm was back again, the "trouser-burning-demonstration" could be dropped as being groundless.

The following Sunday, another pastor, Winiyam from Manayiyo, made Wilhelm wonder, when he said in his address that the day posed only half a joy for him, even though he had tears of joy in his eyes. And then he calls out into the gathered congregation, "I want to tell you why it is only half a joy: His wife and children aren't here with him!"

Wupwiini: Always Good for a Surprise

It goes without saying that wherever Wilhelm is welcomed back, there will be one sumptuous banquet after another. Some islanders make it less sumptuous than others, but all the more warmhearted.

One afternoon, around four o'clock, Wupwiini appears once again at his door to bring him a special surprise. Out of an old paper bag he digs out two freshly baked and still warm loaves of bread and a can, telling Wilhelm, "You go ahead and set the table. I have brought something good for both of us."

What comes oozing out of that can is not quite recognizable to Wilhelm in those circumstances, but he assumes it should really first be cooked before it would be ready for human consumption. But he goes along with what Wupwiini is doing. Both of them smear the contents of the can, some kind of mush, on their pieces of bread. Since it is quite spicy it makes them thirsty. Wilhelm, however, does not yet have any drinks stored in his house. This lack is remedied by Wupwiini, who goes to the rainwater tank and draws two glasses of water. After this "small talk over coffee," as Wilhelm calls it, Wupwiini packs the remains of the meal back in his paper bag, throws it over his shoulder and shuffles back through the bush to his nearby hut.

Memories

Wilhelm himself lives in the same house he had built in 1963, shortly before his trip home. He really feels at home in it and likes his work very much. He prepares the Sunday school lessons for 1969 and other theological support material for the pastors. And he is back in the past of long ago.

The third day after his return to the islands he is already on his way to Wútéét, where he had been interned together with his family twenty-three years ago. Early in the morning everything is still quiet around here. He walks along by the ocean, recognizing individual trees as he remembers them from days past, until he comes to the swamp where all those rats had come from. He even finds the place again, where he and his family and the other missionaries had to set up camp under such wretched circumstances and where together they had survived the American Air Force bombing raids. He is overcome by deep gratitude, as he lets the events of that time pass before his inner eyes.

The conditions of the youth work on Chuuk had on occasion been described to him in rather gloomy terms. Now he is pleasantly surprised to find seventy young people sitting in front of him, listening to what he has to say. The following week there are eighty of them, from only two congregations, and in the village of Féwúpé a few days later even two hundred and fifty! "Some of them have had to walk for two and a half hours, over rough and smooth, rock and swamp, uphill and downhill, through high wet grass, as the rain had been pouring down the night before."

An Oceangoing Motorboat

In April, he visits Pwolowót once again, and later he is picked up from there and brought back to Toon under special circumstances – in a brand new, oceangoing, roomy motorboat; its history goes back to Hong Kong.

On May 1, 1969, the sky over the giant city is overcast with rain clouds. Despite this, many friends of the Mission have come to attend the launching of the new Mission ship meant for Chuuk. With a coconut it is christened *Chen*. Under the strains of "Praise God from whom all blessings flow" it glides into the water.

A few weeks later, the *Chen* arrives on Pwolowót after a voyage of over 3,100 miles (5,000 km). Under the command of a Canadian captain, missionaries Peter Ermel and Ernst Seng had picked the ship up in Hong Kong.

Chen means "Love," as described in John 3:16. With this ship, built of fibreglass and equipped with two diesel engines, work on Chuuk becomes much easier. Outlying stations can be serviced much better and the churches on the islands can be visited regularly. Wilhelm gets acquainted with the ship and learns to appreciate it during the last year of his stay on Chuuk.

A few days after Wilhelm's return from Pwolowót on the *Chen*, the ship is on its first voyage to the Mortlock Islands. It goes without saying that Wilhelm is also on board.

Close to Nómwuluuk that memorable date of May 4, 1954, comes to his mind, when he had changed canoes at the last moment and stayed alive. Now, fifteen years later, he no longer travels back and forth among the islands by outrigger canoe but with a robust, seaworthy vessel, especially built in Hong Kong for the purpose.

Nobody has any inkling at this time of the dark fate that awaits the boat. Four years later, the *Chen* will come to a tragic end during a mission trip to the Central Carolines – Wilhelm's "Road of Islands." In the early morning hours of August 5, 1973 it is dashed to pieces on a coral reef (Müller 1975:41).

The Mentor

On August 27, 1969, an Air Micronesia Boeing 727 lands on the island of Wééné. My wife and I and our two children have arrived on Chuuk from Guam. From Wééné we take the *Chen* to Toon where Wilhelm meets us at the dock. We live in the same house that Wilhelm had built for his family years before, next to the Girls' School building.

During the coming weeks he gradually introduces me to the churches as the new teacher at the Philadelphia School. For this I accompany him on Sundays when he goes to the villages to hold church services and he familiarizes me with the simple life of the islanders.

On one of the first Sundays, we take a hike around all of Toon – for five hours. With trouser legs rolled up we march through the bush wet from the rain. Not far from the village of Wóónipw we look for a place to sleep. In a *wuut*, a hut constructed of four posts covered with a roof of leaves, we each find a rough beam to lie on, with a smaller piece of wood for a pillow. For a while we twist and turn, and all of a sudden sleep overcomes us so deeply that we forget all about the hard wood. Later, we are just in time for the church service.

On another Sunday, we are going to Éét. The weather is very nice, but the trade wind from the north is blowing full strength today. It is the start of the stormy season, and the waves have white crests. Wilhelm and I are sitting on the wooden engine cover of an old Japanese fishing tub. If there had been something like a harbour police or coastguard service on Chuuk, it would long have been withdrawn from operating. At the slightest swell of the waves the boat tilts from one side to the other, so much so that it seems better to either change the concept of over and under or cease using the words altogether.

The boat is equipped with a diesel motor. The exhaust pipe sticks out on deck and is already totally riddled with holes from the rust. If it is anchored anywhere, a tin can is clapped over the exhaust so the rain can't get in. As he starts the motor, the skipper forgets to take the tin can off. At the first ignition, the thing is forcibly flung into the air and – to our great delight – lands some place in the water.

We have barely passed the reef via a narrow channel, when we feel as though we are on the open ocean. The waves are six feet high (two meters), and soon get even higher. The boat climbs up the crest of a wave every time, instead of splitting through it, then it rests there for a brief moment until the wave has passed underneath it, only to fall full force into the next trough. The impact, as it hits the water, is very hard. But we can't do anything except crawl deeper into our raincoats so that the spurting spray won't get us wet right from the start. It takes only a few minutes and I am so seasick that I can barely hang with both arms over the bamboo pole along the middle of the deck. The effort makes me break out in sweat.

Arriving on Éét, I am so exhausted that I fall asleep right away in a hut made of palm fronds. Wilhelm starts the service without me. It is almost over when I finally wake up from my stupour. But I still get to speak. With my hands I mimic the movements of our boat on the way to Éét. Getting more expressive still and putting my hand over the area of my stomach, I can hear a comprehending murmur going through the rows of people sitting there before us in the sand. They know this. South Sea islanders also get seasick when the ocean is restless.

Over Easter of 1970, we are taking our third trip together. This time we are going to Wútéét. Until now, Wilhelm has always translated for me. Today he suggests I should try to speak in the language of the islanders.

While I am speaking, the people's behaviour is noticeably quiet and attentive. I become aware of that tension among listeners when someone does not quite know how to express himself in their language or can only do so as a beginner.

I realize at that moment that Wilhelm Friedrich Kärcher, both as a person and as missionary, has become my mentor. He has confidence in me that my talk in the Chuukese language won't be totally awry, in spite of my amateurish bungling. The sovereign attitude he radiates gives me the feeling that I am not as bad as I think I am at the moment. And he urges me again and again to consign as much as possible of what I experience to writing, and learn from working together with the islanders. In doing so, neither he nor I have any idea how his advice will impact the direction of my life in a decisive way. It is really and essentially due to him as mentor that I later became a university teacher.

On our way we come via Romónum. The first buildings that one can make out on approaching an island like this one are small huts of a somewhat square design, spaced irregularly along the beach on stilts. These stilt houses are easily recognized as toilet structures. Their water flushing is regulated by nature itself during high tide.

As we approach the beach through the shallow water, a young woman comes toward us among the palm trees across the sand. It is Florita, a former Philadelphia student. She carries her baby in islander fashion on her hip. Suddenly she bends down, scoops up ocean water in the hollow of her hand and rinses her mouth with it. This she does in the immediate vicinity of an outhouse. Wilhelm's dry remark is merely: "That's not a real problem; everything is already somewhat diluted."

Wilhelm Kärcher as "Senior Missionary"

He is reminded daily of the truth that he has come very close to the age of a grandfather. He certainly enjoys his work, but a little bitterness is mixed in as well. In a letter to Richard Neumaier he laments the fact that walking is now quite strenuous for him, especially when he has to go through the reef waters between Téé and Satawan.

The children's work, he finds, is in bad shape. Many of the younger pastors and church helpers are either of the opinion that such an hour does not need any special preparation, since it concerns "only" children and young people, or else they think, children's clubs can be run following the same monotonous routine as is often done for adults.

This is not necessarily a question of any laziness or bad intentions of the people responsible. Often it is because of handed down ideas already embedded in the language of the islanders that make them think and act that way. Little children are called *semiriit*, which means "unreasonable." If that is how children are, why should they be made to think? A similarly biased concept is *tipáchchem*. This word means "intelligence." If someone is credited with intelligence, he is literally said to be "endowed with a good memory." That makes even the teachers believe that a person only needs to learn as much as possible off by heart in order to understand facts. Thus, children are mostly taught to memorize what the teacher tells them. They, and young people too, then only need to repeat things. But often this only amounts to a mindless shouting of things told and things repeated. There is, then, nothing to offer any stimulation whatsoever for creative thinking that could help them to associate certain concepts and to understand and apply them.

But then again, Wilhelm expresses his satisfaction that nobody is "throwing a spanner into the works" as had been the case in the years of 1963 to 1968 in Germany: "Nobody wants to squeeze me against the wall here."

He is very concerned about the fact that once again he has left his children and that Ernst had written to him: "I have no father to talk with about important matters."

The work of the younger missionaries and workers also troubles him. He does acknowledge that they want "to do the right thing in the right way." But they obviously give him the feeling that he and Richard Neumaier have "not done it right." In his insecurity he feels out of place, speaks of the "indigenous" but of himself as "out-digenous," but then ends with the rather conciliatory statement, "That's how it is in life; we probably thought in the same way sometimes."

Occasionally, there is evidence of a certain misjudgment on his part as to what should be done with Micronesia in the future. Several procedures in class really run against his grain. He can be especially suspicious towards Americans in relation to the teaching techniques and didactic concepts.

There is one of his character traits his younger missionaries at the mission station appreciate above others. If something has to be repaired, they only have to ask him once for his advice and expert knowledge in craftsmanship. They can be sure that he will be there the next morning in his working shorts, lugging his tools along. As a reward he, as a "bachelor," only expects to be invited to breadfruit salad and other good things – preferably fried chicken! – as he cannot prepare these himself. At his place he most often just has rice and sauerkraut (pickled cabbage) from a can, almost his standard meal. He usually cooks for himself for several days in advance.

One accusation concerning the educational program he devised years ago for the Philadelphia School hits Wilhelm very hard.

The development of life on the islands has meanwhile progressed to the stage where only those possessing a good knowledge of English and ability to speak it can play a role in public life. Those who have these are considered well educated and will go far in public service or in jobs related to business. Wilhelm and Elisabeth did not foresee that things would develop in this direction, and possibly could hardly be faulted for not doing so. At the time of the founding of the Philadelphia School totally different topics were uppermost in their thinking. Thus, for example, the preparation of young people for the ministry in the churches must have seemed far more important to them than their qualification for eminent positions in public life. For that reason classes were exclusively taught in the vernacular.

The consequences are only coming to light now, ten years later. Among other reasons, Philadelphia students are not yet to be found in official positions because of their rather poor knowledge of English. And Wilhelm gets to hear that his students have not achieved anything. This accusation he sees as unjust, and it really bothers him.

On one of the stormy trips from Woneyopw to Chuuk he wonders again and again whether his students have really come to nothing. On the surface this impression almost seems to be true, he thinks. He tries to comfort himself with the challenge to the farmer in James 5:7 to be patient and wait for the "valuable crop." But this comfort only comes over him gradually.

On the Hall Islands he learns with great interest that things have become brighter. One islander tells him how the chiefs in the earlier days used to live a despotic life: Women simply had to do their bidding; disputes over land were always settled in their favour, just like between Ahab and Naboth in 1 Kings 21. This has changed, but many things still haven't.

His experience time and again, even now, is that islanders do indeed respond to the Word of God easily and quickly. But he warns himself not to get his hopes up too quickly just because of this and not to get carried away in unrealistic expectations.

It disturbs him that many men laze around idly in the shade of their huts, playing cards, or simply getting drunk. Employment on the islands is indeed only available for all on a temporary basis, for example, when there are larger community projects, when a pathway or dock has to be built, or the land must be protected against erosion from the sea through a wall of coral blocks. Hardly anyone among the adults has trained for a profession; and jobs with corresponding income are practically nonexistent and they cannot be created.

He is also disturbed by the transistor radios that have invaded every household in the meantime, constantly making noise. He himself does not have one. When an aged church elder discovers this, he asks him right away whether he should bring him his radio. Exposing everyone to a constant stream of musical entertainment has become so normal that at a child's funeral he has to expressly ask for the radios to be switched off.

His reports sound an increasing note of pessimism. As he sees it modern civilization is forcing itself more and more into the world of the islanders. This, he feels, is threatening the work that he as a missionary has built up, together with others. The islanders are now conducting their economy in ways that he cannot accept. Meanwhile, on many islands, copra – the dried flesh of the coconut – is no longer paid for in money but exchanged for a quantity of beer. This, he is sure, will one day bring Micronesia much misery.

Occasions arise where Wilhelm demonstrates his readiness to speak up and present his opinions without regard for social norms. For the islanders this is sometimes hard to take; and many discussions follow. But it also shows that in the islanders' view Wilhelm possesses a measure of authority allowing him to do this without risking his right to live among them; one essential factor being an attitude that is unspoiled by any arrogance, since he himself is not afraid of criticism. Everything he demands of others, he also demands of himself.

Since he regularly holds meetings with the pastors, church elders, or church helpers these occasions happen at a different church each time. The respective members will then also take care of the food for those attending. It is customary among the islanders to honour higher-ranking persons, primarily those who have specific positions, to present them with as much food as possible. This is especially the case if they are guests. We know this already.

Usually the participants get a meal consisting of breadfruit and fish. For some time now, the normal competition among the islanders, whenever they visit each other and food is served, has extended also to these gatherings. Some conferences do not just end with a sumptuous feast, they even start with one. Wilhelm disapproves of such gluttony – and rightly so!

One day, another such conference is taking place in the village of Neechééché on Toon. In the community hall the tables are bending under masses of open sandwiches and bowls full of *tempúra*, some kind of doughnut. The pastors help themselves as they are wont to, before their meeting as well as afterwards. The villagers, including numerous children, are just looking on.

Already on earlier occasions of this kind Wilhelm has wanted to say something about this, but he restrained himself as it would mean criticism of the pastor of the host congregation who also would be jeopardizing his prestige if his people could not muster some "decent" food. But now Wilhelm has had enough. He rebukes his fellow brothers: "You act just like the Pharisees did when they elevated themselves far above all others. While you sit here feasting yourselves, your fellow Christians sit outside and have to look on. You are feeding yourselves but you do not feed the flock. You only think about yourselves but you do not think of others." Harsh words for the islanders; their behaviour seems perfectly normal and correct to them. After all, they have always done it that way.

Stunned self-consciousness is spreading among them; several pastors stop eating. Others refrain from taking any of the leftovers on the tables home after the conference, even though that is the custom: Islanders are to clear the tables after the meal and are allowed to take home the remainders for their relatives.

The next pastors' conference takes place in Wóónipw. Food is served only after a time of prayer and Bible study. At the start of the afternoon ministerial discussions, one of the pastors makes the point of including the item of "food at our meetings" in the agenda. As his reason he states, "Our missionary has criticized us for eating twice, while our fellow Christians only eat once."

Later, when the item is up for discussion, Wilhelm is asked to present his point of view. He knows that his criticism has stirred up a hornets' nest with the islanders. He starts with well thought-out and moderate words, calmly explaining that the Bible does not condone things like this. After all, pastors are not *samwoon*, i.e. they are not chiefs and privileged office bearers but disciples of Jesus Christ who are to serve others, instead of allowing others to fatten them.

A long period of silence follows, after he finishes his argument. People are thinking. Are pastors really not *samwoon*? If not, are they not, at least, office bearers with a certain status and claim to privileged treatment, also in relation to food? If again the answer is no, isn't it simply a pity to enjoy such good food only once instead of twice? All these are questions that island pastors don't find easy to answer!

Finally someone tries to find a solution that at least allows for eating twice, even though it might not be totally biblical: "Wouldn't it be best if in future we also made *tempúra* for the others?"

This suggestion does not find a majority. What is to be done? At last, the chairman – not Wilhelm – takes the floor: "It is best for us to vote on this point democratically. I myself get the impression that our missionary is right. If the church members visiting from other places can only eat once, then it is indeed not right that we as pastors should eat twice."

The vote in the assembly is unanimous. In future, there will only be one meal during a pastors' conference, just like at any other gatherings.

Is it a need felt by elderly people to rebuke others, that prompts Wilhelm to speak up in this manner? Is it an ageing man's lament over the bad times and the decline of morals? Be that as it may. The real cause for his attitude is probably to be found in the experiences he has gained with people whose shattering fate has also gone to his heart.

Wilhelm F. Kärcher as Senior Missionary

Women in the So-Called South Sea Paradise

During the turn of the year from 1968 to 1969 he spends some time in the village of Woney. The old pastor of the church has been bedridden with tuberculosis in the government hospital now for almost a year. His young colleague, who has only been in office for weeks at this time, is also suspected of having tuberculosis. The two church elders are likewise sick, and the little church of Woney is sick in every respect.

On New Year's Eve, Wilhelm sits together with Asako and her husband in their hut. The two of them have twelve children. Asako has to take care of them by herself, for her husband is an alcoholic. He doesn't work and is about to leave his family. Asako herself does not want to hold him back, for life with him is nothing but a burden for her and the children. Wilhelm tries to talk sense into him, to stir his conscience, to point out the futility of his life, and to pray with him.

In the neighbouring house lives Siyeko. At the moment she is incapable of walking even one step. Soyichi, her husband, has abused her, thrashed her, and totally beaten her up in his drunken stupor. She can only lie there. And yet she should be taking care of her eight children. Half drunk, Soyichi is seeking help by talking with Wilhelm. He does feel terribly ashamed of what he has done and also promises to change. But that is easier said than done. He is so bound by liquor that he is constantly backsliding.

In another village lives Machiko. She is a faithful Christian. As a girl she attended Philadelphia School and proved to be a talented and industrious student. Then she married a young government employee, also talented. Five days after the wedding he was transferred to Guam. Since then she hasn't heard from him. He has found another woman and has lived with her ever since.

In consequence, Machiko married a second time. This marriage seemed to be stable. She brought five children into the world. But her second husband, too, left her and married another.

Her third husband took to drinking. She was constantly beaten up. In his drunkenness he broke the few things Machiko needed to take care of her household. On a rampage one day, he even caused the hut to collapse. He, too, finally left her.

Machiko has had enough of men. By now her oldest boy is able to climb trees and pick coconuts. From now on she will just fend for herself alone with her children. She offers her hut as a place for meetings. This gives her a task that will lend extra meaning to her life. That also means she won't have to walk that long and difficult path to church anymore with her youngest son whenever she wants to attend a service.

In Proverbs 23:29–30, Wilhelm finds a sarcastic commentary relating to these women's fates: "Who has anguish? Who has sorrow? Who is always fighting? Who is always complaining? Who has unnecessary bruises? Who has bloodshot eyes? It is the one who spends long hours in the taverns, trying out new drinks."

He could speak on this topic every day in this place.

The "Beatles of Chuuk"

In an earlier chapter it was already pointed out that in the island society girls have a more privileged position, experience more affection than boys and, therefore, develop a stable personality earlier than the boys. As children the boys are mostly left to themselves. They are regarded as unreliable, and people don't think much of them. They sense this, of course. In order to develop a little bit of self-esteem, they like to band together in gangs; and to quench their thirst for action they plot all kinds of adventures, sometimes with dire consequences, especially when alcohol is involved.

Wilhelm gets acquainted with such a group on Toon. These are about thirty young guys, among whom several show the typical signs of parental neglect. They leave their hair long, unkempt, and full of lice. In order to impress the girls they decorate their tangled heads with lush wreaths of flowers, even though there is no festivity in sight. They wear their trousers purposely full of holes and frayed. With this, they demonstrate that typical deviant behaviour of young people trying to demonstrate self-confidence and gain the attention of people around them. In reality, they just increase their distance between them and isolate themselves even more as a group.

Most of them hang around all day long on the pathways, in the bush, and in the huts, busily drinking beer, bothering the girls, and making the neighbourhood unsafe. Sometimes they appear at night around the Girls' School, steal the students' underwear from the clothesline and cause trouble. Occasionally, they even disturb the Sunday services. If they are peaceful they perch themselves some place in the shade of a tree and play guitar.

What happens next is characteristic of Wilhelm's way of doing things. He doesn't simply complain about the wayward young men but tries to win them over. As he is having a weeklong series of meetings in Fóósón he invites them for the Saturday evening. And they come. He is amazed at how many come. The questions they ask him are impressive, to do with life after death. Some men are considering whether it is proper to live such a reckless life as they do at the moment, and then quickly repent when the time comes to die, according to the motto: "Live as you please and then die as God's child, that way the devil's design will be spoiled."

The result of this invitation makes a great impact. When Wilhelm asks them whether they would like to come together for another evening like that, they spontaneously suggest: "Let's come together every evening." But because he knows that good intentions of this kind do not usually last long, he proposes instead to try it first on Saturday and Sunday nights. In the end, his proposal is accepted on condition he includes Wednesday nights as well.

Amazingly, up to thirty-five young men come to the evening meetings, though sometime this dwindles to half the number. The reason for meeting at night is obvious: Many of their peers have to work during the day, so that they only have time to come at night.

The fact that so many of these *énúwén*, as the young men between fourteen and thirty-five are called, come together in one place at night, leads to a situation on Toon that meets with general enthusiastic approval on the part of the inhabitants. The reason for this is obvious.

Most people go to bed when it gets dark. Troublemakers and hooligans, however, tend to get wide-awake at this time to do their mischief. During those days, when the gangs are normally intent on their annoying activities, but are meeting with Wilhelm instead, the whole neighbourhood remains peaceful. While they are sitting together with their missionary and singing, it seems that all rabble-rousers are out of commission.

Apparently, they enjoy the singing even though the songs at these gatherings have a totally different content than what they are used to when they sing among themselves. Of course, they want to determine their style of singing, to reflect their own liking. It is not supposed to sound like in church, rather more like the soulful love songs they like to proffer. They also have their models. In those years, young people idolize a few long-haired, guitar-playing, and powerfully attractive singers from England. Wilhelm's new "entourage" call themselves the "Beatles of Chuuk."

Often they sing for a whole hour or longer, because time plays hardly any role in their lives. In this way they learn so many songs that Wilhelm decides one day to put the idea of a performance at a church service to them. Well, this needs to be discussed first of all, as they are painfully aware that their reputation is not the best. In reality it is so bad that they wouldn't even dream of showing up in church. But then, several of them do agree, and the missionary appearing with the "scoundrels of the whole area" becomes an important event. After the sermon, several of these young fellows even get up from their seats. They mean to indicate by this that they have realized how their lives need to change and that they are willing to break with their former lifestyle. Some of them confess to Wilhelm that they were the ones to cause trouble at the mission station at night and that they had also stolen things.

Quite a number of them are taking the matter so seriously, they suggest to him that they should accompany him to the services in different churches and sing. He responds to their suggestion by pointing out that he will only take along those who agreed to be on their best behavior from now on; at the next opportunity they must refuse to participate in any further booze-up. In order to place his gang under an obligation to cooperate Wilhelm gets a bright idea.

He puts a notebook on the table. In this are to be written down the names of all who promise not to participate in any beer-drinking bouts for the next four weeks. He purposely chooses such a brief time span because he knows his guys. Again there is a big discussion, for quite a few of them feel that to promise this would be demanding too much of them. But then some do promise not to get drunk again.

It goes without saying that he, too, Wilhelm Kärcher, expressly promises by his own signature that he will not get into a drunken stupor during the next four weeks!

With the registration of the names in the notebook, a sort of "Young Men's Christian Association" has been founded. Its members are between fourteen and thirty-five years old; and the missionary, by now sixty-two-years old, is the oldest of them.

Sure enough, a little later, his "fine fellows" are revealed as the people who are just the way he knows. Of the original fifty plus young men of the "Beatles of Chuuk" only about fifteen to twenty remain, and among these there are perhaps five who mean business and have stuck with the decision they once made. The rest have fallen back into their rotten old lifestyle. For Wilhelm this is no reason for resignation. He knows that spontaneous enthusiasm in a group often raises great hopes among the islanders, but afterwards it becomes reality in only a few lives.

It is the faithful remnant of the five that counts for Wilhelm.

Even after a gathering of almost four hundred young people from eight congregations in the church in the village of Féwúpé, it is clear he no longer has any illusions. At the close of the meeting, thirty of the participants get up to testify that they want to live their lives as Christians. To this he responds as years of experience have taught him: "Someone else may perhaps report this as a revival. But I won't do it. I rather think of looking at blossoming trees in May-time when there, too, not every blossom results in a healthy apple. Still it is a hopeful sign to see trees blossoming at all. Where nothing blossoms there will certainly not be any harvest whatsoever."

"The Tables Have Been Turned"

In the spring of 1970 a missionary conference takes place on Wééné; Wilhelm is taking part. In the meantime, quite a number of alumnae of Philadelphia School have settled on the island with their husbands.

Since Wilhelm needs offers of accommodation during the conference he has someone inquire of Akiko whether he could live with her and her family during that time. Akiko at once offers him her guest room. When he gets to the house in the evening he is surprised. Akiko and her husband no longer live in a hut covered with leaves but in a modern house. In the guest room there is a freshly made double bed, a wardrobe with a light bulb on so that the clothes won't get mouldy; also a table, a chest of drawers, a typewriter desk, a wicker chair, and a fan.

Akiko's husband, Erimes, is a government employee; the house comes with his job; and his father is pastor on one of the Mortlock Islands. Wilhelm remembers at this moment that he knew them as children before when they used to play naked on Kútú. Now he is living with them, enjoying the comfort and their generous hospitality after having lived in much more modest fashion during the past weeks and months. Undisturbed, he can receive visitors that want to talk to him here in his room. But he is already thinking of having to return to the village of Mwúnniyen on Toon in three days' time, where he won't have this comfort. In any case, Erimes and Akiko now live in much nicer surroundings than he does, and without envy he sees the "the tables have turned." Talented islanders willing to work can do very well for themselves. So then, some of his former students, male and female, have accomplished things in life.

And there is something else he is impressed by. At six o'clock in the morning the whole family gathers together for devotions at home. Erimes is sorry that his father can't be there, too, for Wilhelm's visit to his son's house would have been a very special honour for him.

Things Are Different Than They Used to Be

On the Hall Islands, where Wilhelm is on visitation during these weeks, he has nostalgic memories of the beginning of his missionary activity. He is arriving now almost thirty-two years to the day after his first visit to the islands. Comparing his reception at that time with the way he is being welcomed now, he is just amazed. This time, people are expecting him and come to greet him; at that time they still ran away from him into the bush. Now they flock to the meetings that he has up to three times a day. But the things he now emphasizes are different from earlier times. In those days, the missionaries were eager to get the people to come to church mornings and evenings. Now it has become more important to have the Bible read and discussed in the homes and families. On Nómwiin this is especially often the case, as Wilhelm can see.

The best for him are the children's clubs. He has hardly started to ring the bell at 2:30 in the afternoon when the children come running out of their houses as if there were a house on fire somewhere. The teachers dismiss the children that are still at school at this time.

In all the churches he speaks about the return of Christ. One morning after devotions someone suggests to him that he should stay with them on Nómwiin until that time. After a brief consideration, Wilhelm declines his request, pointing out that his family was still waiting for him to come back to Germany before this event happened, and he would not want to disappoint them.

Wilhelm and His Family Become Members of a Clan

Towards the end of 1969, something unusual happens. Wilhelm and his family are being highly honoured. The inhabitants of the island of Woneyopw elevate them to the status of fellow islanders. Customarily this means being accepted into an *eyinang*, a group of relatives corresponding to what Europeans would regard as a clan. With this, Wilhelm, Elisabeth, Hannelore, Waltraud, Anneliese, Ernst, and Helmut become something like honorary citizens of the community of Woneyopw, possessing the right to live and dwell on the island, along with the claim to being supplied with everything they need to the end of their lives. The document that has been written on a simple piece of paper with a pencil contains the following words:

Taropween pwpwon

Eey taropwe aa pwááráátá lóón eey ráán Tiisamper 5, 1969 wusun aa mmak asan pwe eey mwáán itan Mr. Kaercher emén ree Tooyis. Aa pwpwon pwe iiy epwe fiti are pachelong lóón eey eyinang itan Sowumwóóch me wóón eey fénú Woneyopw lóón Mwóchulók, Chuuk District, pwal pwááráátá chék lóón eey ótun aa mmak asan etiyan me néwún repwe fiti are pachelong lóón ewe eyinang itan Wuwáánikar, pwal chék wóón eey fénú Woneyopw wusun aa mmak asan.

Nge reen chóón pwááráátá pwe Mr. Kaercher me aan faamili raa toongeni makkeeló pwe iir chóón ikkeey oo raa emén Sowumwóóch me Wuwáánikar.

Ikkeey iteer raa mmak faan:

> *Wuwáánpóron Carl Derem*
> *Samwoon Kawaichy Philip*

The English translation would be something like this:

Binding Obligation
With this writing, dated December 05, 1969, we confirm that Mr. Kärcher is a German and that, from now on, he is accepted into the clan of *Sowumwóóch* on the island of Woneyopw in the Mortlocks, district of Chuuk. We further affirm that his wife and children are, from now on, accepted into the clan of *Wuwáánikar*, likewise on the island of Woneyopw, as described above.

We, the undersigned, testify, that Mr. Kärcher and his family have the right to call themselves residents of our island and may sign their names with the clan designation of *Sowumwóóch* and *Wuwáánikar* respectively.

Certified as accurate by the undersigned:

Pastor: Carl Derem
Mayor: Kawaichy Philip

For us as Europeans it may seem strange that the family should have become members of two different family groups. Especially noteworthy is the fact that Wilhelm is the only one belonging to the clan of *Sowumwóóch*, whereas his wife and all the children belong to the clan of *Wuwáánikar*. That is exactly according to the express will of the rules governing the islanders' relationships: A man can only be properly married to a wife from another clan, and he is not regarded as related to his children. They automatically belong to the mother's clan. This rule applies, of course, also to honorary citizens.

Once Again: the Mentor

One morning in February 1970, Wilhelm is standing on the airport of Wééné waiting for an airplane. His nephew Klaus W. Müller is arriving with it as a new coworker to become part of the team of Liebenzell missionaries and to be the next leader of the work that his uncle had taken over from his predecessors.

Klaus spends the first weeks with his uncle as his mentor, starting on Toon and then on Woneyopw in the Mortlock Islands.

For the islanders, these two are interesting yoke fellows. According to their understanding, they are not uncle and nephew but father and son. There is no term for grandfather and great-grandfather in the Chuukese language. In listing relational ties the islanders only count fathers, just as it used to be in Israel in Old Testament times. Accordingly, the language does not differentiate between father and uncle or mother and aunt, brother and (male) cousin, sister and (female) cousin.

Wilhelm F. Kärcher and his nephew Klaus W. Müller

Boundary Markings

During those two years that Wilhelm spends on Chuuk, he visits every congregation on all the islands in order to fulfill the important task that had made him depart for the islands once again. The issue has to do with clarifying and securing the title claims for all properties; these are then to be listed in a legal register as the future property of an independent, self-governing, indigenous church.

With a few helpers Wilhelm pours boundary markers of concrete and sets them in place after having surveyed the church properties in the presence of chiefs, pastors, and adjoining neighbors. He prepares documents, plans, and drawings and has them signed by all the eyewitnesses.

Barely ten years later, in the fall of 1980, it will be shown quite how important this work is that Wilhelm accomplished for the churches. By then, Chuuk is one of the states belonging to the "Federated States of Micronesia," as they are now called. A mere three months after the declaration of independence, their government legally decrees that foreigners may not possess any landed property within its national boundaries. All Mission properties have to be either transferred to an independent national church or to one that is officially recognized; if not, they are to revert to the original owner on the respective islands. At that time, the "Evangelical Church of Chuuk" is the only organization called into being by a mission that can document its titles of ownership and so does not lose any claim to its landed property.

Final Farewell from Chuuk

During the final months, Wilhelm lives in a little house with two rooms on the campus of Philadelphia School. He calls it his *"Ausdinghaus"*. That was the term used in the olden days in Germany for a building reserved as a dwelling place for the old farmer and his wife after they had given their farm over to a son or some younger relative. Here he is again "setting up camp" a bit like he used to do earlier as a bachelor on the Mortlock Islands. For example, his wife had sent him a can of honey. He has to empty it urgently because the ants are getting interested in it. It is already teeming with them and he can't fish them all out of the sticky mess by hand. It is altogether too good for him to throw it out. So he pours boiling tea over the honey: "Then it tastes nice and sweet, and I haven't found or seen any more of the little ants in the tea. Apparently, they have simply dissolved into thin air. Even Wupwiini who just arrived at my place likes the taste of the ant-honey tea very much. He thinks my wife is really spoiling me with such good tea."

The old head chief, to whom he owes so much, comes to visit him more often now in order to talk with him, borrow money from him – just a few dollars that he regularly pays back.

How little thought Wilhelm spares for himself and his welfare is evidenced on January 27, 1970. Just in time, before the day is over, he remembers that it is actually his birthday, making him sixty-three years old.

He still won't be able to celebrate. When he comes home at eight in the dark of the evening, an old man is sitting in front of his door, asking him to pull one of his teeth. He already had done this with three other patients the night before; and if anyone turns out to be skilled as a dentist, word gets around among the islanders pretty fast.

During his stopovers in the villages, he is constantly being badgered by people with a toothache. For this purpose he always carries pliers with him so he can remove the offending objects. Given the circumstances, he does this without anaesthesia. It sometimes happens that a patient tells him after the operation that it was the wrong tooth he pulled out. Wilhelm can only reply calmly: "Well, then we'll just have to pull out the right one now."

Most of his patients then find that the second tooth is indeed the right one.

Unexpectedly, a recording team from the *Zweites Deutsches Fernsehen* (Second German TV) comes to Toon. The whole mission station and the school are hurriedly made spick and span. It hadn't seen such order and cleanliness in a long time.

First, the TV people record on film the work of the boy and girl students in the pineapple and taro fields. The central part of the report is the interview with Wilhelm Kärcher as the founder of the school. They film this scene between the Boys' School building and the house he is presently living in. The girl students, demonstratively busy with crochet work, form the background, sitting on the lawn. Before the filming, a little problem occurs. For the recording Wilhelm has put on a brand new white shirt, the most beautiful he owns, given to him by his wife for his return trip to Germany. But the cameraman doesn't like this white shirt at all because it causes interfering colour spots together with the luscious green of the lawn. What is to be done?

I myself am standing close by, wearing a bright yellow shirt telegenic enough to be elevated to the honour of appearing on screen. Wilhelm's brief instructions to me: "Take your shirt off. I'll do the interview in it."

Wilhelm then recounts his experiences in Micronesia. After a very short time, the team leader, Herr Westermann, gives up interrupting his voluble speech with questions. He just lets him talk on.

Almost every day another family group or alumnus comes to announce a banquet in his honour: "My whole house here is full of the smell from the frying pan." The congregations on Toon also try to outdo each other inviting the old missionary to elaborate feastings in order to show him their deep gratitude.

Obviously, he cannot take everything he has back to Germany. So whatever he doesn't want to take, he distributes among the people. Of the two pairs of trousers he still possesses he keeps one for his trip home. The other one he gives away, dirt and all. The recipient is overjoyed, as it is a high honor to be able to call a pair of trousers one's own that once belonged to Wilhelm Kärcher. There are even people who ask if they could have his glasses, as they think that he only needed them on Chuuk but not in Germany.

The very last farewell gathering Wilhelm attends on his mission field takes place in Wóónipw. The rain is pouring down. Despite this, the church is full to bursting. Even outside a vast crowd is sitting in the rain listening. The Philadelphia School choir and the men's choir of Wóónipw with more than fifty members are performing. Even the "Beatles of Chuuk" are present with twenty of their young men.

Wilhelm is preaching from John 4:16. This verse is the inscription over the platform in the church: *"Ngaang aan me nnet me manaw"* – "I am the way, the truth, and the life." He tries to impress this word once again as deeply as possible on the minds and hearts of the islanders, in the way he had experienced it himself during his long missionary life. It is his legacy to them.

At night, on his return home from the farewell party around ten thirty, the "Beatles" are sitting there and want to sing to him. Because he is so tired he tries to persuade them to go home. But they refuse: "Tonight, we are not going home." All right then. He prepares himself patiently for a whole night of having to endure their singing. But soon they are also overcome with tiredness. One after another just keels over wherever they sit. Not long after, they are all lying among their guitars in deep slumber.

Old Wupwiini had once said to him that he would sleep in Wilhelm's house for his last night. He does actually turn up now in the dark to keep his promise. The scene before him is like a biblical one: Jesus in Gethsemane, and his disciples asleep around him. Only the roles are distributed differently. Wilhelm Kärcher, in the midst of the "Beatles of Chuuk"! Wupwiini takes a look, turns around without a word and goes back to his own house for the rest of the night.

Early the next morning, all who manage to wake up are starting to sing again, of course. After a short devotion in the church of Chukiyénú, the *Chen* casts off from the dock. Many people want to be present when Wilhelm's plane leaves from Wééné, and there would not have been sufficient seats available on the boat if they had not been limited to three per congregation. Despite this, it takes some doing this morning to keep the boat from being overloaded. Many who still want to go along, simply have to be turned away.

Some are really getting mad about this. One woman from Chukiyénú starts to make a fuss because she is not allowed on board. Scolding loudly she clings to one of the ropes tying the *Chen* to the dock, and refuses to let it go.

At his first farewell in 1963, Siyales Amewel, the pastor from Kútú, had already pointed out to the leaving missionary that, although Liebenzell Mission had been working on the islands of Chuuk since 1907, not one island pastor had ever visited Germany and met the Christians there who had ensured that the gospel would come to be known in Chuuk also. At the time, Siyales had suggested to him: "For this reason I would like to go with you to Germany and express my gratitude." Wilhelm had not been able to fulfill his desire that year.

Meanwhile things have totally changed. On Wééné, not only is Siyales Amewel, the pastor from Kútú, prepared for the trip with Wilhelm, but also Kumo Epineyiser, the pastor from Wóónipw. They will accompany him to Germany. The three of them are saying their good-byes via WSCZ, the radio station, reaching more than thirty thousand inhabitants of the islands in the Chuuk District.

At the airport, a high-ranking government delegation as well as crowds of singing people are gathered together. At times, three giant choirs are singing three different songs simultaneously. Small wonder then, that the "Beatles" also want to be heard loudly once more.

Because the "Air Micronesia" plane arrives late once again, the three have to scramble to get aboard. This short farewell suits Wilhelm very much. It makes it easier for him. The plane takes off and disappears in a huge cloud of dust.

The cloud, as he always liked to quote, had risen once again. It is April 13, 1970.

Three Islanders on a World Trip

On Guam Wilhelm is faced with a difficult problem. It is really unbelievable. The Liebenzell missionary and his wife stationed on Guam, where Wilhelm and both pastors have to stay until they can catch their onward flight to Germany, do not want to have the two islanders in their house. Their reasoning is more than peculiar: If they were both Palauans, they could enter the house, but not as islanders from Chuuk. It goes without saying that Wilhelm cannot accept this. At first he tries amicably to persuade the objectors of the impossibility of what they are saying. Never would any islander on Chuuk have refused him entrance into their house or a place to sleep. On the contrary; they would move out themselves and sleep in the cooking hut so he could have a comfortable place. But his arguments fall on deaf ears.

The missionary colleague even has the gall to accuse Wilhelm of arrogance by not respecting the instructions of the Liebenzell Mission house administrator, as he calls himself. Only Wilhelm Kärcher would be allowed to enter the guest apartment; the two island pastors – officially guests of the Liebenzell Mission – would have to sleep in the shed.

Wilhelm doesn't know what to make of it!

He continues to insist that either all three will stay in the apartment overnight, or he also will go and sleep in the shed.

For his two companions it is the first time in their lives that they are on a world trip; they are not used to it and find it quite arduous. Even on Guam they are overcome by homesickness. Understandably so, considering the fact that Rev. Siyales alone is father of fifteen children. Their depressed mood leads Wilhelm to forget his own pain of parting he is dealing with; for now he needs to take care of these two.

On Guam, Wilhelm finds plenty of opportunities to acquaint the two pastors with the life of Westerners. For them it is sheer horror to cross over a street with four lanes of traffic. Siyales is suffering badly: his feet are not used to wearing shoes. Coming from a remote Mortlock Island where there is no hustle and bustle, and no noise from airplanes, he is totally confused. One night, Wilhelm hears him pray: "Lord, help me, for I know not what to think anymore!"

Also, they are not used to the portions they get to eat on the plane; they appear to them to be fearfully small: little bowls, little cups, and buns instead of big bowls, cans of liquid, and loaves of bread. These miserly quantities seem to be a threat to the very existence of an islander who has never experienced anything like it. Siyales, who had already gained the impression in the airplane from Chuuk to Guam that they mean to let him starve, expresses his opinion before they fly on from Guam: "Now we must eat our fill once more, so it will last until we get to Germany."

After a long flight via Okinawa and Taiwan, the three of them have a stopover in Hong Kong. All the busyness, the coming and going of people at the international airport of the Chinese city of millions leaves a lasting impression on the two islanders. They ask themselves why there are so many people on the go.

From Hong Kong a Lufthansa aircraft takes them via Bangkok, Karachi, and Kuwait to Frankfurt. For the first time the two pastors see snow, on the peaks of the Lebanon Mountains.

After landing in Frankfurt on April 14, 1970, Wilhelm once again has to explain in detail to an immigration official where exactly Micronesia is located and that it really exists. He surveys the two dark-skinned men rather suspiciously. However, when Wilhelm tells him about them and what they will be doing in Germany, it finally makes sense to him. The three of them may pass through the checkpoint.

In Stuttgart-Echterdingen everything Wilhelm had experienced already in 1963 is now repeated. His family and friends are there to welcome all three. On the trip to Bad Liebenzell the magnificent Black Forest pines cause the two islanders to be amazed again and again, and the reception on the "Mission Hill" is no less impressive to them.

In his greeting, Rev. Kumo Epineyiser is reminded regarding Wilhelm's return to his family that it must have been quite similar to that of the prodigal son's in Luke 15, when the father received him back after his repentance. For the listeners it sounds a bit far-fetched. Kumo, of course, does not intend to characterize the missionary who returned home as a son who was lost (the German designation for the prodigal) and who had acted wickedly; rather, he is thinking of the splendid reception and generosity of the father towards the returning son.

Kumo Epineyiser, Wilhelm F. Kärcher, Siyales Amewel

Both islanders are wondering about that pale springtime sun standing high in the sky and not giving off any appreciable warmth.

The next weeks and months are filled with travels; Wilhelm is accompanying the pastors and translating their messages. Kumo has to have an eye operation in Pforzheim, and since he speaks neither German nor English it is necessary to take special care of him there.

In his closing message at the Fall MissionFest 1970 in the tent in Bad Liebenzell he addresses the *samwoonun misin*, i.e. the "chiefs of the Mission," as he calls the missionary leaders in his language, to express his thanks to them in touching words for having made it possible for him, who was already strongly visually handicapped when he arrived, to have this operation.

At the farewell for Siyales and Kumo on October 13, 1970, Wilhelm Friedrich Kärcher has his last immediate contact with people from his field of service. He will never again set foot on Chuuk.

16

Twilight Years in Pforzheim-Eutingen
(1970–1993)

Retirement

Back in Germany, as an early retiree, Wilhelm can now determine and schedule his days as he likes. This is not easy for him. He struggles with the feeling of being "out of the action." He has to get over the fact that his knowledge and experiences are not sought by others in the way he had expected.

He is still fulfilling his function as mentor in supplying his nephew Klaus W. Müller with information he needs for a paper to finish his studies in the United States (Müller 1981 and 1985). Wilhelm also supports him in his efforts to start a missiological doctoral dissertation. Wilhelm's contributions to this are found in a voluminous correspondence he sustains with Klaus Müller. In a letter dated June 10, 1977, he warns him not to report too critically on the early years or the mistakes made by others, "… for in old age, when you stand before the gates of eternity, many things will look different."

In these last years again and again we find statements that show how much he is preoccupied with memories of his activities as a missionary. He often used to pray for the islanders, he says occasionally. However, he does not become euphoric and bask in glorified memories; on the contrary he remains self-critical.

He has no inclination to go back to Chuuk anymore, as he freely admits. Yet he cannot let go of his past: "I think and pray and dream about the islands a lot. Last night, too, I dreamed. But I really do not want to go back. I gladly think of those who have finished the race by faith in Jesus Christ, as far as I can see. I also like to think of the many times God protected us on the ocean and during the war. But then again, there are times when I see everything in black and think to myself: Surely, you did most of it the wrong way. If you read about defeat here and there, you are overcome by deep pain and start accusing yourself of all kinds of things."

He finds fulfillment by participating eagerly in many evangelistic campaigns and retreats.

Visitors expressing their impressions of Wilhelm and Elisabeth speak about a married couple radiating a light of harmony in their old age. They complement each other in every respect: She dials the phone number, he does the phoning; she reads aloud, he listens.

Wilhelm F. und Elisabeth Kärcher in retirement

Children and Grandchildren

Wilhelm and Elisabeth do not live alone in the Brömachweg in Eutingen. Their oldest son and his family live in the same house. The other children live not far away from them.

Hannelore Kärcher, married to Werner Stein, is a nursery-school teacher. Originally she also planned to return to Chuuk and work where she had spent her childhood, but these plans did not come to fruition. Her children's names are Stefan André, Thorsten Michael, and Anke Mirjam. She lives in Backnang near Stuttgart.

Waltraud Kärcher, married to Gerhard Rist, is a secretary by profession. She worked at the Deutsche Bank and for the city of Pforzheim as head of administration at a school. Her children are called Beate and Holger. She lives with her husband in Beimerstetten in the vicinity of Ulm.

Anneliese Kärcher, married to Frieder Carle, is an elementary and junior high school teacher by profession. For twelve years she worked as a teacher for missionary children in New Guinea, first on a remote mission station in the area of the Sepik River, and then at the Lutheran Mission boarding school in Wau (Papua New Guinea). She lives with her husband in Künzelsau (east of Heilbronn).

Ernst Kärcher, married to Brigitte (Gitte), is a junior high school teacher of religion and physical education. For five years he worked at the "South Sea Evangelical Church Secondary School" in Brugam, a town in the Sepik River area of New Guinea, then for a brief time also on Manus, one of the Admiralty Islands. His children are Michael, Jennifer, Anja, and Ingo. He lives with his wife in the parental home in Pforzheim-Eutingen.

Helmut Kärcher, married to Brigitte, is a teacher of German and geography. His children are called Monika and Peter. He lives with his wife in Jettingen close to Nagold.

The children of Wilhelm and Elisabeth Kärcher
with their spouses in 2005 (left to right):
Helmut and Brigitte Kärcher, Waltraud and Gerhard Rist,
Anneliese and Frieder Carle, Hannelore and Werner Stein,
Brigitte (Gitte) and Ernst Kärcher

The End of His Earthly Life

After he turns seventy Wilhelm begins to reduce his workload. Occasionally he has to cancel an engagement to speak at an evangelistic campaign. There are physical signs of aging. A slight paralysis in his left arm improves after some time.

Years go by.

One of his last services is held in Pinache, a village close to Mühlhausen. In the course of his message he happens to lose his thread and cannot find it again. He has to break off. This is a difficult situation for a usually active speaker like him.

On May 21, 1993, he replies to a letter from his daughter Anneliese. Wilhelm cannot write the letter himself anymore and dictates it to his wife. It is addressed to Anneliese in Wau on New Guinea, but she doesn't get it there because she is on her way home. She receives it instead weeks later when she is already back in Germany. Wilhelm calls it his "second to last letter" and announces that he will write "next week the last" letter to her. He talks about his grandchildren and remarks: "Otherwise we are doing fairly well." Elisabeth adds a sentence at the end concerning herself: "It will be good to have you here soon because my writing is getting more and more scraggly."

This letter, which was to be the second to last one, is in reality the last one. One day later, on May 22, 1993, the missionary Wilhelm Friedrich Kärcher dies after a fulfilled life at the age of eighty-six.

The Liebenzell Mission newsletter announcing his death starts with the words: "On Saturday morning, May 22, 1993, the Lord called his faithful servant, our dear brother Wilhelm Kärcher, from this earthly life to his eternal home."

The funeral takes place on May 29, 1993, at ten o'clock in the morning at the cemetery in Pforzheim-Eutingen. At the beginning of the funeral message, given by Rev. Helmut Geggus, is the statement prayed by the ageing Simeon when he saw Jesus: "Sovereign Lord, as you have promised, you now dismiss your servant in peace. For my eyes have seen your salvation" (Luke 2:29–30).

His wife Elisabeth, from whom he had been separated for a total of seven years, continues to live for several years in Pforzheim-Eutingen together with her son's family in the *imwen kinamwmwe*, the "House of Peace." The last period of her life is spent in the nursing home "Friedensheim" (Home of Peace) belonging to the Liebenzell Mission in Calw-Stammheim. There, on March 31, 2000, her earthly life comes to an end.

On April 5, she is buried next to her husband in the Pforzheim-Eutingen cemetery.

Life Achievements

Back in 1957 Wilhelm Friedrich Kärcher had been honored by the then Federal President Theodor Heuß for his *"Verdienste in der Schular-beit"* (meritorious contribution to school education) – as it says in the document.

In his old age, this man who had been totally committed to life of mission, had at times to deal with the question of how he himself would evaluate his life's work. In spite of all the difficulties and inadequacies that he saw – and suffered from – in his own person, he was not disappointed; his work had been effective. What he started often took a totally different direction from what he had first thought; but something lasting had become of it.

More light had come to the living world of the islanders of Chuuk.

Through his practical knowledge of their language, his familiarity with the details of their culture, his intimate acquaintance with their norms of behaviour and their pre-Christian animistic form of religion, through his extensive itinerant teaching and preaching ministries (full of wise and relevant guidance for their culture) and, lastly, through his love for these island people, he had laid the practical and theological foundation for the "Evangelical Church of Chuuk," which gained its independence in 1975 with over thirty member congregations.

Without the help of his wife Elisabeth, he would not have been able to achieve all this in such a comprehensive way. God visibly blessed the life and work of both of them.

Epilogue

The life of missionary Wilhelm Friedrich Kärcher has not only decisively affected the people on the islands around Chuuk. It has also influenced the life's work of at least two of his fellows in a manner he presumably never imagined. Without his influence, neither the professional career of his nephew Klaus W. Müller nor that of the author, i.e. my own, would have taken the direction that they did take. His ideas, the impact of his personality, and the fact that he had confidence in us hesitant beginners (to the extent that, after our ministry on the islands around Chuuk, we had the wherewithal to plan a career as university teachers), all this means we owe a great debt of gratitude to him and his wife Elisabeth. Our thanks cannot be more aptly expressed than with the words of Matthias Claudius in his poem "at the grave of my father," whose first verse here (translated from German and slightly altered) runs:

May peace surround his grave,
God's peace gently conveyed;
A good man there to earth was laid
Yet more to us he gave.

Klaus W. Müller   Lothar Käser

Bibliography

Publications by Wilhelm Friedrich Kärcher

Und vergiss nicht, was er dir Gutes getan hat. Bad Liebenzell 1950.

Krimen, ein treuer Insulaner-Prediger. Lahr-Dinglingen 1960.

Durch die Brandung. Aus den Erlebnissen eines Südsee-Missionars. Bad Liebenzell 1965.

His numerous contributions to mission and other journals have not been recorded here.

Works by Other Authors

Bollig, P. Laurentius: *Die Bewohner der Truk-Inseln. Religion, Leben und kurze Grammatik eines Mikronesiervolkes.* Anthropos Ethnologische Bibliothek 3, no. 1. Münster 1927.

Eggert, Johanna: *Missionsschule und sozialer Wandel in Ostafrika. Der Beitrag der deutschen evangelischen Missionsgesellschaften zur Entwicklung des Schulwesens in Tanganyika 1891 bis 1939.* Bielefeld 1970.

Grünzweig, Fritz; Thoma, Traugott (ed.): *Gottes ewige Treue. Bekannte Persönlichkeiten berichten aus ihrem Leben.* Bad Liebenzell (VLM) 1989.

Hofmann, Rebecca: *Situating Climate Change in Chuuk. Navigating Belonging through Environmental and Social Transformations in Micronesia.* Diss. München 2014.

Kärcher, Anneliese: *Vernarbte Wunden.* In: Kleemann (ed.) 1996:55–67.

Kleemann, Joachim (ed.): *Lebensschicksale, die jeden treffen können.* Lahr ²1996.

Lehmann, Friedrich Rudolph: *Mana. Der Begriff des „außerordentlich Wirkungsvollen" bei Südseevölkern.* Leipzig 1922.

Lehmann, Friedrich Rudolph: *Die polynesischen Tabusitten.* Leipzig 1930.

Müller, Klaus W.: *Kurs 330 – Südseemissionare unterwegs.* Bad Liebenzell 1975.

Müller, Klaus W.: *Die evangelische Missionsarbeit auf den Trukinseln (Mikronesien) – Eine missiologische Analyse* – Ann Arbor, Michigan 1981. (Englisch: *The Protestant Work on the Truk Islands in Micronesia: A Missiological Analysis and Evaluation.* M. A. Thesis, Fuller School of World Missions 1981, University Microfilms International. Ann Arbor, Michigan 1985).

Neumaier, Richard: *Al en Manaü are longolong ün souläng in Chuk me Fanäpi.* Lahr-Dinglingen 1961.

Neumaier, Richard: *Uruwo mi pin seni lon toropwe en Pipel fanasängesin soulängin Chuk me Fanäpi.* Lahr-Dinglingen (no date).

Neumaier, Richard: *Von Christus* ergriffen. In: Grünzweig, Fritz; Thoma, Traugott (ed.) 1989:102–112.

Neumaier, Wilfried: *Sing, mein Herz! Neun Lieder für Singstimme und Klavier von Richard und Wilfried Neumaier.* Metzingen 1988.

Pagel, Arno: *Sein Ruf hat sie getroffen.* Bad Liebenzell (VLM) 1989.

Petersen, Glenn: *Traditional Micronesian Societies. Adaptation, Integration, and Political Organization.* Honolulu, Hawai'i 2009.

Scheu, Adolf: *Aus der Vergangenheit des Dorfes Mühlhausen a. E.*, O. A. Vaihingen. Plieningen 1907.

Schibel-Yang, Gwi-bun: *Koreanische Frauengruppe in Deutschland: In die Prostitution gezwungen: koreanische Frauen erinnern sich. Zeugenaussagen aus dem japanischen Asien-Pazifik-Krieg.* Osnabrück 1996.

Foreign Cultures

by Lothar Käser

An Introduction to Ethnology
for Development Aid Workers and Church Workers Abroad

In recent decades foreign cultures have not just loomed large for Europeans seeking holiday destinations. Since the 1960s increasing numbers of professionals such as teachers, doctors, agronomists, and other professional workers and missionaries from Europe and America have been partnering local churches in Africa, Asia and Latin America whose fellowships are often very differently organised. When preparing these specialists, development agencies and missions often overlook the knowledge and insights that ethnology and cultural anthropology have to offer, help that makes it easier for professionals to take their bearings, to be well integrated, and to go about their work more effectively. This book deals with such issues.

For future theorists dealing with foreign cultures (ethnologists, anthropologists, etc.) there is now a whole range of brilliantly written textbooks. However, for development aid practitioners, whether secular workers or church workers, these introductory works are overloaded with theory and are thus difficult to digest. What has been missing until now is a simple introduction to the basic concepts which could enable a European working in foreign surroundings to come to terms with the ethnological literature relevant for his activities overseas, to recognise these essential concepts woven into the daily cultural reality of life and work, and to work with them and to bring to bear his or her own analysis. This book is a simplified introduction along these lines, not just written for the target readers just mentioned, but also for students of ethnology/cultural anthropology and for those who frequent ethnological museums.

The author is a professor of anthropology with relevant experience of the issues. He spent five years working in the South Pacific, and has visited Africa, Asia and South America on many occasions for research.

Pb. • pp. 290 • £ 22.50 • $ 37.50 • € 24.95
ISBN 978-3-95776-113-2

VTR Publications • Gogolstr. 33 • 90475 Nürnberg • Germany
info@vtr-online.com • http://www.vtr-online.com